COMPASSIONATE THINKING
An Introduction to Philosophy

WERNER J. KRIEGLSTEIN

KENDALL/HUNT PUBLISHING COMPANY
4050 Westmark Drive   Dubuque, Iowa 52002

Front Cover Photo "Minoan Dolphins" by Gregory Carnevale
Back Cover Photo of Author by Rich Malec

ISBN 13: 978-0-7575-3141-5
ISBN 10: 0-7575-3141-5

Printed in the United States of America
10 9 8 7 6 5 4 3 2 1

ACKNOWLEDGEMENTS

Words cannot express my gratitude to the many teachers, colleagues, and friends who have assisted me in shaping my philosophy and in writing this book. I can only mention a few. I would like to thank my colleagues at the International Society for Universal Dialogue who have over the years inspired me and made me see new horizons. Above all I like to thank Professor Janusz Kuczynski for his tireless support and for his guiding wisdom. Over many years Riane Eisler has been my mentor and friend as well. She and Maryann, my partner for more than 35 years, have shown me what true feminism is all about.

A special thank you goes to both. I like to thank my colleagues at the College of DuPage, above all Keith and John, who helped me with their critical questions and encouragement. Special thanks to my illustrator Tim Butcher, who not only provided the cartoons for the book but gave me support in countless other ways. Intellectual discussions with him were invaluable in bringing this project to fruition. I like to thank my graphic designer Annette Thurston and my editor Hal Temple. Both of them spent numerous hours to shape this book. Finally I like to thank my students at the College of DuPage. They have taught me much about philosophy and life; above all they have forced me to keep things simple.

Philosophy is like a grape vine with many roots and many branches. Mine is only one of the many possibilities. We are all nourished by those who went before us. We must admire their thoughts even in criticizing them. They were our roots, and our branches. Thanks to all of them.

– Werner Krieglstein

TABLE OF CONTENTS

I. THE ROOTS OF PHILOSOPHY	**1**
1. SO THIS IS PHILOSOPHY	1
2. THE DILEMMA OF MODERN PHILOSOPHY	1
3. THE BEGINNING OF PHILOSOPHY	3
4. THE GOLDEN AGE	4
5. THE END OF THE GOLDEN AGE	4
6. THE SPREAD OF THE DOMINATOR MODEL	5
7. EARLY POLYTHEISM AND THE DEVELOPMENT OF MONOTHESIM	6
8. THE SHIFT FROM MATRIARCHY TO PATRIARCHY	7
9. ONCE MORE THEN: WHAT IS PHILOSOPHY?	8
10. LOOKING EVEN FURTHER BACK IN TIME: THE MYTH OF ORIGIN	9
11. AN EGYPTIAN MYTH OF ORIGIN	9
12. GREEK MYTHOLOGY	10
13. THE STORY OF CHAOS IN SOME NON-WESTERN PHILOSOPHIES	11
14. MATHEMATICS, THE MOTHER OF ALL SCIENCES	11
15. FROM ISAAC NEWTON TO ALBERT EINSTEIN: THE CONTEMPORARY CONFUSION	12
16. DEMOCRITUS, THE FOUNDATION FOR ATOMISM	15
17. WHY IS ATOMISM IMPORTANT IN OUR DISCUSSION ABOUT DOMINATION?	17
18. PYTHAGORAS AND THE PYTHAGOREANS	18
19. THE SOPHISTS	19
20. PARTNERSHIP TO THE RESCUE: CO-CREATING A VISION FOR THE FUTURE OF HUMANITY	20

II. The Greek Masters	**25**
1. FROM PLATO'S APOLOGY	25
2. SOCRATES, THE FATHER OF ALL PHILOSOPHERS (470-347 BCE)	38
3. PLATO (427-347 BCE)	41
A. THE ALLEGORY OF THE CAVE	41
B. THE DIVIDED LINE	46
C. PLATO'S SOCIAL PHILOSOPHY: A BLUEPRINT FOR AN IDEAL STATE	48
D. THE PERFECT STATE	51
E. AND HERE COMES THE MUSIC	52
4. ARISTOTLE (384-322 BCE)	54
A. MAN AND STATE, ARISTOTLE'S THEORY OF HAPPINESS	54
B. DON'T WORRY, BE HAPPY	54
C. TELEOLOGY	55
D. A FIRST LESSON ON LOGIC	58
E. ON LANGUAGE	60
F. SOME MORE ON LOGIC	61
G. THE FOUR CAUSES AND THE ROLE OF ART	64
H. A FEMINIST CRITIQUE OF ARISTOTLE	66
III. MEDIEVAL PHILOSOPHY	**67**
1. AUGUSTINE (354-430)	67
2. THE END OF THE MIDDLE AGES AND THE RISE OF SCIENCE	71
3. THOMAS AQUINAS (1224-1274)	74
4. THE FIVE PROOFS OF GOD	75

IV. Renaissance and Reformation — 77

    1. The Renaissance — 77

    2. The Rise of the Middle Class — 82

    3. The Reformation — 82

V. The Age of Reason — 85

    1. René Descartes (1596-1650) — 85

    2. Isaac Newton (1642-1727) — 87

    3. Spinoza (1632-1677) — 88

    4. Empiricism Versus Rationalism — 89

    5. Immanual Kant (1724-1804) — 92

        A. The European Enlightenment — 94

        B. Kant's Ethics: A Categorical Imperative — 96

        C. Kant's Plea for World Peace — 98

VI. The Post Kantian Era and Modernity — 101

    1. Georg Wilhelm Friedrich Hegel (1770-1831) — 101

    2. Existentialism — 103

        A. Sören Kierkegaard (1813-1855) — 104

        B. Jean Paul Sartre (1905-1980) — 105

    3. Pragmatism — 106

    4. Marxism — 108

    5. Neo-Marxism — 112

    6. Nietzsche – My Fear, My Trembling and My Exaltation — 117

    7. Lessons Learned at the Frankfurt School — 120

    8. The Feminist Voice? — 121

VII. TRANSCENDENTAL PERSPECTIVISM — 127

   1. TRANSCENDENTAL PERSPECTIVISM — 127

   2. A PERSPECTIVIST MANIFESTO — 127

   3. TOWARD A UNIVERSALIST FUTURE? — 128

VIII. APPENDIX — 133

   1. IS THE UNEXAMINED LIFE REALLY NOT WORTH LIVING? — 133

   2. COMPASSION AND THE WISDOM OF NATURE — 142

   3. TOWARD A NATURALISTIC FOUNDATION OF COMMUNITY — 152

IX. GLOSSARY — 173

FOREWARD

This book is not just another introduction to philosophy; it is a book with a special purpose in mind. It is a personal account of how a contemporary teacher of philosophy came to value philosophy both as a tool for liberation and simultaneously could see philosophy as a tool for oppression and domination. You can use the book as an introduction to the most important ideas and thinkers of Western philosophy. But it is my hope that you will use it long after your school experience as a guide book for life. My twelve years as an organic farmer and my life experience as a father of five boys have taught me to see the hidden connections behind things. There are many things in life we can analyze and understand, but some things we must just do. Understanding the origins of ideas and concepts enables us to make changes if the need arises.

We must trust in intuition, but in order to shape our subconscious mind we must train our intellectual mind. Critical philosophy, as taught by the Frankfurt School, helps both, intuition and critique.

I have included a short list of recommended films that will help you to follow the material better. They are available in any good library. But I do not believe they are essential to enjoy and benefit from the book.

My intention is to make philosophy available again at the street corners, in coffee houses, and the public forum. I deeply believe that the pursuit of a critical philosophical mind is one of the most vital corner stones of a free and democratic society.

CHAPTER I: THE ROOTS OF PHILOSOPHY

■ 1. SO THIS IS PHILOSOPHY

View the film: *So This Is Philosophy*. After you see the film and before you start reading this unit you should answer the questions of Activity One in the accompanying *Activities Book*.

BRANCHES OF PHILOSOPHY
(Love of Wisdom)
ONTOLOGY (METAPHYSICS)
study of what is real
EPISTEMOLOGY
study of how we know
LOGIC
study of accurate statements
ETHICS
study of what is good/right
AESTHETICS
study of what is beautiful

The short film you viewed in preparation for this first learning unit demonstrates that **modern philosophy** is a complicated affair. In the beginning of the movie, the two young girls casually roll a dice. They talk with each other in the complex language of modern linguistics. We have the impression that they do not really know what they are talking about. Academic philosophy often seems to shroud itself in mystery by using big and complicated words. Modern philosophy usually is written for highly trained experts. In this book we will try to make philosophy simple.

Philosophy must once more capture the imagination of ordinary people like you and me, as it once did. In Athens, some four centuries before our time, a simple-minded and stubborn philosopher named Socrates stood on street corners and addressed passersby by asking them questions. He mostly attracted young people, ordinary youth with average parents. This is what philosophy should do again.

The goal of philosophy: To live a good life.

The film also makes clear that philosophy deals with ethics, or doing the right thing. *So This Is Philosophy* deals with the question: What reasons do people give to **justify** their actions?

The story is simple. A teacher discusses with his students the case of a factory owner. The owner found out that the plastic bottles his company produced might cause cancer in his workers. Now the owner faces the **dilemma** of whether he should tell his workers of this potential hazard or keep it to himself. He is taking the risk of being sued later on. Does the owner have a moral obligation to let his workers know? Should he inform them, regardless of the consequences?

In the course of the film, different actors give various justifications for their actions. Have you made a list of these justifications? Try to order them according to what you think is of greater or lesser importance. Compare your list with your neighbors. Have you come to the same conclusions? What are some reasons why different people come up with different orders?

Did you find that the order depends on your **values**? What values would you have if you were a worker in the factory? What would be your values if you were the owner?

■ 2. THE DILEMMA OF MODERN PHILOSOPHY

Looking over the whole body of two-and-one-half-thousand years of Western philosophy, the question "What makes an action right?" has always been a central theme. Thus morality is the main concern of philosophy. A systematic investigation into morality is called ethics.

This term goes back to the Greek philosophers. Aristotle wrote one of his major works on ethics. The two Greek philosophers – Plato and Aristotle – invented most of the terms we use today to discuss philosophical topics.

Systematic philosophy started with the Greeks. A systematic, logical approach to problems is called a **discourse**.

> *Question:* Why do we start philosophy with the Greeks and not with some other civilization, i.e., the Egyptians or the ancient Chinese?
>
> All civilizations, ancient or modern, have developed ways to understand the world and the meaning of our life in the universe. The Greeks were the first to treat these questions systematically. Thus the terminology used to discuss philosophical ideas around the world goes back to the ancient Greeks. The Greeks developed a systematic way of thinking about life, its meaning, and our place in the universe.
>
> Most other civilizations used a more narrative approach. They told stories in order to convey meaning and pass this meaning on to the next generation. In a discourse we do not use storytelling, but develop an argument logically. To develop this rigor in thinking, the Greeks used the rigor they had learned in mathematics, especially in geometry.

Besides ethics philosophy also deals with **ontology**. Ontology, the science of being, asks the question, "What is?" or "What exists?" This is actually often seen as the first major field of philosophy. You might ask, "But don't we all know what exists?" As we will soon see, this is not at all a simple question. We need only to listen carefully to two or three people describing the same event. Take a car accident for example.

Original drawing Tim Butcher

Witnesses often come away with completely different, sometimes contradictory stories. Or consider a suicide bombing in an Israeli café. One observer calls it a terrorist act, the other an act of martyrdom, or a selfless act of liberation. Here the observers see the same event, but interpret it completely differently. Our language models what we believe reality to be. Mathematics also expresses a model of reality. The Greeks believed that mathematics was a more accurate way to express what is real than using language and words.

Philosophy also deals with beauty. This philosophical field is called **aesthetics**. Aesthetics asks the question: "What is beautiful?" For the Greeks the world appeared to be beautiful. They felt a divine mission to restore beauty where it was lacking. Where there was beauty there was also truth and goodness, because the highest God on Mount Olympus represented these qualities: truth, goodness, and beauty. The lack of complete truth, goodness, and beauty was caused by lower gods or by **chaos**.

Greek artists believed that they could be closer to the gods and imitate them by creating beautiful things. Think about what it could mean, when Einstein said, "God is beautiful mathematics."

At the end of our film the students appear to be frustrated. Their philosophical investigation does not lead them to any conclusions. Their frustration continues, even though the teacher asserts, "We have gotten somewhere." He assures them that they have found out what they cannot use as a justification. In the words of the teacher, "We cannot say, 'It's my opinion and that makes it right.'"

Did two thousand years of philosophizing lead only to this? When we ask the question what makes something right or wrong, is all we can come up with a set of negative notions? Is philosophy really just "too long a story," as the elderly gentlemen in the film says? As we will learn, philosophy has not produced any real conclusions because a major part of the reason why people started to philosophize has never been told.

■ 3. THE BEGINNING OF PHILOSOPHY

In the middle of the Twentieth Century, when I went to school, first in Germany and then in Chicago, I learned that philosophy started with the Greeks for three reasons:

- The Greeks traveled a great deal and on their travels encountered many other cultures. Their polytheism allowed them to adopt other people's beliefs and stories.

- The Greeks produced much surplus. Their surplus economy allowed some of them to sit around and think about the meaning of life. The Greeks were a creative bunch of people.

- The Greeks did not have a strong priestly class to control their thoughts.

This explanation is only partially correct. It misses one crucial point – the early Greeks were painfully aware that they had lost something important. Their poets talk about a **Golden Age**, a time when people could still communicate with the gods, a time when people lived in harmony with each other and with nature. Similar to the old Hebrew Bible which begins with the story of the Garden of Eden, Greek **mythology** talks about such a peaceful and harmonious time as well.

For a long time stories about a Golden Age were dismissed as wishful thinking, as nothing but stories. When the Greek historians and philosophers compared and contrasted their memory of the Golden Age with their current reality of war, conflict, and strife, the world to the Greeks not only seemed beautiful, but also appeared full of contradictions, pain and misery. Their mythologies were meant to give life a meaning and to solve the contradictions of daily living. But now the Greeks found that these old stories failed to fulfill this purpose. For many modern Greeks they had outlived their usefulness.

■ 4. THE GOLDEN AGE

By classical Greek times, only a memory remained of what was then called the Golden Age. It was the memory of a time when life was harmonious and communication flowed easily between human beings and their nature gods. As artworks from these times and regions testify, rich cultures flourished for thousands of years, long before the ancient Greeks and Romans laid the foundations of our current civilization. These prehistoric peoples lived in advanced, city like settlements, and developed a high standard of living. Free and open sexuality constituted a large part of their daily lives. They worshiped primarily earth connected goddesses and gods.

In her book *Sacred Pleasure,* Riane Eisler brings forth numerous examples for the way our ancestors revered sexuality as both the source of life as well as a wellspring of sacred power.

> *"Our ancestors celebrated sex not only in relation to birth and procreation, but as the mysterious – and in that sense, magical – source of both pleasure and life. In other words, I am proposing that prehistoric erotic myths and rites were not only expressions of our ancestors' joy and gratitude for the Goddess's gift of life, but also expressions of joy and gratitude for the Goddess's gift of love and pleasure – particularly for that most intense of physical pleasures, the pleasure of sex."*

> *– Riane Eisler*

The **Minoans** were one of those civilizations that preceded the classical Greeks by several thousand years. They lived on the island of Crete. Around one-thousand years before our time, a mysterious event made them all but disappear from the face of the earth.

Minoan Vase
1600 - 1200 BCE
© 2006 JupiterImages Corporation

Minoan art provides a rich testimony to the Minoan appreciation of beauty, harmony and play. Their daily life continuously celebrated living in accordance with nature. Unrepressed sexuality was part of this celebration. The Minoan civilization provides a well-documented example of an ancient society that showed no marked difference in the social treatment of men and women.

Anthropologists had long suspected that the Greek male-dominated civilization had been preceded by a gentler and more egalitarian civilization. Evidence mounted that on the island of Crete in the Mediterranean Sea, a civilization once flourished in which men and women had an equal chance to advance into higher positions. Most of all, their artworks did not glorify violence. One can imagine how the daily life of those early people must have appeared to the later Greeks as a Golden Age indeed. In contemporary times, Greek society moved from war to war, from one battle into another, and political regimes changed often. One question remains: Why and how did the Golden Age disappear?

■ 5. THE END OF THE GOLDEN AGE

As the newest discoveries indicate between approximately 4500 BCE and 1200 BCE, waves of invaders from the steppes of Central Asia conquered much of Europe and advanced as far as India, perhaps even to China. Due to their common language these people became known as **Aryans**. German fascists falsely claimed that Aryans were one homogeneous tribe and the ancestors of the Germanic race. Little is known about the true origins of those Aryans.

These Aryans were nomadic and semi-nomadic peoples who brought with them tamed horses, chariots, and war tools. Their society was ranked hierarchically. A male chieftain was their leader and the gods in their heavens followed an equally **hierarchical** structure.

According to their belief, a male god presided over the other gods in the sky. Living as nomads in the northern steppes, Aryans brought with them the **dominator model** and war gods that lived in the sky. We will never know for sure, but the Aryans might have adopted their religious and social hierarchical structures from their observation of the wild herds of horses they eventually tamed.

The lead male in a herd of horses has nearly absolute power. The stallion has to defend his ruling position against competitors. This social model became the norm for later dominator societies. We can easily see that such a hierarchical social model worked quite efficiently for wandering animal herds. It also proved to be an efficient model for nomadic peoples.

■ 6. THE SPREAD OF THE DOMINATOR MODEL

Traveling by horse, Aryan tribes could cover large territories. Once they learned to mount, break, and tame horses, they had a distinct advantage over all other peoples. The horse proved to be the first human fighting machine. Fighting from horseback, Aryan tribes subdued many groups of people. On horseback, nomadic Aryans roamed and conquered most parts of the ancient world in relentless search for treasure and gold. Agricultural tribes they encountered often were not at all prepared to defend themselves, since traditionally they had few enemies.

As recent archeology shows, pre-Aryan settlements and villages were often unfortified and unprepared to fend of enemies. Before the Aryans came they had most likely lived in peace with their neighbors for many thousand years.

As these militant Aryans migrated into many places in the ancient world, they affected the local, peaceful, agrarian societies in profound ways. The new dominator system infected the old earth and life-centered religions like a virus. The agricultural and trading people of Old Europe had little resistance against the new dominator culture.

A group of those Aryan invaders made their way to India. As in other regions, the invading Aryans quickly subdued the earlier civilization living in the Hindus valley. **Hinduism** assimilated the original Indian tribal religions into the dominant Aryanism. The introduction of the **caste system** put the invaders into the position of rulers and dominators, while declaring the original inhabitants as the lower castes.

This is how the dominator model spread around the world and infected nearly all societies.

Only few groups of people, the indigenous people of the Americas and Australia, for instance, preserved a more gentle relationship with nature and with each other.

■ 7. EARLY POLYTHEISM AND THE DEVELOPMENT OF MONOTHEISM

Hindu God Ganesh
© 2006 JupiterImages Corporation

By classical Greek times, only a memory remained in Europe of what was then called the Golden Age. It was the memory of a time when life was harmonious and communication flowed between human beings and nature gods.

Between 1400 BCE and 800 BCE, **Zoroastrianism** developed in the area of Persia. Zoroaster was the son of an old priest family, who were most likely direct descendants of the Aryan nomads. The prophet Zoroaster founded a religion that instituted a monotheistic male god in the sky. He ultimately turned against polytheistic nomads whom he called "the perpetrators of lies."

Some major features of the lost polytheistic beliefs remained part of Zoroastrianism. Zoroaster's male god, Ahura Mazda, initially presided over other gods (mazdas) in heaven, but was the most powerful god. Zoroaster proclaimed that the other gods were not deserving of worship and sacrifice. Eventually they were forgotten. Thus, human beings first conceived of monotheism.

When the ancient Hebrews were released from Babylonian captivity, they brought with them the **monistic** idea of a single, most powerful male god, whom they called Yahweh. Initially other less powerful gods accompanied the Hebrew god as well, but they were eliminated when Moses brought forth the Ten Commandments. Only one God was to rule Israel. Early Hebrew religion continuously attempted to discredit and eradicate its polytheistic roots. For example, they condemned the snake, which virtually all early religions considered to be a mysterious and even holy animal.

Some of the ritual practices of the Golden Age survived the invasion. But in line with dominator thinking, Greek **mythology** adopted Zeus, a male god, as the head of the pantheon of many gods. With Zeus, a militant, often violent attitude became popular in the Greek heaven and in Greek culture.

Gentler ritual practices of the earlier culture survived in popular festivals such as the **Eleusinian Mysteries.** With their origins in Minoan culture, this cult was devoted to creativity, fertility, sexual pleasure, regeneration, and rebirth. Many of the early Greek philosophers were educated by and remained in contact with female priestesses, from whom they learned the mysteries of nature and of the gods.

Pythagoras founded a community to which men and women were accepted as equals. Plato still allowed women to become members of his academy and was an advocate, at least among the ruling class, for the education of women. Education for women in those days did generally not exist anymore. According to Riane Eisler's careful documentation, as male domination took a firmer hold, Greek mythology systematically changed to reflect the new reality.

■ 8. THE SHIFT FROM MATRIARCHY TO PATRIARCHY

As societies became increasingly more organized, the focus began to shift from partnership and equality to treating people as mere property. In the center of this development was a momentous change in the practice and understanding of sexuality.

In earlier tribal societies, here we will call them primal, most things were owned communally. Even in modern families today the question often does not arise as to who owns the family home. But as families loose their traditional cohesion, the lines are often drawn with ever increasing clarity. Especially in divorce cases, property is divided up and unfortunately the toughest fight often centers on the question of who owns the children.

Zoroaster
© 2006 JupiterImages Corporation

In ancient societies this question did not come up. Children belonged to the mothers who birthed them. A mother bore the child and was the main focal point for the child, at least in its early stages of development. Everyday the child grew older, the community took on more and more of the task of caring for the child. At an early age, perhaps around five or six, a male child was given a male relative to be its caretaker. Often this was a brother of the mother or another close relative.

Sexual procreation had little to do with this whole process. In fact, for most of human history the question of who was the biological father was all but inconsequential and often not known at all. People practiced sex with each other at an early age of maturity. As mentioned earlier, this was often connected with religious ceremonies. As a matter of course, women became pregnant and mothers of children for whom the group then cared. In the minds of early people, these two facts, sexual procreation and pregnancy, were often not put together. Today there are still some tribes who believe that pregnancies are the result of women being exposed to the moonlight.

Advances in the domestication of animals and animal husbandry most likely made people aware of the inevitable connection between breeding and childbirth. Training of animals, especially of large animals such as horses, made people aware of the value present in living property, not only in that of an animal but also in that of people. Slavery was invented.

A well-trained young man was suddenly seen as a quite useful object to own, since he could perform many necessary tasks around the house. An experienced woman was seen as a quite valuable breeding asset for future offspring. As male domination became fashionable and accepted, women were increasingly more enslaved and used as property by wealthy men.

Once the connection between sexual intercourse and having children became a popularly known fact, males also became interested in owning the property they had created. Just like animals, children, too, were beginning to be seen as valuable resources to be owned and exploited. In order for the male to be sure that the child a woman bore was actually his child, the access to many women had to be limited. This was achieved through the phasing out of rituals that resulted in promiscuous sexuality, such as the Dionysian ritual and many of the old mystery rites.

This was also accomplished through the institution of monogamy and marriage. Men now were asked to limit their sexual activities to one woman. In order not to limit the male's desire for unlimited sexual access, one woman had to be subdued to endure the male's advances whenever he felt it necessary and desirable. Thus male domination became the norm.

As said earlier, Greek mythology and early history demonstrates this shift in public morality; and at the center of this shift was a devaluation of women as property and an enforcement of male dominance as ruler of the world. The establishment of a male God in heaven was the most visible expression of this development.

■ 9. ONCE MORE THEN: WHAT IS PHILOSOPHY?

Philosophy is the search for happiness, for a harmonious and peaceful life. Since our Greek ancestors had a feeling of having lost that former harmony, they set out to search for it.

Their first answer was this: perhaps if we live again according to nature, as the ancient people did, we again find happiness. Therefore the question of highest importance is this: what is nature really like? Since the Gods made the natural world according to definite laws, our obligation is clear: we must find out what nature is really like and discover its lawfulness.

A. **Ontology** investigates the true nature of everything. Ontology is the first major field of philosophical inquiry. What is nature really like? On the surface everything seems to be constantly changing. In an ever changing world, how can we discover any laws?

One of the early philosophers, Heraclites, thought of everything being like fire. But isn't there anything that is permanent? Is there indeed something that does not change, that is the same in everything?

Ontology investigates these kinds of questions. Literally ontology means the science of what is (**ontos** is the Greek word for being.)

B. Ethics is the second major field of philosophy. Since knowing what is or exists does not seem to produce happiness by itself, it soon became evident that one must also live in accordance with the laws and rules of nature. We have to adjust our lives to live in accordance with nature. This attempt to live in harmony with nature is called ethics. The Greek word is connected with habit forming, doing the right thing over an extended period of time. The Greek philosophers were convinced that if we can live an ethical life, a life in accordance with nature, then we will also live a happy life.

C. **Aesthetics** is the third major field of philosophy. The Greeks actually did not use the term aesthetics; it was invented in the 17th century and has remained popular ever since. Aesthetics deals with **theories** of art and beauty. Behind the surface world of appearances, the Greeks suspected that there was another world, more permanent and more perfect. That is the world these early philosophers tried to uncover. It is supposed to reveal to us the very laws and rules created by the gods, which would we but live by them, would make our lives more peaceful. One of the characteristic of these laws is that they are expressions of extreme beauty and harmony. They observed symmetries and balanced relationships in nature, which they believed were signs of divine creation. To this day, Greek buildings and artworks are admired for their style and beauty.

Look at some Greek artworks and observe their beauty. Describe their symmetrical structure. Think about how this could be connected with God. We can also look at some Islamic art found in many mosques. Do you see similarities here with early Greek art? Muslim artists, who are not permitted to paint faces or figures, are allowed to express their admiration of God (Allah) through geometrical designs. And remember that Einstein once said that, "God is beautiful mathematics."

■ 10. Looking Even Further Back In Time: The Myth of Origin

Why is it that we first see order as totally positive and chaos as completely negative and, only after some reflection, we find that each of these ideas somehow contains the opposite aspect?

Order and chaos are two very elemental aspects of our world. By this I mean that every culture somehow observed the fact that order and chaos are present in this world. Each civilization, in their **creation myth,** tried to find a place for order and chaos.

Which creation story or creation myth is most familiar to you? If you were raised as a Christian, Muslim or Jew, you most likely will share the same creation myth. The Hebrew Bible, which for Christians became the Old Testament and was worked into the Koran by Muhammad, contains in its first pages the account of how God created heaven and earth. According to this ancient story, God is a powerful and creative spirit who brings order into a chaotic world. In the beginning, the world is formless and empty. In the beginning "the earth was formless and empty, darkness was over the surface of the deep, and the Spirit of God hovered over the waters." God's spirit brings order to the darkness. Later, under the influence of Christian philosophers, darkness became the symbol for Satan.

The value a culture puts on order and chaos defines that culture's relationship to the universe and to the natural world. It determines the way people relate to God, nature, animals, and each other. Human beings first formulated the story of order and chaos in the oldest mythologies and then continued on in religions. Order and chaos eventually became part of the scientific world as well.

■ 11. An Egyptian Myth of Origin

Chaos, in Egyptian mythology, occupied a prominent place and was experienced as a living and creating power. *The Book of the Dead* is one of the oldest documents in existence dating back to about 2000 BCE. According to that mythology, in the beginning there was Nun, a chaos like primordial fluid. Nun with its snake body lifted itself into being, becoming *Atum and Ra*, the sun and the rising and setting of the sun.

Egyptian Book of Dead
© 2006 JupiterImages Corporation

Egyptians called **Chaos** "the father of the gods." It was the creative beginning of everything. Chaos brought forth a line of gods and pharaohs who ruled the destiny of the country for thousands of years. Atum, formless in the beginning and residing within Nun, bore the seed for everything. In later worship, Egyptians considered Atum the father of the human race. Atum, by the effort of his will, rose from the abyss and presided as Ra over the universe. Ra brought forth eight gods. The first human beings grew from his tears and from them came all other living creatures.

Ra at first reigned peacefully over creation. As he aged, however, his divine offspring, Isis, took advantage of his senility and made him reveal his name. By knowing his name, Isis gained magical powers over Ra. From this point on, conflict and strife entered the peaceful heaven of the Egyptians. On orders of Nun, Ra withdrew angrily into a distant heaven and created a new, less perfect world, in which human beings were condemned to live.

■ 12. GREEK MYTHOLOGY

From the beginning in Greek mythology, chaos played a lesser, mostly negative role. Gaea, the mother goddess of Earth, created the gods and human beings. According to the classical Greek writer Hesiod, Chaos was in the beginning, vast and dark, but Gaea appeared (unrelated to Chaos) and so did Eros. They resided over the formation of all things. In the Greek mind, chaos never had a creative power; instead, the Greeks thought of it as an open space which could be filled with objects. Later still, the idea of disorder was attached to the word chaos. Some scholars speculate that this was the result of a "false derivation from a word meaning 'to pour'." After this change, chaos meant a confused, unorganized mass of elements scattered through space.

Erebus and Night were born from Chaos. Under the reign of *Chronos*, Night gave birth to a long list of miseries: Doom and Death, from which later came Sleep and Dream. From the same source came the Fates, responsible to apportion good and evil at the birth of every child. Night also bore Nemesis, Fraud, Old Age, Incontinence, Sorrow, Forgetfulness and Hunger. Disease, Combat, Murder, Massacres, Lies and Injustices were, according to classical Greek mythology, also the direct creation of Chaos. No wonder the Greeks did everything they could to stay away from chaos.

The whole body of Greek philosophy, which, in turn, has influenced all of Western civilization, represents a persistent attempt to escape and diminish the power of chaos. For the Greek mind, chaos was a defect, a mistake, an absence of order that had slipped into the world as a result of the dabbling of some lower celestial gods who didn't know any better.

Had the whole universe been the sole creation of the *demiourg*, the master god of Aristotle, chaos would not have existed. God, however, endowed us human beings with a rational, ordering mind, so we can fix chaos and provide order. In this classical universe, once human beings had achieved total order, they could finally overcome fate, which ruled even the gods of the Greek pantheon. They could know and predict everything. The future would be ours to tell, and this would represent the ultimate triumph of reason.

As the Greek myth would have it, nothing useful could ever come from chaos, only misery and death. Under the influence of this classical preference for order, and aided by a similar message of the Judeo-Christian God, Western human beings set out to eliminate chaos and bring order everywhere. In reality, this mentality has managed to eliminate a great number of species, which had developed as a result of the chaotic self-organization existing in natural systems. In our ignorance we human beings felt the need to eliminate all those things in nature for which our limited view saw no immediate use. Life on earth would have perished long ago, had it depended on the limited imagination and ability of human beings to create order.

"The fact that mathematics works is nothing less but a miracle."

– Eugene Wigner, Modern physicist

Though the idea of chaos as a positive and constructive energy has been present since early civilizations, the Western mind mostly perceived its negative aspects. We realize now that those civilizations that lived in harmony with chaos fared better in their interaction with nature. While the West harmed and has possibly irreversibly damaged the environment and the earth, other so called primitive cultures lived in greater harmony with nature. In the next chapter we will deal with the role of chaos in some Eastern mythologies.

13. THE STORY OF CHAOS IN SOME NON-WESTERN PHILOSOPHIES

In Hinduism, for instance, the god Shiva is the destroyer and the creator. Chaos and order are two aspects of the same god. Taoism also tries to find a balance between the opposing principles of Yin and Yang.

In Native American stories, chaos was often represented by the cunning coyote, a mere trickster who turns things upside down. This has a distant similarity to the popular Western name for Satan, the devil. The word devil goes back to the Greek word *diaballein*, which means tumbling things upside down, quite a difference from the awesomely dangerous Satan, the father of Evil that has so much destructive power in the Christian mind.

14. MATHEMATICS, THE MOTHER OF ALL SCIENCES

Plato said that a good philosopher must study eight years of mathematics before engaging in philosophy. Several early philosophers are remembered today more for their contributions to mathematics than to philosophy. When you hear the name Pythagoras, what comes to mind first?

If you thought of the **Pythagorean Theorem** you were right. Many students learn about this famous law in geometry long before they know of any philosophical ideas. Thales, another ancient philosopher, developed a theorem that is still known and taught today, yet few people are familiar with the significance of geometry to the early development of philosophy.

Both **Thales** and Pythagoras were intrigued by the stunning correspondence of natural phenomena and their representation in mental images such as circles, angles, and graphs.

A story is told of Thales that in his wanderings he had come to the Pyramids in Egypt where he observed the length of his body's shadow on the ground. He measured the angle of the sun in the sky and again measured the shadow of the pyramid. With these three measurements he was able to calculate the height of the pyramid without actually having to climb to its top. He reasoned that there was a definite and calculable relationship between these three numbers and the height of the pyramid.

If some things in the world are connected by logical necessity, the Greeks reasoned, then can one not also assume that all things in the world, indeed that the whole universe is logically connected, and therefore understandable and predictable? If God is the embodiment of all order, is it not logical to assume that the world God created is also ruled by order? If the mind can recognize order in the familiar neighborhood of the world around us, can we not also assume that the mind will be able to recognize a consistent order in the far reaches of the universe?

This optimism that all things in the universe are knowable, understandable and ultimately predictable propelled the Greek mind and brought forth a scientific faith. To this day, most scientists still firmly believe in a universe that is understandable and free of contradiction.

> When we realize that something that appears connected to the mind is also connected in the real world, then we begin to grasp the essence of philosophizing and ultimately the essence of science. For science and philosophy to be possible, we must believe that events are causally connected, and that the human mind can grasp these connections.

Before we continue let us examine several discoveries that in the course of the 20th century, severely undercut this scientific belief and gave rise to a new sense of unpredictability and chance in the fabric of the universe.

■ 15. FROM ISAAC NEWTON TO ALBERT EINSTEIN: THE CONTEMPORARY CONFUSION

Isaac Newton was born on December 25, 1642 in Lincolnshire, England. He was born the same year Galileo died. Newton is clearly the most influential scientist who has ever lived. His accomplishments in mathematics, optics, and physics laid the foundation for modern science and revolutionized the world. As a mathematician, Newton invented integral calculus, and, jointly with Leibnitz, differential calculus. Newton also had a huge impact on theoretical astronomy.

He defined the laws of motion and universal gravitation which he used to predict the precise motions of stars, and the movement of the planets around the sun. Newton left the field of science with a unified system of laws that could be applied to an enormous range of physical phenomena, and could be used to make exact predictions. Newton published his works in two books, namely Opticks and Principia. Newton died in London on March 20, 1727 and was buried in Westminster Abbey, the first scientist to be accorded this honor. An eighteenth century poem written about Sir Isaac Newton by Alexander Pope states it best: "Nature and Nature's laws lay hid in night: God said, Let Newton be! and all was light."

The modern scientific age began with Isaac Newton in the seventeenth century. The influence of Newton's formulation of the laws of motion on the modern world cannot be underestimated. Today we talk about the Newtonian universe. Scientist believed Newton's description of natural laws to be universally true until the beginning of the twentieth century when Einstein developed his laws of relativity.

What did the Newtonian Universe, or the world of classical science, look like? The futurist Alvin Toffler compared it with a world built out of giant tinker toys. Toffler depicted the world of classical science as "a world in which every event was determined by initial conditions that were, at least in principle, determinable with precision. It was a world in which all the pieces came together like cogs in a cosmic machine."

During the nineteenth and throughout most of the twentieth century, the image of a "simple, uniform, mechanical universe" not only shaped the development of science, but also influenced most other areas of human development. We shaped even our social orders, the large bureaucracies that governed most modern industrialized nations, like giant machines with their "checks and balances clicking like parts of a clock." The achievements of the technological mind confirmed, as Toffler said' "the image of the universe as an engineer's giant Tinker toy."

In the mind of those optimists this universe would eventually become totally predictable because all events evolve according to eternal laws made by god. The philosophers of those days promoted a philosophy which became known as Deism, the belief that God wound up the world like a clock and now it runs like clockwork. Newton's world, therefore, is also known as the **clockwork universe**.

Scientists assumed that if one knew all the conditions or causes that had produced an event, one could completely predict that event. As we understand the universe better and better, we would ultimately be able to predict everything. This was indeed an incredible trust that was put into the ability to reason. Out of this optimism grew what became known as the **European Enlightenment**, a complete trust in the power of human reason.

The first indication that all was not well with this kind of optimistic thinking came in the form of a scientific discovery made during the nineteenth century. This discovery, in a new science called thermodynamics, resulted in the formulation of what became known as the Second Law of Thermodynamics.

This law states that in the natural world things always evolve from order to disorder. Drop a perfectly fine cup on a stone floor and it will shatter into pieces. This is a perfectly normal occurrence. To visualize the pieces of the cup flying upward, coming together and forming a cup, is unrealistic; only a video running in reverse can produce this. Everyone watching it would know that it could not be real. Or think of the pieces of a sunken ship coming up out of the ocean and forming a ship. Nonsense! Ships are built by workers in a shipyard.

The Second Law of Thermodynamics tells us that order in natural systems always dissipates, a fancy word for disappearing. Scientists call this entropy. According to the Second Law, the universe will inevitably end up in total equilibrium, meaning that all differences between differently ordered systems will have disappeared and the temperature will be evenly lukewarm everywhere. Such a universe would of course be totally inhospitable to life of any kind.

Recognizing this fate of the universe, the general mood of people suddenly went from optimism to pessimism. The glorious universe of classical physics began to make way for a universe condemned to a slow death. In addition, remember that the God of the Deists was a God, who was separate, detached, and uninvolved. This was a God who did not influence the course of events. To the contrary, perhaps this God himself was condemned to die.

At the turn of the twentieth century, a young patent clerk in an office in Switzerland was about to change the course of history once more. In a few highly publicized papers, young Albert Einstein was able to prove that the two constants that once forged the absolute background for Newtonian science, space and time, were deeply involved with each other and were an integral part of the most fundamental processes of nature. People so far had seen space and time as an absolute backdrop for all that exists. Einstein suggested that these ancient categories were far from being absolute. Space and time changed, according to Einstein, depending on the viewpoint of the observing scientist. If a scientist were able to travel close to the speed of light, time would practically extent to near eternity, and at the speed of light it would actually stand still.

Now to be perfectly honest, Einstein had no way to try this out. Our daily experience tells us that we do things in time and also in a definite place. A clock placed in a moving train runs with the same speed as the clock in the train station that never moves. At least, this is how it appears to us; and we are pretty convinced that this is how it is. When contemplating Einstein and his Theory of Relativity, we can perhaps finally appreciate the radical doubt of philosophers who ask us not to assume that the world is the way it appears. Hang in there, we will explain more.

Einstein could not try this out himself. Nobody can come close to the speed of light, at least not with any currently known technology. Einstein derived this from his knowledge of mathematics and from his peculiar equations. Remember that we have called mathematics the mother of philosophy. By the time Einstein used the mathematics of his time, science, too, had progressed in ways that early philosophers and mathematicians, such as Thales and Pythagoras, could have never imagined.

Mathematical language, remember, is a precise representation or model of the world. Often we can predict outcomes of experiments only by calculating their model in mathematical languages. Even modern wars are fought that way: computers calculate the trajectory of a missile from the beginning to its target, before they actually are deployed. Rockets are propelled into orbit in a similar fashion. Behind all of it is mathematical calculation.

Now this same mathematical calculation, in the brilliant brain of Einstein, indicated that space and time change when trajectories move close to the speed of light. In fact anytime something moves, the speed of those objects changes the space through which it moves. The faster it moves, the more time slows down, and space condenses.

For most people, still today, this invention of Einstein is incomprehensible. It seems to contradict our daily experience. But Einstein had an explanation: at the speeds with which we move, the changes in space and time are so small that we cannot perceive them. Even in our mathematical calculations they are so small that they can be neglected as classical, Newtonian physics did. And that is why Newtonian physics by and large still works when applied to processes here on earth. But as we develop projectiles that move faster and faster, we have to take these subtle changes into account. And, once we try to calculate the speed of light itself, we need to know the rules of **Einstein's Theory of Relativity.**

Anything or anyone who falls through the event horizon will soon reach the region of infinite density and the end of time.

– Stephen Hawking

Einstein's insight, that space curves in the vicinity of large moving objects was actually confirmed when astronomers in 1917 observed the light of a distant star being bent around the sun during a full eclipse. This proved that the speed of light had a profound impact on space.

A second implication resulted from Einstein's calculations. His formulas suggested, that in some areas of the universe there could be odd structures in which all the known laws of the universe cease to exist. This phenomenon became known as a black hole. Black holes, too, were ultimately experimentally confirmed.

Why are black holes important to the topic of this introductory philosophy book on partnership and domination? Black holes were proof that the so called universal laws of nature are not as universal as we first thought. This is an important implication of Einstein's Theory of Relativity. Since moral laws took their universality by referring to natural laws, the whole argument was now undermined. The Deists believed that God had created nature following an eternal and universal set of rules. If nature was constructed in that way, the rules of human conduct could be seen in a similar way. There was a set of logical, rational rules that each individual could follow and would have to follow if one wanted to consider oneself rational. But if the natural law was not quite universal and allowed for exceptions, then perhaps moral law was similarly not universal and open to exceptions.

In a nineteenth century story called "The Dream of a Ridiculous Man," by Fyodor Dostoyevsky, the hero looks at a distant planet and wonders out loud, if a murder committed out there would also be a sin, and if suffering would be considered suffering in that distant place of the universe.

■ 16. DEMOCRITUS, THE FOUNDATION FOR ATOMISM

In Denmark, there is a place called Legoland, where whole cities are made out of legos. Legoland is a world made of tiny plastic blocks. Mr. Lego, who invented the world famous lego blocks, was a creative mind and a philosopher. He wanted people to be able to imagine what a world that is made up of tiny little block of material, just like the real world we live in would look like. So he invented lego blocks as the atoms of his imaginary world. Today most children have played with lego blocks and have built fantastic structure.

Ancient philosophers pondered many kinds of questions, some connected to things in the real world, others to questions of a logical nature. Let's try to define the difference between these two types of questions.

One early philosopher, Zeno, for instance, pondered this famous problem: If one wants to get from point **a** to point **b**, one first has to get through half of that space, to a point exactly half way between **a** and **b**. But to get to that point one needs to get to the new halfway point.

The new line can again be divided into half and so on and so on. You guessed it: there are infinitely many points between **a** and **a** that one would have to reach first before one can get to point **b**, a seemingly impossible task. This is a problem obviously in logic only. In reality one simply walks from **a** to **b** and forgets about all the infinite points in between.

Zeno's paradox is indeed puzzling to the mind, but reality does not seem to pose the same problem. The philosopher Democritus saw a different problem when dividing a spatial distance. Legend has it that he explained the smallest particles of space like this: when one divides a piece of cheese into ever smaller pieces, one will eventually come to a point when the last piece is too small to divide any further. The knife is simply not sharp enough. Democritus called this final piece an atom, which is Greek for indivisible. According to Democritus, nature is a composition of such smallest building blocks or atoms. The world is constructed in a similar way Mr. Lego had envisioned his Legoland.

Fast-forward to the beginning of the Twentieth Century. Scientist still believed that the smallest particles of the material world were atoms, just as Democritus had proposed. Of course, they knew by now that these smallest particles were much, much smaller than a piece of cheese. Actually they knew that a piece of cheese contained many trillion atoms. This is how small an atom is. One way to visualize this is to imagine the whole earth as being the last little piece of cheese that a knife can't cut any smaller. An atom, of course, is in reality immensely much smaller than Democritus had envisioned. Democritus' piece of cheese would be the size of the earth in comparison to the real atom.

Given this reality, it is easy to imagine how hard it was for scientists to develop tools that can probe into the world of these tiny little atoms.

In *A Brief History of Time,* **Stephen Hawking** speculates about a space traveler approaching a black hole. The event horizon, the boundary of the region of space-time from which it is not possible to escape, acts rather like a one way membrane around the black hole. Objects, such as unwary astronauts, can fall through the event horizon into the black hole, but nothing can ever get out of the black hole through the event horizon.

Remember that the event horizon is the path in space-time of light trying to escape from the black hole, and that nothing can travel faster than light.

One should well say of the event horizon what the poet Dante said of the entrance to Hell, "All hope abandon, ye who enter here." Anything or anyone who falls through the event horizon will soon reach the region of infinite density and the end of time.

■ 17. WHY IS ATOMISM IMPORTANT IN OUR DISCUSSION ABOUT DOMINATION?

For much of Western development, atomism had little impact. Most philosophers followed the idealistic views of Plato and Aristotle. While atomism claimed that the smallest building blocks of the world are tiny material objects, those two Greek philosophers claimed that what really matters is ideas. One may also call the primary substance spirit, soul, or mind. The message spread by the Bible supported this idea: In the beginning there was a powerful spirit, which in Christian Judeo belief is called God.

Atomism became important when science began to take hold. Science is based on a philosophy called materialism. Materialism states that everything began with matter, and everything, including consciousness, emerged from the material world.

Toward the end of the Middle Ages people began rejecting, more and more, the influence and power of the Church. This rejection of religious authority was often combined with a trust in scientific inquiry. Through careful experimentation, science often proved that the old ideas propagated by the church were wrong. It was this trust in the ability to prove things by experimentation that made a belief in atomism and materialism so appealing. Spiritual ideas, however, were hard to prove using the tools of science. If the whole world were composed of tiny Lego blocks without any discernable ordering principle, perhaps it would be easier to make sense of it.

In some ways perhaps this new trust in science and the material world went far overboard. There are some philosophers today who would look at science as just another type of faith. Science, too, has underlying principles, that are not questioned. But all in all, the scientific method is still a more reliable method for ascertaining truth and sometimes, when truth cannot be established, science at least can show us, which beliefs are false.

As we learned earlier, much support for domination came from traditional science or Newtonian science. During the nineteenth century, another area of science, biology, also developed support for relentless domination. Charles Darwin proposed the theory that in nature, at least in principle, domination rules. Change in nature happens as a result of the survival of the fittest. For the social interpreters of Darwin's ideas this meant that nature is a giant arena of one species dominating the other, all in the name of progress and survival. Today some scientists believe that Darwin did not really intend to be so lopsided in favor of domination, but rather used cooperation, love, and compassion to explain many biological processes, especially when he talked about human development and the evolution of culture. Nevertheless, his theories of domination and survival of the fittest became standard scientific thinking during the Nineteenth and most of the Twentieth Century.

Thus theories of atomism and materialism are important concepts in understanding the development of modern science and its intricate connection with the evolution of the modern dominator culture.

■ 18. PYTHAGORAS AND THE PYTHAGOREANS

Pythagoras and the Pythagoreans are important for several reasons. As an ancient mathematician, Pythagoras had a tremendous influence on the development of science. The theorems he developed are still taught and memorized by millions of young people around the world. His unwavering belief that the fundamental structure of all reality consists of numbers and relationships may still prove to be a prophetic insight.

As always we must ask the question: What is the importance of Pythagoras and his philosophy for the topic of this book, domination and partnership?

As a philosopher Pythagoras marks a cultural transition. He represents a link to the early egalitarian history of humanity when truth was based on experience. In prehistoric times truth was the result of ritual practice, which often utilized insights gained from altered states of mind. Pythagoras had much in common with those ancient ways, believing that philosophical activity was purifying just like a religious ritual might be. Few philosophers would have believed this at any later time. This experiential aspect of truth was reminiscent of the ancient ways of finding truth. It is preserved today in religious and spiritual experiences of the divine. As a philosopher in transition, Pythagoras perhaps realized the shortcomings and problems of that kind of experiential truth. Such truth was difficult to communicate often taking a lifetime of practice.

Mathematical and logical truth in contrast was easy to communicate. Everyone with a clear and logical mind could understand the truth of a mathematical thorem. Provided then that the universe was arranged in a mathematical way everything in the universe made sense. This new philosophical way of thinking could provide access to truth for everyone.

One of Pythagoras' central beliefs was that the universe was composed of mathematics, or more precisely, of numerical relations that could be expressed in sounds. Some of his followers believed that their master could hear the music of the spheres. This might have been a different way to express the state of deep meditation which Pythagoras undoubtedly had learned in his travels. Walking by a blacksmith shop, Pythagoras is said to have observed the different sounds made when the smith banged his hammer against the metal rods.

Pythagoras realized that there was a harmonious relationship between the length of a piece of metal and the sounds it produces. From this observation he developed his ideas about musical harmony that are still valid today.

Sensing the importance of balance and logic was perhaps behind Pythagoras' refusal to accept the possibility of irrational number relations in the universe. Legend has it that Pythagoras was on a boat ride on the Mediterranean when one of his disciples challenged the master with the question: "What is the square root of the number two?" Pythagoras of course eventually realized that there was no rational answer to this simple but tantalizing conundrum. But refusing to admit defeat, he supposedly pushed the man over board and drowned him. It took humanity more than eight hundred years to raise again the question about irrational numbers.

Still today, Pythagoras' influence on the development of mathematics and science is unquestioned. Physicists look back at Pythagoras and recognize his influence. In fact, the question whether numbers are not indeed at the basis of all reality is considered again in all seriousness. Einstein had deep insights when he said that, "God was beautiful mathematics." Many Muslim artists and mathematicians, who were not allowed to express their visions of Allah in pictures, did so in mathematical and geometrical forms. Go into a mosque in the Middle East and admire the gorgeous decorations on the walls, often made out of mosaic tiles. These images were often not just playful decorations, but deep speculations about the secrets of the universe.

Many scholars believe that Pythagoras might have traveled in his youth to India. Here he would have come in touch with Hindu philosophy and early Buddhist teachings. This might also have caused his belief that society is divided into three groups, a division later used by Plato.

During his early travels Pythagoras was also introduced to several ancient ritualistic practices, which in many cases continued the reverence to the great mother Goddess and other earth centered spirits in secrecy. The Pythagoreans thus represents a transitional community form in some ways still practicing an egalitarian life style. Women and men were equally admitted to become members. Like the ancient Hindus the Pythagoreans were vegetarians and believed in reincarnation.

Knowledge for the Pythagoreans was an intellectual pursuit and as it was the result of ritual experience. The activities in the Pythagorean community thus were a mixture of religious exercises, meditative practices to purify the mind, and intellectual discussions. Followers of Pythagoras who wanted to become members of his school had to pass a three year waiting period. They then could enter an outer order or cycle. At that first level members were allowed to keep their possessions and did not yet have to become vegetarians. The second circle, or inner order, required a more ascetic way of life. These people lived permanently within the society, had to renounce all possessions, and had to become vegetarians.

Within that inner society there was a still more select inner circle, which was called *electi*. This highly secretive group of people was instructed in the occult rituals of the Great Mystery Schools of antiquity. They learned the process of psychic transmutation, and they learned how to use different sounds to heal people.

■ 19. THE SOPHISTS

We often imagine that Greek philosophers pursued a solitary quest for truth. We know them as isolated seekers, submersed in their own thoughts, or leaders of semi-religious communities shrouded in secrecy, far from the bustle of public

---

PYTHAGORAS TEACHINGS IN A NUTSHELL:

- all reality is mathematical in nature,

- philosophy is useful as spiritual purification,

- souls transmigrate and can live in union with the divine,

- numbers and symbols have a mystical significance,

- members of the community should be loyal to each other and protect the secrets of the group.

life. In a single minded pursuit they struggled to extract the last secrets of nature and understand the riddles of the gods.

But there was another group of seekers, much more involved in public life, and to some extent, almost modern in their beliefs. This group has become known as the sophists. They were teachers who trained young people for political positions and for public life. As Greek society became increasingly more organized, these sophists became more and more influential.

In contrast to main stream philosophers, the sophists, being firmly grounded in daily life, had no esoteric notion of truth. They believed in their own abilities more than in any divine laws imbedded in nature. What they knew best and could teach best could be described as a technique rather than a lofty idea. Truth, for the sophists, was like a commodity that could be acquired and learned, and they charged a fee for their services. They knew that a good teacher was valuable and should be paid well. They knew how to use words in their favor and make an argument look right. All one needed to be successful was to be an eloquent speaker.

The sophists taught mostly speech or **rhetoric**, as it was called. Their philosophy was quite simple: Man is the measure of all things. If truth does exist, it could not be communicated: but most probably there is no such thing as truth. What we believe to be truth, is a historical construction. Those who have power in history have always promoted, and succeeded in convincing others, of the truth of their argument. What really exists is interests and power. You can easily understand why many people today can identify with the sophists' point of view.

Today we still use the word **sophisticated** to describe a person who is refined in manner and style, but relatively hollow inside. The sophists, especially during the time of Plato and Aristotle, were even aware of the emptiness of their arguments. Since truth was not attainable, one could defend any point of view. The only thing that made a difference in the end was how well one could present a case. In this game the sophists were quite clever, purposefully aiming to confuse the opponent. They had one goal in mind: win and get ahead.

A contemporary American philosopher, Richard Rorty, quite famously called truth a mere party game. Needless to say, the sophists had many followers. Their cynical philosophy has perhaps become one of the most successful models of all times. Sadly enough it most often is used to defend the dominator ideology.

■ 20. PARTNERSHIP TO THE RESCUE: CO-CREATING A VISION FOR THE FUTURE OF HUMANITY

Under the dominator system, we are socialized from childhood to accept domination as the natural law. Greek dualism located the origin of reason and mind in the Absolute. For Greek philosophers, the divine craftsman was the highest principle of order. Since God had created this world in a logical manner, wherever logic was missing or not evident, it was the result of mistakes made by lower gods or a case of absence of order. The ancient Greeks believed they could discover logic within things. Wherever it was lacking, human beings had the duty to supply it. Hence, human beings were called upon to supply order to the world. This mission to create ordering became the cornerstone of early Christianity. The Hebrew story in the

Biblical book of Genesis asserted this dominator prototype as well. A thousand years later, science also claimed to be the expression of an ordering mind that dominated nature. Again and again from Aristotle to Hume, philosophers equated the logical mind with masculinity. For this reason, modern feminism has rightly put into question the very core of Western philosophy, which is characterized by an insistence on objectivity and reason.

The dominator model, which is currently practiced in virtually all civilizations around the world, requires a huge amount of violence to maintain itself. A dominator society is characterized by rigid, top-down control, with unyielding domination by the male half of humanity over the female half of humanity. There are also other kinds of domination in society: for example, that of masters over slaves, as in ancient Greece; race over race, as in fascist Germany; and human beings over nature, as in traditional Western science. This type of organization, according to Riane Eisler, requires a high level of built-in violence in order to maintain hierarchical rankings. An unimaginable amount of wife beating and child beating is often used to enforce the husband's superiority in the family; and on a global scale, chronic warfare is used to establish the superiority of one nation over another.

Minoan Goddess
© 2006 JupiterImages Corporation

In her ground breaking book *The Chalice and the Blade*, Riane Eisler developed a picture of the world organized along the lines of a partnership model. In her vision of a future world, Eisler boldly projects the spread of such a model but only if enough people around the globe will join the partnership movement.

In this partnership future, we will find a more democratic and equitable social organization of all aspects of life, both on the large scale and on the small, individual scale. As such, an equal partnership will finally exist between male and female, the two halves of humanity. In such a society, people will no longer require built-in violence in order to maintain rigid, hierarchical ranking in society.

In the world of today, there is no society that completely orients itself toward partnership on one hand or outright violent domination on the other. Most societies are a mixture of both models. Fascist societies as one extreme utilize a high degree of violence to maintain their superiority and often defend violence as a legitimate method for solving problems. Democracies tend to prefer negotiation and other peaceful means in order to resolve conflicts. In any case, the degree to which societies tend toward domination molds all human relationships within the society, from intimate to international, and all social institutions, from the family, to education and religion, and politics and economics.

- Societies oriented toward the dominator model justify this form of organization with their own beliefs, stories, and myths. For example, these societies may worship a punitive, supreme god who is said to be the final judge of an inherently sinful humanity that must be controlled from the top down.

- Societies oriented more toward the partnership model have different beliefs, stories and myths. Such societies emphasize mutual respect, caring, and creativity and give equal value to women and femininity and men and masculinity.

21

To the careful observer of human beings, it is clear that humans have the potential both for caring and cruelty, non-violence and violence, or mutual respect and insensitive control. In projecting humanity's course into the future, now is the time to make a clear stand. Instead of focusing on cruelty, violence, and destruction, our educational systems, from the family to the schools, must once again emphasize the human qualities of caring and creativity over violence and domination. During periods of extreme disequilibrium such as ours, human beings can turn chance into choice.

The new values of partnership-living will include intuitive thinking and a spiritual relationship with nature as partner. Even science can be practiced in an empathic way, rather than in a domineering way. Rather than finding power in our ability to dominate others, we must find power in affiliation with others and in the empowerment of others. In a well-functioning family, members link with each other and develop a strong sense of solidarity. Such a family allows all of its members to advance themselves, without limiting the ability of each other.

In contrast to the dominator model, which sees love as a complete loss of self, in the partnership model love can be agape or selfless love. This is the kind of love a truly loving mother has for her child, similar to the divine love of the Great Mother for her human children. In contrast to the symbol of the dominator god, the goddess returns as a symbol of spiritual transformation and of birth and the celebration of life. The goddess, of course, embodies stereotypically feminine qualities, such as caring and nurturing

Eisler must be credited with turning the ethical principles of partnership into a new model for politics and economics, in which both women and men can identify their own humanity with the values of caring and nurturing. Once these stereotypically feminine values are universally accepted and asserted as core values, they will bring about a social ethos that will reshape our relationship to the natural world and will redirect the use of natural resources. It will not be an ideal world, but in this new world, human beings will balance competition – now the highest value in the dominator world – with a new sense of care and cooperation. Love and care will eventually counteract the unyielding individualism so characteristic of our times as well as the repressiveness of earlier cultures where conformity was brutally imposed. Human beings will overcome a relentless conquest of nature and will learn again to live in harmony with nature. Global cooperation will evolve as a free partnership between peoples. And satisfactory emotional relationships will replace our cultural obsession with taking, buying, building, wasting, and discarding things.

In the current dual economy, care-giving work, so stereotypically associated with women, is generally nearly invisible. A shared economy, in which the sexes are equal in position, will eventually replace it. This new economy will no longer underpay and thereby alienate the labor of caring and helping. Machines and computers will be used to assist in minimizing alienating labor and repetitive tasks.

Eisler predicts that this truly monumental transformation will bring out the best in people. As a result, a new, human striving for truth, beauty, and justice will ensue. Instead of creating another utopia, humanity will evolve as the co-creator of what Eisler has called a pragmatopia.

Instead of creating an insubstantial utopia, this new world will enact a quite practical scenario built on the principles of partnership.

- It will finally be possible for humanity to live free of the fear of war and global destruction. Neither war between nations nor the war of the sexes will be built-in, as they are in the dominator model.

- We will be able to bring the birthrate in balance with available resources, as women will have reproductive freedom and access to equal education and work.

- We will develop rational measures to reduce hunger and poverty as women and children are no longer, as they are today, the mass of the world's poor and the poorest of the poor.

- As the result of fundamental psychic changes, people will fully accept cultural diversity and will celebrate it.

- Having learned to find happiness within themselves and within their relationships with others, people will no longer need to rely on the production and consumption of things as a primary source of wish fulfillment and happiness.

Tremendous social and technological breakthroughs will accompany this new age of cooperation.

- For example, corporations will allow for greater worker participation and offer paid parental leave, childcare and other ways for people to balance work and family.

- Hierarchies of actualization, where accountability, respect, and benefits flow both ways rather than just from the bottom up, as they do in hierarchies of domination, will become the norm in families, governments and business organizations.

- Mutual companionship, sexual pleasure, and love will be the primary purpose of human bonding.

- Societies will allow for diverse models of caring relationships and no longer insist on the traditional, heterosexual model as the only one sanctioned by law.

- This new society, based on the principles of partnership, will put its greatest emphasis back again on the human child.

- Public education will include good nutrition, combined with both physical and mental exercises.

- Instead of relying on largely competitive sports, schools will teach advanced yoga and meditation as a standard part of their curriculum.

- Learning itself will become a lifelong process. This will fully maximize human flexibility and insure creativity at all stages of life.

CHAPTER II: THE GREEK MASTERS

■ 1. FROM PLATO'S APOLOGY

Instead of reading the following original text by Plato, you may also watch the movie: Man and State, The Trial of Socrates, from the famous Encyclopedia Britannica film series. The film quite authentically portrays Socrates in his final hours and gives most of the words spoken by him and his friends, as written down by his student Plato who was a mere 18 years old when his beloved master died.

Before proceeding, answer the questions on Socrates in the ACTIVITIES BOOK.

How You, O Athenians, have been affected by my accusers, I cannot tell; but I know that they almost made me forget who I was — so persuasively did they speak; and yet they have hardly uttered a word of truth. But of the many falsehoods told by them, there was one which quite amazed me; — I mean when they said that you should be upon your guard and not allow yourselves to be deceived by the force of my eloquence. To say this, when they were certain to be detected as soon as I opened my lips and proved myself to be anything but a great speaker, did indeed appear to me most shameless — unless by the force of eloquence they mean the force of truth; for if such is their meaning, I admit that I am eloquent. But in how different a way from theirs! Well, as I was saying, they have scarcely spoken the truth at all; but from me you shall hear the whole truth: not, however, delivered after their manner in a set oration duly ornamented with words and phrases. No, by heaven! but I shall use the words and arguments which occur to me at the moment; for I am confident in the justice of my cause: at my time of life I ought not to be appearing before you, 0 men of Athens, in the character of a juvenile orator — let no one expect it of me. And I must beg of you to grant me a favor: — If I defend myself in my accus-

tomed manner, and you hear me using the words which I have been in the habit of using in the [market], at the tables of the moneychangers, or anywhere else, I would ask you not to be surprised, and not to interrupt me on this account. For I am more than seventy years of age, and appearing now for the first time in a court of law, I am quite a stranger to the language of the place; and therefore I would have you regard me as if I were really a stranger, whom you would excuse if he spoke in his native tongue, and after the fashion of his country: — Am I making an unfair request of you? Never mind the manner, which may or may not be good; but think only of the truth of my words, and give heed to that: let the speaker speak truly and the judge decide justly.

Well, then, I must make my defense, and endeavor to clear away in a short time, a slander which has lasted a long time. May I succeed, if to succeed be for my good and yours, or likely to avail me in my cause! The task is not an easy one; I quite understand the nature of it. And so leaving the event with God, in obedience to the law I will now make my defense.

I will begin at the beginning, and ask what is the accusation which has given rise to the slander of me, and in fact has encouraged Meletus to prefer this charge against me.

Well, what do the slanderers say? They shall be my prosecutors, and I will sum up their words in an affidavit: 'Socrates is an evildoer, and a curious person, who searches into things under the earth and in heaven, and he makes the worse appear the better cause; and he teaches the aforesaid doctrines to others.' Such is the nature of the accusation: it is just what you have yourselves seen in the comedy of Aristophanes, who has introduced a man whom he calls Socrates, going about and saying that he walks in air, and talking a deal of nonsense concerning matters of which I do not pretend to know either much or little — not that I mean to speak disparagingly of any one who is a student of natural philosophy. I should be very sorry if *Meletus* could bring so grave a charge against me. But the simple truth is, 0 Athenians, that I have nothing to do with physical speculations. Very many of those here present are witnesses to the truth of this, and to them I appeal. Speak then, you who have heard me, and tell your neighbors whether any of you have ever known me hold forth in few words or in many upon such matters. . . . You hear their answer. And from what they say of this part of the charge you will be able to judge of the truth of the rest.

As little foundation is there for the report that I am a teacher, and take money; this accusation has no more truth in it than the other. Although, if a man were really able to instruct mankind, to receive money for giving instruction would, in my opinion, be an honor to him. There is *Gorgias of Leontium,* and *Prodicus of Ceos* and *Hippias of Elis* who go the round of the cities, and are able to persuade the young men to leave their own citizens by whom they might be taught for nothing, and come to them whom they not only pay, but are thankful if they may be allowed to pay them. I dare say, Athenians,

that some one among you will reply, 'Yes, Socrates, but what is the origin of these accusations which are brought against you; there must have been something strange which you have been doing? All these rumors and this talk about you would never have arisen if you had been like other men: tell us, then, what is the cause of them, for we should be sorry to judge hastily of you.' Now I regard this as a fair challenge, and I will endeavor to explain to you the reason why I am called wise and have such an evil fame. Please to attend then. And although some of you may think that I am joking, I declare that I will tell you the entire truth. Men of Athens, this reputation of mine has come of a certain sort of wisdom which I possess. If you ask me what kind of wisdom, I reply, wisdom such as may perhaps be attained by man, for to that extent I am inclined to believe that I am wise; whereas the persons of whom I was speaking have a superhuman wisdom, which I may fail to describe, because I have it not myself; and he who says that I have, speaks falsely, and is taking away my character. And here, 0 men of Athens, I must beg you not to interrupt me, even if I seem to say something extravagant. For the word which I will speak is not mine. I will refer you to a witness who is worthy of credit; that witness shall be the God of Delphi—he will tell you about my wisdom, if I have any, and of what sort it is. You must have known *Chaerephon;* he was early a friend of mine, and also a friend of yours, for he shared in the recent exile of the people, and returned with you. Well, *Chaerephon,* as you know, was very impetuous in all his doings, and he went to Delphi and boldly asked the oracle to tell him whether— as I was saying, I must beg you not to interrupt — he asked the oracle to tell him whether any one was wiser than I was, and the *Pythian* prophetess answered, that there was no man wiser. *Chaerephon* is dead himself; but his brother, who is in court, will confirm the truth of what I am saying.

Why do I mention this? Because I am going to explain to you why I have such an evil name. When I heard the answer, I said to myself, What can the god mean? and what is the interpretation of his riddle? for I know that I have no wisdom, small or great. What then can he mean when he says that I am the wisest of men? And yet he is a god, and cannot lie; that would be against his nature. After long consideration, I thought of a method of trying the question. I reflected that if I could only find a man wiser than myself, then I might go to the god with a refutation in my hand. I should say to him, 'Here is a man who is wiser than I am; but you said that I was the wisest.' Accordingly I went to one who had the reputation of wisdom, and observed him — his name I need not mention; he was a politician whom I selected for examination — and the result was as follows: When I began to talk with him, I could not help thinking that he was not really wise, although he was thought wise by many, and still wiser by himself; and thereupon I tried to explain to him that he thought himself wise, but was not really wise; and the consequence was that he hated me, and his enmity was shared by several who were present and heard me. So I left him, saying to myself, as I went away: Well, although I do not suppose that either of us knows anything really beautiful and good, I am better off than he is—for he knows nothing, and thinks that he knows; I neither know nor think that I know. In this latter particular, then, I seem to have slightly the advantage of him. Then I went to another who had still higher pretensions to wisdom, and my conclusion was exactly the same. Whereupon I made another enemy of him, and of many others besides him.

Then I went to one man after another, being not unconscious of the enmity which I provoked, and I lamented and feared this: But necessity was laid upon me, — the word of God, I thought, ought to be considered first. And I said to myself, Go I must to all who appear to know, and find out the meaning of the oracle. And I swear to you, Athenians, by the dog I swear! — for I must tell you the truth — the result of my mission was just this: I found that the men most in repute were all but the most foolish; and that others less esteemed were really wiser and better. I will tell you the tale of my wanderings and of the 'Herculean' labors, as I may call them, which I endured only to find at last the oracle irrefutable. After the politicians, I went to the poets; tragic, dithyrambic, and all sorts. And there, I said to myself, you will be instantly detected; now you will find out that you are more ignorant than they are. Accordingly, I took them some of the most elaborate passages in their own writings, and asked what was the meaning of them — thinking that they would teach me something. Will you believe me? I am almost ashamed to confess the truth, but I must say that there is hardly a person present who would not have talked better about their poetry than they did themselves. Then I knew that not by wisdom do poets write poetry, but by a sort of genius and inspiration; they are like diviners or soothsayers who also say many fine things, but do not understand the meaning of them. The poets appeared to me to be much in the same case; and I further observed that upon the strength of their poetry they believed themselves to be the wisest of men in other things in which they were not wise. So I departed, conceiving myself to be superior to them for the same reason that I was superior to the politicians.

At last I went to the artisans, for I was conscious that I knew nothing at all, as I may say, and I was sure that they knew many fine

"I have concealed nothing, I have dissembled nothing. And yet, I know that my plainness of speech makes them hate me..."

– Plato

things; and here I was not mistaken, for they did know many things of which I was ignorant, and in this they certainly were wiser than I was. But I observed that even the good artisans fell into the same error as the poets; — because they were good workmen they thought that they also knew all sorts of high matters, and this defect in them overshadowed their wisdom; and therefore I asked myself on behalf of the oracle, whether I would like to be as I was, neither having their knowledge nor their ignorance, or like them in both; and I made answer to myself and to the oracle that I was better off as I was.

This inquisition has led to my having many enemies of the worst and most dangerous kind, and has given occasion also to many calumnies. And I am called wise, for my hearers always imagine that I myself possess the wisdom which I find wanting in others: but the truth is, 0 men of Athens, that God only is wise; and by his answer he intends to show that the wisdom of men is worth little or nothing; he is not speaking of Socrates, he is only using my name by way of illustration, as if he said, He, 0 men, is the wisest, who, like Socrates knows that his wisdom is in truth worth nothing. And so I go about the world, obedient to the god, and search and make enquiry into the wisdom of any one, whether citizen or stranger, who appears to be wise; and if he is not wise, then in vindication of the oracle I show him that he is not wise; and my occupation quite absorbs me, and I have no time to give either to any public matter of interest or to any concern of my own, but I am in utter poverty by reason of my devotion to the god.

There is another thing: — young men of the richer classes, who have not much to do, come about me of their own accord; they like to hear the pretenders examined, and they often imitate me, and proceed to examine others; there are plenty of persons, as they quickly discover, who think that they know something, but really know little or nothing; and then those who are examined by them instead of being angry with themselves are angry with me: This confounded Socrates, they say; this villainous misleader of youth! — and then if somebody asks them, Why, what evil does he practice or teach? they do not know, and cannot tell; but in order that they may not appear to be at a loss, they repeat the readymade charges which are used against all philosophers about teaching things up in the clouds and under the earth, and having no gods, and making the worse appear the better cause; for they do not like to confess that their pretense of knowledge has been detected — which is the truth; and as they are numerous and ambitious and energetic, and are drawn up in battle array and have persuasive tongues, they have filled your ears with their loud and inveterate calumnies. And this is the reason why my three accusers, *Meletus* and *Anyrus* and *Lycon*, have set upon me; Meletus, who has a quarrel with me on behalf of the poets; Anyrus, on behalf of the craftsmen and politicians; Lycon, on behalf of the rhetoricians: and as I said at the beginning, I cannot expect to get rid of such a mass of calumny all in a moment. And this, 0 men of Athens, is the truth and the whole truth; I have concealed nothing, I have dissembled nothing. And yet, I know that my plainness of speech makes them hate me, and what is their hatred but a proof that I am speaking the truth? — Hence has arisen the prejudice against me; and this is the reason of it, as you will find out either in this or in any future enquiry.

I have said enough in my defense against the

first class of my accusers; I turn to the second class. They are headed by Meletus, that good man and true lover of his country, as he calls himself. . . He says that I am a doer of evil, and corrupt the youth; but I say, 0 men of Athens, that Meletus is a doer of evil, in that he pretends to be in earnest when he is only in jest, and is so eager to bring men to trial from a pretended zeal and interest about matters in which he really never had the smallest interest. And the truth of this I will endeavor to prove to you.

Come hither, Meletus, *and let me ask a question of you.* You think a great deal about the improvement of youth?

Yes, I do.

Tell the judges, then, who is their improver; for you must know, as you have taken the pains to discover their corrupter, and are citing and accusing me before them. Speak, then, and tell the judges who their improver is. — Observe, Meletus, that you are silent, and have nothing to say. But is not this rather disgraceful, and a very considerable proof of what I was saying, that you have no interest in the matter? Speak up, friend, and tell us who their improver is.

The laws.

But that, my good sir, is not my meaning. I want to know who the person is, who, in the first place, knows the laws.

The judges, Socrates, who are present in court.

What, do you mean to say, Meletus, that they are able to instruct and improve youth?

Certainly they are.

What, all of them, or some only and not others?

All of them.

By the goddess Her_, that is good news! There are plenty of improvers, then. And what do you say of the audience, — do they improve them?

Yes, they do.

And the senators?

Yes, the senators improve them.

But perhaps the members of the assembly corrupt them? —or do they too improve them?

They improve them.

Then every Athenian improves and elevates them; all with the exception of myself; and I alone am their corrupter? Is that what you affirm?

That is what I stoutly affirm.

I am very unfortunate if you are right. But suppose I ask you a question: How about horses? Does one man do them harm and all the world good? Is not the exact opposite the truth? One man is able to do them good, or at least not many; — the trainer of horses, that is to say, does them good, and others who have to do with them rather injure them? Is not that true, Meletus, of horses, or of any other animals? Most assuredly it is; whether you and Anytus say yes or no. Happy indeed would be the condition of youth if they had one corrupter only, and all the rest of the world were their improvers. But you, Meletus, have sufficiently shown that you never had a thought about the young: your carelessness is seen in your not caring about the very things which you bring against me.

And now, Meletus, I will ask you another question — by Zeus I will: Which is better, to live among bad citizens, or among good ones? Answer, friend, I say; the question is one which may be easily answered. Do not the good do their neighbors good, and the bad do them evil?

Certainly.

And is there any one who would rather be injured than benefited by those who live with him? Answer, my good friend, the law requires you to answer — does any one like to be injured?

Certainly not.

And when you accuse me of corrupting and deteriorating the youth, do you allege that I corrupt them intentionally or unintentionally?

Intentionally, I say.

But you have just admitted that the good do their neighbors good, and evil do them evil. Now, is that a truth which your superior wisdom has recognized thus early in life, and am I, at my age, in such darkness and ignorance as not to know that if a man with whom I have to live is corrupted by me, I am very likely to be harmed by him; and yet I corrupt him, and intentionally, too — so you say, although neither I nor any other human being is ever likely to be convinced by you. But either I do not corrupt them, or I corrupt them unintentionally; and on either view of the case you lie. If my offence is unintentional, the law has no cognizance of unintentional offenses: you ought to have taken me privately, and warned and admonished me; for if I had been better advised, I should have left off doing what I only did unintentionally—no doubt I should; but you would have nothing to say to me and refused to teach me. And now you bring me up in this court, which is a place not of instruction, but of punishment.

It will be very clear to you, Athenians, as I was saying, that Meletus has no care at all, great or small, about the matter. But still I should like to know, Meletus, in what I am affirmed to corrupt the young. I suppose you mean, as I infer from your indictment, that I teach them not to acknowledge the gods which the state acknowledges, but some other new divinities or spiritual agencies in their stead. These are the lessons by which I corrupt the youth, as you say.

Yes, that I say emphatically.

Then, by the gods, Meletus, of whom we are speaking, tell me and the court, in somewhat plainer terms, what you mean! for I do not as yet understand whether you affirm that I teach other men to acknowledge some gods, and therefore that I do believe in gods, and am not an entire atheist — this you do not lay to my charge, — but only you say that they are not the same gods which the city recognizes — the charge is that they are different gods. Or, do you mean that I am an atheist simply, and a teacher of atheism?

I mean the latter — that you are a complete atheist.

What an extraordinary statement! Why do you think so, Meletus? Do you mean that I do not believe in the godhead of the sun or moon, like other men?

I assure you, judges, that he does not: for he says that the sun is stone, and the moon earth.

Friend Meletus, you think that you are accusing Anaxagoras: and you have but a bad opinion of the judges, if you fancy them illiterate to such a degree as not to know that these doctrines are found in the books of *Anaxagoras the Clazomenian,* which are full of them. And so, forsooth, the Youth are said to be taught them by Socrates, when there are not unfrequently exhibitions of them at the theatre (price of admission one drachma at the most); and they might pay their money, and laugh at Socrates if he pretends to father these extraordinary views. And so, Meletus, you really think that I do not believe in any god?

I swear by Zeus that you believe absolutely in none at all.

Nobody will believe you, Meletus, and I am pretty sure that you do not believe yourself. I cannot help thinking, men of Athens, that Meletus is reckless and impudent, and that he has written this indictment in a spirit of mere wantonness and youthful bravado. Has he not compounded a riddle, thinking to try me? He said to himself — I shall see whether the wise Socrates will discover my facetious contradiction, or whether I shall be able to deceive him and the rest of them. For he certainly does appear to me to contradict himself in the indictment as much as if he said that Socrates is guilty of not believing in the gods, and yet of believing in them — but this is not like a person who is in earnest.

I should like you, 0 men of Athens, to join me in examining what I conceive to be his inconsistency; and do you, Meletus, answer. And I must remind the audience of my request that they would not make a disturbance if I speak in my accustomed manner:

Did ever man, Meletus, believe in the existence of human things, and not of human beings? . . . I wish, men of Athens, that he would answer, and not be always trying to get up an interruption. Did ever any man believe in horsemanship, and not in horses? or in flute playing, and not in flute players? No, my friend; I will answer to you and to the court, as you refuse to answer for yourself. There is no man who ever did. But now

please to answer the next question: Can a man believe in spiritual and divine agencies, and not in spirits or demigods?

He cannot.

How lucky I am to have extracted that answer, by the assistance of the court! But then you swear in the indictment that I teach and believe in divine or spiritual agencies (new or old, no matter for that); at any rate, I believe in spiritual agencies, — so you say and swear in the affidavit; and yet if I believe in divine beings, how can I help believing in spirits or demigods; — must I not? To be sure I must; and therefore I may assume that your silence gives consent. Now what are spirits or demigods? are they not either gods or the sons of gods?

Certainly they are.

But this is what I call the facetious riddle invented by you: the demigods or spirits are gods, and you say first that I do not believe in gods, and then again that I do believe in gods; that is, if I believe in demigods. For if the demigods are the illegitimate sons of gods, whether by the nymphs or by any other mothers, of whom they are said to be the sons — what human being will ever believe that there are no gods if they are the sons of gods? You might as well affirm the existence of mules, and deny that of horses and asses. Such nonsense, Meletus, could only have been intended by you to make trial of me. You have put this into the indictment because you had nothing real of which to accuse me. But no one who has a particle of understanding will ever be convinced by you that the same men can believe in divine and superhuman things, and yet not believe that there are gods and demigods and heroes.

I have said enough in answer to the charge of Meletus: any elaborate defense is unnecessary; but I know only too well how many are the enmities which I have incurred, and this is what will be my destruction if I am destroyed; — not *Meletus,* nor yet *Anytus,* but the envy and detraction of the world, which has been the death of many good men, and will probably be the death of many more; there is no danger of my being the last of them.

Some one will say: And are you not ashamed, Socrates, of a course of life which is likely to bring you to an untimely end? To him I may fairly answer: There you are mistaken: a man who is good for anything ought not to calculate the chance of living or dying; he ought only to consider whether in doing anything he is doing right or wrong — acting the part of a good man or of a bad.

Strange, indeed, would be my conduct, 0 men of Athens, if I who, when I was ordered by the generals whom you chose to command me at *Potidaea* and *Amphipolis* and *Delium,* remained where they placed me, like any other man, facing death — if now, when, as I conceive and imagine, God orders me to fulfill the philosopher's mission of searching into myself and other men, I were to desert my post through fear of death, or any other fear; that would indeed be strange, and I might justly be arraigned in court for denying the existence of the gods, if I disobeyed the oracle because I was afraid of death, fancying that I was wise when I was not wise. For the fear of death is indeed the pretense of wisdom, and not real wisdom, being a pretense of knowing the unknown; and no one knows whether death, which men in their fear apprehend to be the greatest evil, may not be the greatest good. Is not this ignorance of a disgraceful sort, the ignorance which is the conceit that man knows what he does not know? And in this respect only I believe myself to differ from men in general, and

may perhaps claim to be wiser than they are: — that whereas I know but little of the world below, I do not suppose that I know: but I do know that injustice and disobedience to a better, whether God or man, is evil and dishonorable, and I will never fear or avoid a possible good rather than a certain evil. And therefore if you let me go now, and are not convinced by Anytus, who said that since I had been prosecuted I must be put to death — if you say to me, Socrates, this time we will not mind Anytus, and you shall be let off, but upon one condition, that you are not to enquire and speculate in this way any more, and that if you are caught doing so again you shall die; — if this was the condition on which you let me go, I should reply: Men of Athens, I honor and love you; but I shall obey God rather than you, and while I have life and strength I shall never cease from the practice and teaching of philosophy, exhorting every one whom I meet and saying to him after my manner: You, my friend, a citizen of the great and mighty and wise city of Athens, are you not ashamed of heaping up the greatest amount of money and honor and reputation, and caring so little about wisdom and truth and the greatest improvement of the soul which you never regard or heed at all? And if the person with whom I am arguing, says: Yes, but I do care; then I do not leave him or let him go at once; but I proceed to interrogate and examine and crossexamine him, and if I thank that he has no virtue in him, but only says that he has, I reproach him with undervaluing the greater, and overvaluing the less. And I shall repeat the same words to every one whom I meet, young and old, citizen and aliens but especially to the citizens, inasmuch as they are my brethren. For know that this is the command of God and I believe that no greater good has ever happened to the state than my service to the God. For I do nothing but go about persuading you old and young alike, not to take thought for your persons or your properties, but first and chiefly to care about the greatest improvement of the soul. I tell you that virtue is not given by money, but that from virtue comes money and every other good of man, public as well as private. This is my teaching, and if this is the doctrine which corrupts the youth, I am a mischievous person But if anyone says that this is not my teaching, he is speaking the untruth. Wherefore, O men of Athens I say to you, do as Anytus bids or not as Anytus bids, and either acquit me or not; but whichever you do, understand that I shall never alter my ways, not even if I have to die many times.

And now, Athenians, I am not going to argue for my own sake, as you may think, but for yours, that you may not sin against the God by condemning me, who am his gift to you. For if you kill me you will not easily find a successor to me, who, if I may use such a ludicrous figure of speech, am a sort of gadfly, given to the state by God; and the state is a great and noble steed who is tardy in his motions owing to his very size, and requires to be stirred into life. I am that gadfly which God has attached to the state, and all day long and in all places am always fastening upon you, arousing and persuading and reproaching you. You will not easily find another like me, and therefore I would advise you to spare me.

Perhaps it may seem strange to you that, though I go about giving this advice privately and meddling in others' affairs, yet I do not venture to come forward in the assembly and advise the state. You have often heard me speak of my reason for this, and in many places: it is that I have a certain divine sign, which is what Meletus has caricatured in his indictment. I have had it from childhood. It is a kind of voice which, whenever I hear it, always turns me back from something which I was going to do, but never urges me to act.

It is this which forbids me to take part in politics. And I think it does well to forbid me. For, Athenians, it is quite certain that, if I had attempted to take part in politics, I should have perished at once and long ago without doing any good either to you or to myself. And do not be indignant with me for telling the truth. There is no man who will preserve his life for long, either in Athens or elsewhere, if he firmly opposes the multitude, and tries to prevent the commission of much injustice and illegality in the state. He who would really fight for justice must do so as a private citizen, not as an officeholder, if he is to preserve his life, even for a short time.

I will prove to you that this is so by very strong evidence, not by mere words, but by what you value highly, actions. Listen then to what has happened to me, that you may know that there is no man who could make me consent to do wrong from the fear of death, but that I would perish at once rather than give way. What I am going to tell you may be a commonplace in the law court; nevertheless it is true. The only office that I ever held in the state, *Athenians*, was that of Senator. When you wished to try the ten generals who did not rescue their men after the battle of Arginusae, as a group, which was illegal, as you all came to think afterwards, the tribe *Antiochis,* to which I belong, held the presidency. On that occasion I alone of all the presidents opposed your illegal action and gave my vote against you. The speakers were ready to suspend me and arrest me; and you were clamoring against me, and crying out to me to submit. But I thought that I ought to face the danger, with law and justice on my side, rather than join with you in your unjust proposal, from fear of imprisonment or death. That was when the state was democratic. When the **oligarchy** came in, the Thirty sent for me, with four others, to the councilchamber, and ordered us to bring

33

Leon the Salaminian from Salamis, that they might put him to death. They were in the habit of frequently giving similar orders, to many others, wishing to implicate as many as possible in their crimes. But, then, I again proved, not by mere words, but by my actions, that, if I may speak bluntly, I do not care a straw for death; but that I do care very much indeed about not doing anything unjust or impious. That government with all its powers did not terrify me into doing anything unjust; but when we left the councilchamber, the other four went over to Salamis and brought Leon across to Athens; and I went home. And if the rule of the Thirty had not been destroyed soon afterwards, I should very likely have been put to death for what I did then. Many of you will be my witnesses in this matter.

Now do you think that I could have remained alive all these years if I had taken part in public affairs, and had always maintained the cause of justice like an honest man, and had held it a paramount duty, as it is, to do so? Certainly not, Athenians, nor could any other man. But throughout my whole life, both in private and in public, whenever I have had to take part in public affairs, you will find I have always been the same and have never yielded unjustly to anyone; no, not to those whom my enemies falsely assert to have been my pupils. But I was never anyone's teacher. I have never withheld myself from anyone, young or old, who was anxious to hear me discuss while I was making my investigation; neither do I discuss for payment, and refuse to discuss without payment. I am ready to ask questions of rich and poor alike, and if any man wishes to answer me, and then listen to what I have to say, he may.

I believe in the gods as no one of my accusers believes in them: and to you and to God I commit my cause to be decided as is best for you and for me.

[The vote is taken and he is found guilty by 281 votes to 220.]

There are many reasons why I am not grieved, O men of Athens, at the vote of condemnation. I expected it, and am only surprised that the votes are so nearly equal; for I had thought that the majority against me would have been far larger; but now, had thirty votes gone over to the other side, I should have been acquitted. And I may say, I think, that I have escaped Meletus. I may say more; for without the assistance of Anytus and Lycon, any one may see that he would not have had a fifth part of the votes, as the law requires, in which case he would have incurred a fine of a thousand drachmae.

And so he proposes death as the penalty. And what shall I propose on my part, O men of Athens? Clearly that which is my due. And what is my due? What return shall be made to the man who has never had the wit to be idle during his whole life; but has been careless of what the many care for — wealth, and family interests, and military offices, and speaking in the assembly, and magistracies, and plots, and parties. Reflecting that I was really too honest a man to be a politician and live, I did not go where I could do no good to you or to myself; but where I could do the greatest good privately to every one of you, thither I went, and sought to persuade every man among you that he must look to himself, and seek virtue and wisdom before he looks to his private interests, and look to the state before he looks to the interests of the state; and that this should be the order which he observes in all his actions. What shall be done to such an one? Doubtless some good thing, O men of Athens, if he has his reward; and the good should be of a kind suitable to him. What would be a reward suitable to a poor man who is your benefactor, and who desires leisure that he may instruct you? There can be no reward so fitting as maintenance in the Prytaneum, 0 men of Athens, a reward which he deserves far more than the citizen who has won the prize at Olympia in the horse or chariot race, whether the chariots were drawn by two horses or by many. For I am in want, and he has enough; and he only gives you the appearance of happiness, and I give you the reality. And if I am to estimate the penalty fairly, I should say that maintenance in the Prytaneum is the just return.

Perhaps you think that I am braving you in what I am saying now, as in what I said before about the tears and prayers. But this is not so. I speak rather because I am convinced that I never intentionally wronged any one, although I cannot convince you — the time has been too short; if there were a law at Athens, as there is in other cities, that a capital cause should not be decided in one day, then I believe that I should have convinced you. But I cannot in a moment refute great slanders; and, as I am convinced that I never wronged another, I will assuredly not wrong myself. I will not say of myself that I deserve any evil, or propose any penalty. Why should I? Because I am afraid of the penalty of death which Meletus proposes? When I do not know whether death is a good or an evil, why should I propose a penalty which would certainly be an evil? Shall I say imprisonment? And why should I live in prison, and be the slave of the magistrates of the year — of the Eleven? Or shall the penalty be a fine, and imprisonment until the fine is paid? There is the same objection. I should have to lie in prison, for money I have none, and cannot pay. And if I say exile (and this may possibly be the penalty which you will affix), I must indeed

be blinded by the love of life, if I am so irrational as to expect that when you, who are my own citizens, cannot endure my discourses and words, and have found them so grievous and odious that you will have no more of them, others are likely to endure me. No indeed, men of Athens, that is not very likely. And what a life should I lead, at my age, wandering from city to city, ever changing my place of exile, and always being driven out! For I am quite sure that wherever I go, there, as here, the young men will flock to me; and if I drive them away, their elders will drive me out at their request; and if I let them come, their fathers and friends will drive me out for their sakes.

Some one will say: Yes, Socrates, but cannot you hold your tongue, and then you may go into a foreign city, and no one will interfere with you? Now I have great difficulty in making you understand my answer to this. For if I tell you that to do as you say would be a disobedience to the God, and therefore that I cannot hold my tongue, you will not believe that I am serious; and if I say again that daily to discourse about virtue, and of those other things about which you hear me examining myself and others, is the greatest good of man, and that **the unexamined life is not worth living,** you are still less likely to believe me. Yet I say what is true, although a thing of which it is hard for me to persuade you. Also, I have never been accustomed to think that I deserve to suffer any harm. Had I money I might have estimated the offence at what I was able to pay, and not have been much the worse. But I have none, and therefore I must ask you to proportion the fine to my means. Well, perhaps I could afford a mina, and therefore I propose that penalty: Plato, Crito, Critobulus, and Apollodorus, my friends here, bid me say thirty minae, and they will be the sureties. Let thirty minae be the penalty; for which sum they will be ample security to you.

[2nd vote: The jury decides for the death penalty by a vote of 360 to 141.]

Not much time will be gained, O Athenians, in return for the evil name which you will get from the detractors of the city, who will say that you killed Socrates, a wise man; for they will call me wise, even although I am not wise, when they want to reproach you.
If you had waited a little while, your desire would have been fulfilled in the course of nature. For I am far advanced in years, as you may perceive, and not far from death. The difficulty, my friends, is not to avoid death, but to avoid unrighteousness; for that runs faster than death. I am old and move slowly, and the slower runner has overtaken me, and my accusers are keen and quick, and the faster runner, who is unrighteousness, has overtaken them. And now I depart hence condemned by you to suffer the penalty of death, — they too go their ways condemned by the truth to suffer the penalty of villainy and wrong; and I must abide by my award — let them abide by theirs. I suppose that these things may be regarded as fated, — and I think that they are well.

Friends, who would have acquitted me, I would like also to talk with you about the thing which has come to pass, while the magistrates are busy, and before I go to the place at which I must die. Stay then a little, for we may as well talk with one another while there is time. You are my friends, and I should like to show you the meaning of this event which has happened to me. O my judges — for you I may truly call judges — I should like to tell you of a wonderful circumstance. Hitherto the divine faculty of which the internal oracle is the source has constantly been in the habit of opposing me even about trifles, if I was going to make a slip or error in any matter; and now as you

see there has come upon me that which may be thought, and is generally believed to be, the last and worst evil. But the oracle made no sign of opposition, either when I was leaving my house in the morning, or when I was on my way to the court, or while I was speaking, at anything which I was going to say; and yet I have often been stopped in the middle of a speech, but now in nothing I either said or did touching the matter in hand has the oracle opposed me. What do I take to be the explanation of this silence? I will tell you. It is an intimation that what has happened to me is a good, and that those of us who think that death is an evil are in error. For the customary sign would surely have opposed me had I been going to evil and not to good.

Let us reflect in another way, and we shall see that there is great reason to hope that death is a good; for one of two things— either death is a state of nothingness and utter unconsciousness, or, as men say, there is a change and migration of the soul from this world to another. Now if you suppose that there is no consciousness, but a sleep like the sleep of him who is undisturbed even by dreams, death will be an unspeakable gain. For if a person were to select the night in which his sleep was undisturbed even by dreams, and were to compare with this the other days and nights of his life, and then were to tell us how many days and nights he had passed in the course of his life better and more pleasantly than this one, I think that any man, I will not say a private man, but even the great king will not find many such days or nights, when compared with the others. Now if death be of such a nature, I say that to die is gain; for eternity is then only a single night. But if death is the journey to another place, and there, as men say, all the dead abide, what good, O my friends and judges, can be greater than this? If indeed when the pilgrim arrives in the world below, he is delivered from the professors of justice in this world, and finds the true judges who are said to give judgment there, Minos and Rhadamanthus and Aeacus and Triptolemus, and other sons of God who were righteous in their own life, that pilgrimage will be worth making. What would not a man give if he might converse with Orpheus and Musaeus and Hesiod and Homer? Nay, if this be true, let me die again and again. I myself, too, shall have a wonderful interest in there meeting and conversing with Palamedes, and Ajax the son of Telamon, and any other ancient hero who has suffered death through an unjust judgment; and there will be no small pleasure, as I think, in comparing my own sufferings with theirs. Above all, I shall then be able to continue my search into true and false knowledge; as in this world, so also in the next; and I shall find out who is wise, and who pretends to be wise, and is not. What would not a man give, 0 judges, to be able to examine the leader of the great Trojan expedition; or Odysseus or Sisyphus, or numberless others, men and women too! What infinite delight would there be in conversing with them and asking them questions! In another world they do not put a man to death for asking questions: assuredly not. For besides being happier than we are, they will be immortal, if what is said is true.

Wherefore, 0 judges, be of good cheer about death, and know of a certainty, that no evil can happen to a good man, either in life or after death. He and his are not neglected by the gods; nor has my own approaching end happened by mere chance. But I see clearly that the time had arrived when it was better for me to die and be released from trouble; wherefore the oracle gave no sign. For which reason, also, I am not angry with my condemners, or with my accusers; they have done me no harm, although they did not mean to do me any good; and for this I may gently blame them.

Still I have a favor to ask of them. When my sons are grown up, I would ask you, 0 my friends, to punish them; and I would have you trouble them, as I have troubled you, if they seem to care about riches, or anything, more than about virtue; or if they pretend to be something when they are really nothing — then reprove them, as I have reproved you, for not caring about that for which they ought to care, and thinking that they are something when they are really nothing. And if you do this, both I and my sons will have received justice at your hands.

The hour of departure has arrived, and we go our ways — I to die, and you to live. Which is better God only knows.

2. SOCRATES, THE FATHER OF ALL PHILOSOPHERS (470 BCE – 347 BCE)

The American philosopher Alfred North Whitehead once said that all philosophy is only a footnote to Plato. I, for one, believe that the great Plato himself was only a footnote to his master Socrates. Ideally we philosophers should all try to emulate Socrates, not because he knew the truth, but because he consistently argued that a known truth is probably not the truth. That makes Socrates the proverbial **skeptic**. Although he never went as far as the sophists to say that there was no truth and that man is the ultimate measure of all things, he came pretty close to it. Socrates never gave up on the truth and ultimately paid for it with his life.

Socrates
(470 - 347 BCE)
© 2006 JupiterImages Corporation

Socrates' father was a sculptor and his mother, a midwife. He received some of his training from a woman called **Diotima of Mantineia**, who apparently was a priestess and a mystic. In *The Symposium,* Plato says that Socrates learned all about love from this mystical woman. Socrates was married and had three sons by his wife, the legendary Xanthippe. Having to deal with four typical males was perhaps the reason why Xanthippe ruled the house with an iron fist. Socrates himself was probably also not much help in the house, but preferred to be out in the market place where he was known for holding so called symposia. These symposia were a harmonious mixture of discussing important topics and getting drunk. Previously in his youth, Socrates had distinguished himself as a soldier, fighting in at least three famous battles.

Socrates is known for inventing a very special kind of philosophical dialogue which was later developed further by his student Plato. It is called the Socratic Method. This is a way of continuing to ask your opponent questions, until you convince your opponent that he – it was usually a male – could not be quite sure of anything, especially not of the ideas he set out to defend.

The Life and Death of Socrates

THE UNEXAMINED LIFE IS NOT WORTH LIVING !

SOCRATES TEACHES HIS ATHENS STUDENTS

SO, MR. BIG, TELL ME THE MEANING OF TRUTH AND JUSTICE, IF YOU CAN!

UMM... TRUTH IS WHAT IS, AND JUST-ICE IS THE PURSUIT OF TRUTH... MAYBE...

WELL, YOUR ANSWER HAS AT LEAST THREE BIG PROBLEMS, I'D SAY...

SOCRATES' FAVORITE HOBBY: EMBARASSING HIS STUDENT'S PARENTS, ATHENS' POWERFUL

THIS IS **NOT** WHAT I MEANT BY 'THE EXAMINED LIFE' !!!

SOCRATES ON TRIAL FOR ANNOYING ATHENS ELITES

One of his famous dialogues, called *Euthyphro,* was reported by Plato. Socrates tells the story of a master who takes his servant to court accusing him of impiety. Socrates succeeds in proving that the master himself had an insufficient concept of piety, one far too vague to convince a court to convict the servant of this crime.

What lesson may we learn from Socrates? In most human affairs we may ourselves be sure of certain truths, but we know nothing so well that we can expect others to come to the same conclusions that we have reached; nor can we feel justified in sitting in judgment over others who see things differently from us. Of course, if we always go around and tell people how stupid they are, we have a good chance of ending up like Socrates, who was accused of impiety and of corrupting the young people of Athens. You can easily understand why Socrates never believed for a moment that his accusers could ever succeed in convicting him of any crime because he felt himself to be so important and so right in his criticism. But when it comes to the truth, you should never underestimate hurt pride. Humility was not one of Socrates' virtues.

The Oracle of Delphi
© 2006 JupiterImages Corporation

Talking about virtues, Socrates promoted the virtues of piety, wisdom, temperance, and justice. Even though he often confessed his own ignorance, humility was not a special virtue that he espoused. A famous anecdote tells about Socrates going to the **Oracle of Delphi** where a priestess, put in an altered state of mind by inhaling fumes that came out of the ground, gave answers to the visitors' questions and advice on how to solve their problems. Her responses were believed to be inspired by the God Apollo. Socrates proceeded to ask the god who he believed to be the wisest of all men. Back came the answer: Socrates, Socrates is the wisest of all men. This puzzled Socrates, at least initially. He started interviewing all kinds of people, mostly politicians, to prove that they were wiser than he. But he found they all believed only in themselves and their superior knowledge, which Socrates, with the help of his Socratic method, could quickly prove wrong. Socrates finally came to realize that he was indeed the smartest man alive after all. Why? Because he knew of his own ignorance. Not much humility there, I should say.

This brings me to another issue I have with the old war hero: his famous saying that, "The unexamined life is not worth living."

Did Socrates really mean that? Did he really mean that the unexamined life is not worth living? This statement is probably one of Socrates' most often repeated phrases, repeated daily by millions of well-meaning philosophers around the world. But think about it for a moment. Who is Socrates to tell anybody that his or her life is not worth living? Isn't that one of the gravest and most damaging judgments anyone can make of another person? Did he really mean to say that; and how does this statement jive with his own Socratic method?

Alas, he did say it, and history has proved that people throughout the centuries took this statement exactly the way I was hoping he would not have meant it. Are you with me and do you get what I am talking about?

For two-thousand years, Western civilization, allegedly following the Greek philosophers, exacted this harsh judgment on the rest of the world. When Western explorers and conquerors came to Africa, they found a rich culture among the various tribes. But these people were different in one important way from Western people: they did not examine their lives in the same way Western people did. So Westerners called them barbarians and set out to "civilize" them. The same thing happened in the Americas.

You say this happened a long time ago in the past? Not so. Right here in America, children of Native Americans were taken away from their families and educated in white schools, mostly run by missionaries, as late as the early 1970s. How about that as an example of believing that one's own language, religion, and ways of doing things are culturally superior!

So keep this in mind: Socrates was a great guy. He taught us all to be critical of our own beliefs. His Socratic method is superb and still useful today. But perhaps not everybody needs it.

This is so important that I have decided to stay with the topic a while longer. I often ask my students if Mother Teresa could have benefited from the Socratic Method. You probably will have to come to the conclusion that she would not have. She was all she could be without skeptically analyzing her life for answers. And similarly I can think of some other cases. Self-doubt and analysis are not the most important cultural values. I believe happiness is near the top, but we will come back to that later.

The Socratic Method is often used to teach students how to think. This is of course a good thing. The Twentieth Century German philosopher Martin Heidegger once said that one of the most discouraging realities about people is that they still have not started to begin thinking. There is of course *thinking* and then there is *thinking*. What do we mean by thinking?

Critical thinking as a discipline is often taught as a sophisticated application of logical rules. Knowing and applying the rules of logic can only be the beginning of good thinking. Don't worry; we will deal with logic in more depth when we come to Aristotle. He invented most of those rules. The rules of logic are a little bit like good etiquette: you need to know social rules in order to occasionally transgress them graciously and not look like a fool. It's similar with the rules of logical thinking.

Of course we need to learn how to make correct logical inferences. But we cannot stop there. A person who always uses all the rules of logic correctly , is precisely the kind of person Socrates would have started to question with his Socratic Method. Today, we say that he would have deconstructed him (or her). Knowing and applying all the rules correctly does not make for a real or deep thinker. What Socrates wanted to teach us, I believe, was something more. Even at the deepest levels, our thoughts are only constructions of a world which first of all exists independently of our thoughts, out there, somewhere.

So when you think, "This time I've really got it, I've found the truth," don't be so sure. Listen to the deeper Socrates, not the one who is teaching you to follow rules; listen to the one who truly believed in the depth of his heart that all his knowledge was vain, and that included the knowledge of logic. Somehow I believe Socrates message was not dissimilar to the message of an unknown Buddhist monk who said, "When you meet the Buddha on the road, kill him." That, too, is a hard one to swallow, but think about it. In fact, keep it in your mind as you read this book, study philosophy, and walk through life on a path that is uniquely yours. believe that this is the ultimate wisdom or something close to it the best that philosophy c offer. The rest indeed may be only a footnote.

3. PLATO (427 BCE - 347 BCE)

Although Socrates may be thought of as a blue collar guy, the son of a working class family, Plato was distinctly upper class; he had wealthy parents and a good education. He didn't drive a BMW, but in today's world he probably would have. He lived from 427-347 BCE. Plato was only 18 years old when Socrates died. After Socrates' death, Plato had some study abroad experiences, mostly in Italy, where he studied with students of Pythagoras' school. This experience exerted a great influence on the young philosopher.

Plato
(427-347 BCE)
© 2006 JupiterImages Corporation

Remember that Pythagoras thought that the universe was made up of numbers. Mathematics was the basis not only for philosophy but also for nature. That was Plato's belief as well.

Plato demanded that everyone who wanted to become a philosopher first had to study several years of math. For good measure he also threw in a couple of years of mandatory military service. The first was good discipline for the mind; the second probably was meant not to lose sight of the need to serve people and your community.

Of course, Plato had great things in mind for his well trained philosophers. They, and only they, were the ones fit to run a country as king or president. Plato made no qualms about this: he preferred a king, but it had to be a philosopher king. He never thought for a moment that democracy would work. Remember, he was a well-to-do kid. You could also call him an elitist or someone who believes that only privileged people have the right to make important decisions. The average person is simply too dumb. Of course, he didn't quite say it that way, but wait and see.

A. THE ALLEGORY OF THE CAVE

An aunt of mine had Alzheimers and lived in a nursing home for the last years of her life. She saw the world around her as an assembly of television sets. My aunt had watched so much television that everything appeared to her as just another program on television. That is a good way to understand Plato's *Allegory of the Cave.*

Average, ordinary people, like you and me, Plato said, live in a state of constant illusion. They believe that what they see is actually real. OK, you say, here comes the crazy philosopher. Does a tree falling in the woods really make a sound when no one is listening? You know this as a real conversation stopper. No one in her right mind would lose sleep over this problem, right? Philosophy is for geeks.

But think for a moment. Plato, and for that matter most philosophers, are not alone. There are millions of Hindus and Buddhists in this world who believe quite similarly. For the

41

devout Hindu, the world as we know it is an illusion. Hindus call this **maya**. Once you have broken through this veil of illusion, you come closer to see the world the way it really is. These ideas developed in India around the same time that Plato had his great insights in Greece, and there is good indication that the two civilizations were already in communication with each other back then. Talk about a global world! Now you know what to say the next time someone insists globalization is a recent phenomenon, invented by McDonald's and MTV.

So here you are tethered to a high chair, staring day in and day out at this giant silver screen. You have no idea that there is a real world outside, with shopping malls and high-speed car races and amusement parks. All that you know of is your high-definition TV. It feeds you and breathes life into you, at least that's what you believe right now and it supplies you with all the goodies you need, like the shopping network channel. Why should you look for more?

Then someday someone not on TV screams into your ear so you can't miss it: "Hey buddy, there is a whole world out there you haven't seen yet. Get off the couch and come with me. Let's give the real world a spin." And off you go for a joy ride in his new, yellow Porsche. Now you know what life is all about or so you think.

Actually, if you were with Plato, you would have given that someone who tried to introduce you to the "real" world a good beating. Let's say it's your old friend Meinrad, whom you have known for a long time as one of the evil characters in a Saturday morning cartoon, on the TV of course. You have no clue how he made it off the screen, but somehow he got out into the world, and now he keeps screaming into your ear. You tell him that you are just fine the way you are. You don't want to change a thing.

"Listen, Buddy," Meinrad insists. "Remember those Miller Light ads? Remember how great the stuff looks and sounds when those pretty girls break open a can? Now tell me, don't you really want to taste the real thing? I'll promise you a high you can never imagine from watching the ads."

Now your friend's got your attention? Let's see for a moment where Plato goes with this? Your friend Meinrad, according to Plato's Allegory of the Cave, is one of the few lucky ones. He's made it off the screen and out of the cave and has seen the light. How he actually accomplished this we will see a little later. For now, just accept the fact: he is outside the cave and sees the way things really are. What is he about to see?

First of all, he is blinded by the light. You thought the images on your HD TV screen were pretty crisp? Wait till you see the real thing. It's a thousand times brighter, more brilliant and breathtaking, so much so that initially your friend Meinrad is simply dumfounded. You know the song: "Blinded by the light." Once Meinrad catches his breath and has a chance to look around, he can't wait to get back into the den and tell his drinking buddies, including you of course, about the incredible things he is seeing. Meinrad is bubbling over. He is bragging, he is boasting. He is so convinced that you all are going to run right out with him and get in on the act.

Nothing like it. You guys are turned off, to say it mildly. Having all you need right in front of you, why should you want to get up and do something, right? Let's be honest: there is a certain satisfaction in it, just sitting on the sofa and doing nothing, just slurping a beer. But Meinrad insists. He keeps nagging you.

Well, according to Plato, the guy who came back from the real world got so obnoxious that the couch potatoes ended up beating the crap out of him. That's what happens when you are so far above the rest. It might be a no-brainer for you, but the rest, well, they just won't put up with you. So you have two choices: get yourself beaten up or keep your wisdom to yourself. Of course when you think you know the real truth, it's darn hard to keep it to yourself, isn't it? So you keep going on preaching the gospel, until someone comes along and puts you up on the cross.

That's certainly not what Meinrad had in mind; but listen up, all you zealous preachers, pay attention to old Plato. He will let you know that he told you so. Do you get the feeling that Plato really had his old master Socrates in mind? Young Plato must have thought many a time, why didn't Socrates shut up for a while and stop nagging everybody? The Athenians would certainly not have put him to death, would they?

PLATO'S CONCEPT OF THE SOUL & HOW IT RELATES TO SOCIETY		
ONTOLOGY	VIRTUE	STRATIFICATION
REASON	WISDOM	LEADERS/PHILOSOPHERS
SPIRIT	COURAGE	SOLDIERS/GUARDIANS
APPETITE	TEMPERANCE	COMMON PEOPLE

From this Plato developed the idea of the **Philosopher King.**

While Socrates kept sort of quiet about what he believed the truth was, Plato was just the opposite. We might believe that what he had different characters express in his dialogues was what he actually believed in; but it's sometimes hard to say what was meant as narrative and what was meant as objective statement. Herein lays the big difference between Plato and Socrates. Plato believed he knew the truth, he had seen it, and any philosopher could do the same. That was the reason Plato believed that philosophers, and only they, were entitled to rule the state.

So here is the full Monty: Once you step out of the cave you realize that what you have taken for reality, the stuff you've been watching on the screen, is really just a bad imitation of actual reality.

Now you say, "Come on, let's get on with it. Let it all out."

Well, what you begin to realize is that outside the cave there is a bright sun, a light so bright that at first it blinds you. Then, after you get your eyes adjusted to the brightness, you realize that the shadows you have been taking for reality are really cast by a long parade of objects, which Plato calls **forms**. In fact, everything in this world is actually an imperfect copy of those forms cast by a powerful sun from beyond our realm, from a place we can conveniently call a heaven of forms.

Here, in this heaven of forms, then, is the real shape – that's what a form is – of every object existing in this world.

I hear you say, "Now you lost me. You mean there is a copy of each and every knife we have here in that other world? A blueprint of every motorcycle?"

Not exactly, but there is an ideal knife, an ideal motorcycle, and an ideal arm chair in that other world.

"Ah", you say, "now I get it. It's kind of like the cookie cutter of the gingerbread man my dad used, when he baked Christmas cookies, or was that my mom?"

Precisely, all you need is such a shape and a lot of dough and you can make a thousand gingerbread men in no time at all. The dough is the raw material from which the world is made and the forms are the shapes everything ultimately turns into.

Let me explain it in another way, because this is really the most important concept Plato left us as his legacy. You have analyzed poems in English class, right? Of course American poems are most often written in a kind of free-flowing style. The verses role like ocean waves or flow like a giant river. But think of a poem by Shakespeare. Remember what your teacher called them? Some of Shakespeare's poems were called sonnets. The crucial point here is that they had to have a very specific format with a particular rhyme scheme, because they were written in a specific style.

In those days young people were often encouraged to write such a poem, a sonnet, as a gift for their parents on special occasions. Their private tutor would show them the format the poem had to be written in and then the child's job was to find words and press them into the format. The words are like the dough or the "world stuff," called **materia** in Greek. The style is the heavenly or divine form developed by the gods to bring shape to an otherwise shapeless world.

"But how do we mere mortals get knowledge of those perfect forms or ideas?"

Great question. I see you are getting the drift. Plato's great gift to posterity is the way that he figured out how we gain knowledge of the true forms. He had learned, probably from Pythagoras, that souls have an independent existence from the body. Pythagoras believed in the transmigration of souls, another belief that he shared with the ancient Hindus. Plato took only the first half of that belief: before your soul came into your body it had a prior existence with the gods where it learned about all those perfect forms. On its way to your body, down from heaven to earth, your soul had to pass through the celestial spheres where lower gods influenced your soul and caused partial amnesia. Yes, that is how Plato explained imperfection in this world.

This all will become extremely important when we learn how Plato's ideas were transformed, when they were absorbed by early Christianity, a religion that had started in nearby Israel and then spread to the rest of the world. In fact, Plato had been dead for more than four hundred years when Christianity began, but we are getting ahead of ourselves.

So your soul has a memory of all the perfect things it saw before it came into your body. Now as you walk through life, whenever the soul sees things in this world, it remembers how they were once in perfection. When your soul sees a sick dog, it remembers that perfect dog in the heaven of perfect forms. When you see a crooked circle, your soul remembers that perfect circle of all circles it once knew when it was still with god.

Talking about a perfect circle, this is why Plato thought it was so important for the philosopher to know mathematics. How do we know about a perfect circle? When you think about it, every circle we see in nature is only approximately round, never perfectly so. Right? A pizza may be round, but is it a perfect circle? No way. Can you think of anything in the natural world that comes close to being perfectly round? Apples? The sun? The moon? Just look closely, and you will see bursting subexplosions on the sun; and the moon, on closer inspection, has protruding mountains and such. No, nothing in this world is quite perfect, not even the most gorgeous girl friend or most handsome boyfriend you have dated. Perfection, Plato concluded, comes from the mind. Incidentally, mind and soul were identical for the Greeks. Back then they weren't quite that sophisticated yet. Everything that moved had a soul; that's why it was called **animate**. Anything that didn't, they called **inanimate**. That's a distinction our scientists have kept until today.

Almost without realizing it, we have just learned the second way Plato thought you could know about perfection and the way things really are. Since not everyone had the guts to leave the cozy den, the second way was through **education**. Education meant leading someone out of the dark cave into the light of true being. A pretty important job for a teacher, wouldn't you think? Through education we are able to find out the true nature of things.

There is one important factor that you have to keep in mind, though. There is no discussion about what the truth is. For Plato there is only one truth. It is true that there is a different truth for each type of thing in this world: a true and perfect apple, a true and perfect spoon,

A Dialogue to Plato

OK **PLATO**, YOU SAY ALL ON EARTH IS BUT A SHALLOW COPY OF SOME **PERFECT FORM** ON HIGH, AND YOUR **FLOWERS** ARE AN EXAMPLE.

SO IS THERE ONLY **ONE** FORM FOR ALL THE FLOWERS, OR DO **ROSES** HAVE ONE PERFECT FORM, AND DAISIES **ANOTHER**?

AND WHERE **ARE** THESE PERFECT FORMS? IN HEAVEN? IN THE MIND OF GOD? IN THE MIND OF **EACH MAN**?

a true and perfect you and me, and so on. Remember the reason why you and I are not perfect now unless of course you personally see nothing wrong with yourself. Some people certainly are this conceited. We are not perfect, Plato says, because on the way down our souls suffered amnesia. Remembering former perfection should be the goal of any noble soul. Plato called this recollection. Trying to become perfect is a true virtue. Bringing the rest of the world closer to perfection is our true vocation. Here you have Platonism in a nutshell.

Let's look all the way back for a moment. Greek society, around the time of the great philosophers, experienced a profound sense of loss. Things weren't going all that well. Athens had lost several wars and there was corruption everywhere. The city was definitely declining. And there was the persistent memory of a time when things were better.

Small wonder then that in such times deep thinking philosophers were in search of some ideal, a guide post if you will,, for people to look toward and adjust their lives accordingly. Perhaps they hoped, if people would follow the ideal, times would become better again and the Golden Age would return.

Plato hoped to find this guidance by an intuitive grasp of another ideal world of forms. It is almost like an act of grace. Some day you get up, leave your comfortable environment, and step out into the unknown. In making this journey, Plato became the foremost promoter of an experience of the divine we generally call mysticism.

Few would expect to return from a mystical journey, which usually involves an altered state of mind, with as clear a vision as Plato did. But Plato saw things only one way and that was his way.

■ B. THE DIVIDED LINE

> Before going on, turn to your ACTIVITIES BOOK and work on ACTIVITY 4. Write a short essay on how the Allegory of the Cave fits in with the Divided Line graph. It will help you understand the following chapter much better.

There is a Buddhist story about two neighbors, two monks, who both had a small body of water in their back yards. One had a modern swimming pool with blue tiles and the other, a Japanese pond with orchids growing in it with all kinds of wild life. Their property was divided by a rather high wall, so in order to communicate with each other they had to shout across the divider. One day they compared the image of the sun appearing in their respective bodies of water. Of course, as you can imagine, they came away with two rather different descriptions, even though both described the reflection of the rays coming from the same sun.

Can you make sense of this story and how it relates to Plato's Allegory? Here is the hitch. When Plato describes the objects at the highest level of the intelligible world he leaves no doubt in your mind that he knows what they look like and what they are. This includes the sun. Plato would want the two monks to stare up into the sky right smack into the sun and then describe what they see. Not only would they come away from that experience with their retinas burned, but they would also each still have a quite different description of what they saw.

Plato thought that the process of recollection, along with a clear thinking mind trained in the discipline of mathematics, could ultimately yield a sure-fire description of what he believed were the objects in the intelligible world, or the ultimate and final truth.

There are several concepts and names we need to learn that go along with this kind of thinking. First of all, such thinking is deeply ideological. **An ideology is a system of beliefs that explains everything.** It's not just one thought, one single proof, or one idea that you hold to be true. It truly does it all. So when something new comes along, an animal you have never seen, a concept about the universe, or an archeological investigation into the life of dinosaurs, your ideology tells you where to put it in your mind.

Assume you are a creationist, for example. A creationist is a person who believes in the literal interpretation of the biblical story. The world was created in six days a little over six thousand years ago. Now you have been vacationing in Dinosaur National Park and your dad found a dinosaur bone laying in the trash next to a bunch of chicken bones left there by irresponsible campers. You have the bone analyzed by the Park Ranger who happens to be a Harvard trained archeologist. He comes back a week later and tells you that the bone is real and that it's the shoulder bone from a dinosaurs rex who lived more than six million years ago. Your immediate response is to throw the bone back with the other chicken bones, because you believe it's a fake: according to your beliefs the world is just not that old. End of story for you. That's the power of ideology.

PLATO'S "THE DIVIDED LINE"		
	ONTOLOGY	EPISTEMOLOGY
INTELLIGIBLE WORLD	MATH, OBJECTS, FORMS, IDEAS, CONCEPTS, UNDERSTANDING	REASON, UNDERSTANDING KNOWLEDGE
VISIBLE WORLD	OBJECTS, IMAGES	BELIEFS, CONJECTURES, OPINIONS

Now granted, we all have our own beliefs and very few of them can actually be proven logically. Lucky for us, we live in a country where we are entitled to believe as we wish. You can believe that Santa Claus is actually a strange imposter, and no one can take that belief away from you. That's part of the freedom we so cherish in this country. But if we start going around and teaching others, especially young, impressionable minds, about the weird things we believe about Santa or that the world is only six thousand years old even when overwhelming evidence tells us otherwise, we have crossed the line. There is nothing wrong with you personally believing weird things, at least no one can really stop you. But when you try to influence others, by manipulation or even by force, you are in the wrong.

Finally, when someone comes and tells you that he or she has seen the "truth" and she wants you to follow and believe in it, use Socratic wisdom and be skeptical. When you believe you have had a mystical experience and now you know the truth, be skeptical still. Experience alone can definitely mislead you. What you should look for is experience enhanced by a critical mind.

Another important concept we can learn from Plato is **dualism**. He was the first to clearly formulate this concept. Dualism entails the idea the there are basically two completely different substances that make up this world. Can you figure out what two substances these are? All

47

you need to do is look at the divided line graph in your ACTIVITIES BOOK. Look for the fat, horizontal line that divides the world into a visible and an intelligible world. The things below the line, the world of automobiles, money, the stock market, and dandelions, are all part of one side of the dualistic divide.

On the other side are mathematical objects, such as circles, parallel lines, triangles and the ideal forms of everything. It's the world of ideas. For this reason Plato is called an **idealist**. An idealist is someone who believes that there were first ideas in the order of things. Everything somehow came from ideas. Can you figure out now what a **materialist** would believe?

Dualism has become one of the great topics in Twentieth Century philosophy, mostly because it was endorsed by the philosopher/mathematician, Rene Descartes, who is considered the father of modern philosophy.

▨ C. Plato's Social Philosophy: A Blueprint for an Ideal State

Perhaps even more influential than anything else Plato wrote was his utopian model of an ideal state. He developed this concept in one of his many books called *The Republic*. Often what really matters is not what a philosopher actually means by an idea that he develops, but rather what becomes of his ideas in the course of history. Plato may never have meant to support dictatorial and even fascist regimes, but unfortunately, hundreds of years later, some dictators took his concepts seriously; and, in his name, implemented some of the most rigid and violent regimes that have ever existed in history.

What Plato must first be credited with is developing a vision of an individual person in an almost "psychological" way. Then he took this vision and applied it to society as a whole. It might perhaps surprise you, but when we talk about what kind of society we live in and why society is the way it is, we are still following a similar process.

First of all to be alive, the Greeks believed that you had to have a soul. The Greek word for soul is **psychae**. Now you know where the word **psychology** comes from – originally, it was the science of the human soul. **Psychae** for the Greeks was everything that gave life to an otherwise dead **materia**. Of course materia is the stuff that things are made of. By itself, materia does not move. The Greeks, of course, had no way to look inside the world of atoms to see that deep inside a rock, for instance, there actually is quite a bit of movement.

Plato saw a deep problem with his concept of the soul. According to his dualistic beliefs the soul came straight from heaven, what he called the intelligible world, into your body when you were born. And that was the problem. Not everything your soul tells you to do is good. Yet as the representative of that other perfect world, all the soul should have told you to do would necessarily have to be good. In other words, Plato was the first philosopher who, in a major way, faced the problem of evil in this world. Why do bad things happen to good people; or more importantly, why do good people do bad things; and even worse, why are there some people in this world who seem to be bent toward always doing bad things, such as criminals?

Let's stop and think about what our modern answer to the question of evildoers would be. Some would certainly say that people do bad things simply because they are just evil. But why are they evil? Scientists have tried to solve this question in many ways. The question of nurture versus nature is right in the center of this scientific debate. The final word is not yet out, even today. Is it in the genes or is it the result of upbringing, family structure, frustration, bad examples? There were times when some scientists believed that one could detect bad character merely by the way your head was shaped or which race or ethnic group you belonged to. Luckily perhaps, such beliefs belong to the past, or at least mostly to the past.

Perhaps this may surprise you, but a good many people would say that people do bad things as the results of the work of the devil. See if you can find any statistics on this for contemporary American society. Compared to this belief, Plato and most Greeks of his time, had a surprisingly enlightened idea when it came to the question of evil. The Greeks did not personify evil. There was no place for a devil or Satan. In Western Civilization this idea came from the Hebrews and from Christianity. The Greeks simply believed that everybody did bad things out of ignorance. If you knew better, you would not have done a bad thing. This of course puts an incredible emphasis on education. Can you think why?

This explanation, neat as it is, does not fully solve the problem Plato faced in regard to the soul. If the soul came straight from god into your body, you should want only to do good things. Why is it that you sometimes decide to do a bad thing?

When you can't think of anything original, revert back to your old beliefs. Plato did just that. Greeks generally believed in the Ptolemaic world view: above the earth are concentric circles of different spheres. The highest and most distant one is the sphere inhabited by the highest god, the one who is all perfect and made your soul. Had it all been up to him, your soul would never guide you to do anything bad. Now comes the hitch. On its way down into your body, the soul has to pass through a number of different, lower level spheres, seven, to be exact. Each of those lower spheres is also inhabited by gods. These gods are of course lower level gods, since they inhabit lower level spheres. What did you expect? But being gods, they also have some influence on each soul that passes by. And yes, you guessed right, the influence is not good. Why couldn't they just leave good things alone?

Well, the damage was done. Blame the gods for it. The good news though, is that your soul has not quite forgotten what it first knew when being created in that upper sphere. It's all there, somewhere. You just have to find it. Remember! Remember! Yes, even Plato believed that somewhere in the depth of your soul you can ace every math test. Calculus is put into every child's brain right at birth. It only takes a good math teacher, of course, to bring it out. And that math teacher better be a philosopher, because the mere belief that you don't know will only enforce your own negative expectations.

So now we have the basics. You have a soul that knows, somewhere, all the good things, but lower gods messed it up. In fact, Plato imagined three different parts to your soul: The highest part, the one shaped by the top god, is the rational part of your soul, always making the right decisions and always being cool and collected. The second part is the spirited one, driving you to action, making you take risks and encouraging you to bravery. Not so bad either. Maybe some lower gods had their act together after all. But woe to the lowest part; it's bad news. It's the part that wants you to have more – more coffee, more cigarettes, more beer, and of course, you guessed it, more sex. Plato called it the appetitive part; I would say it's your addictive self.

How would things be different without the looming danger of addiction? Addiction to alcohol, addiction to drugs, addiction to bad habits, and that, for all practical matters, includes sex. Let's be honest. If you have to take a drink every couple of hours, just to feel normal, it begins to interfere with everything else in your life, right?

Greek Pantheon
© 2006 JupiterImages Corporation

Since we have been talking a lot about Greek gods, here is a short story about the Greek **pantheon**. How did those gods get so lascivious? Well, not all of them are, just the ones in the lowest sphere. The pantheon was a temple in Athens, reminiscent of the real pantheon on Mount Olympus in the north of Greece. The pantheon in Athens, by the way, was the place all the gods were honored; of course, the real one was at the place where the gods lived. Didn't we say before they lived in those different spheres, all divided up by their intellect or lack there of? Well, maybe Mount Olympus was their summer residence. No one knows for sure about gods, not even Plato.

In the pantheon there was always one place kept open for any new god who might come along and need to be honored. Now you might ask, how did the Greeks acquire new gods to put into there pantheon? Good question. The Greeks were of course polytheists, as you already know. As **polytheists they believed in many gods**, and as a good-natured people they did not mind, generally speaking, when other cultures and civilizations that they came in contact with had their own gods and goddesses. In fact, having these new gods meet the old ones made for pretty good soap opera in the Greek pantheon.

A young, single goddess from the island of Samos arrives in search of a suitable lover. Can you see all the eligible young gods queuing up in line to take a look at the new arrival? But before you know it the top god, Zeus, who is married gets wind of this beautiful young goddess and lusts for a little affair. The pretty young celestial gets her own place in the expansive Greek pantheon and not only if the top god approved.

One little footnote here so you don't get confused. By the time Plato wrote *The Republic,* Zeus was already quite discredited, and not just because of his love affairs. The top god that Plato envisioned was a lot more abstract, a noble character who stood high above human affairs. He envisioned him as the Divine Craftsman.

The three parts of Plato's concept of the soul are **reason**, **spirit** and **appetite**. These in turn correspond to the virtues of wisdom, courage, and temperance. Each part of the soul is also represented by a specific metal. Reason is represented by gold, spirit by silver, and appetite by bronze, the most common metal of the time.

We know already how each soul got what it brings into this world, through the influence of all those gods. In other words, you were born with it, and there was little you could do about it, except realize who you are and accept it. Harmony for Plato came to a state when everyone accepted his or her place and lived accordingly. Incidentally, the cast system in India was developed around the same time. This, one could say, was distinctly the opposite of the American dream. No advancement was possible.

D. THE PERFECT STATE

You can already guess how Plato applied this picture of the human soul to the way he looked at society. Society also has three distinct groups. In modern terminology you could say upper, middle, and lower class. This partition of society into three distinct groups goes back to Plato, and as you see, has lasted to this day. Plato believed that this partition, just like the three parts of the soul, was ordained by god and movement from one part to the other was highly unlikely. To Plato's credit, we must say that at birth how much the lower gods messed you up is not written on your forehead. This will not come out until you receive an education. In this way, all people should start out on an equal footing. Plato even admitted women to his academy. But had you asked him if a woman could ever rise to the highest level in society, having been born with a predominantly golden soul, he would probably have denied it.

The three groups that made up Plato's ideal state were defined in a rather practical way – they were represented by their occupation and duties within the state. The higher up you aspired to be, the more obligations you had to accept, and the more restricted your life would appear, judging by contemporary standards.

At the lowest end were the masses of people, comprised mostly of working men and women, those using their hands and their wits to make a living. These average people, endowed with a soul mostly of bronze, were allowed to live out their passions. After all they were born that way – selfish and preoccupied with pleasures and with a lack of restraint. The wise state puts laws into place to channel, guide, and restrain the endless appetite of the masses.

To enforce those laws, to defend the state from without and within, and to educate its citizens was the role of the second class, which Plato called the Guardians. Their silver soul gives them the right amount of courage to stand up and defend what is right. To preclude them from abusing their power and prevent them from becoming greedy, Plato put several restraints on this class of people. They were not allowed to own personal property only communal property was permitted – no Porsche or private yacht to show off your power and influence. Most importantly, these elite groups were not allowed regular sexual activities. They were not to get married and had organized sexual meetings about once a month.

The Philosopher King:
- No property
- No bank accounts
- No getting rich off the backs of other people
- No sex

That's it. Now you know were the idea of **celibacy** came from. On the other hand, our modern day leaders could learn a lot from Plato. The revolving door deal of some politicians would end abruptly. No more president of a corporation one day, president of the United States the next, and then again president of the corporation. By the same token, sex with interns would also be a "no no". Maybe Plato had some good ideas.

▨ E. AND HERE COMES THE MUSIC

The God Dionysus
© 2006 JupiterImages Corporation

Plato's evaluation of music and art in general is perhaps his strangest and most controversial idea. Though in some places he stresses the importance of musical education as part of a balanced curriculum, he generally advocates strict control and censorship of artistic material. You can't help but get the impression that Plato tries to avoid the ancient rivalry between direct experience and logical deduction in the process of finding the truth. Let me add again a little background story so you get the drift of what I mean.

Long before Plato's time, a couple of centuries earlier, there was a little rivalry going on in Greek society. From even earlier times, veneration of the ancient gods had survived. One particular god was **Dionysus**, whom we know as the god of wine, of ecstasy, and of altered states of mind in general. Every so often his followers came together to celebrate this somewhat unruly god. The belief that in total ecstasy it was possible to communicate directly with the gods or the spirits had survived from prehistoric times. It was believed that a person in that state of mind was able to access the truth directly. Remember the Oracle of Delphi!

This experiential access to truth was squarely opposed by the newly emerging philosophers. Pythagoras, though pretty much of a prophetic figure himself, started the process of finding truth through logical deduction – which Plato followed and Aristotle completed. There is one clear advantage to a logically – deducted truth: it can be taught in school and tends to be more democratic. An experiential truth stays forever locked inside of your own experience. You can force others to accept it; you can manipulate them, especially if your audience is young and impressionable. Or best of all, you can live your life according to your truth and invite others to use your example. That is for me the best, if not the only, option. Greek society ultimately relegated the Dionysian mystery cult to the underground.

The mysteries were shunned because of the advances in the desire to control sexual activities. With the spread of male domination, monogamy became the rule for sexual intercourse. You can imagine what happens when a bunch of people get together with a strong inclination toward getting high and feeling ecstatic, with nothing barred. Those mystery gatherings often quickly turned into a group orgy, women got pregnant, and no one knew who the father was. They, of course, had no DNA testing either. Any population control goes out the window. Also, young men who wanted to proudly show off their offspring, as their legitimate property, the fruit of their labor, began asking for stricter controls. And women probably couldn't agree more, at least in the beginning.

So the Greeks did away with the mystery gatherings or pushed them into the underground; but in order not to disappoint the gods – you remember how tolerant and accepting they were in general – they dedicated the Olympic Games to the god Dionysus. Held once a year, the Games included not only sporting events, but also performances of plays and a week-long celebration. They even opened the gates of the prisons and let the prisoners participate.

It was artists, poets, and storytellers who were often the ones who tried to put into words experiences of the unknown, adventures of the darkened mind, and untamed encounters with gods and with devils. These wild practices, too, have lived on in certain festivals, even among modern people. Just think of the festivities surrounding the celebration of Mardi Gras, or what is called Carnival, in other parts of the world. Pagan customs of transformation and role adaptation have survived Christian purges.

So the spirit of Dionysus lives on, still even today, not so much in the Olympic Games, but in art works, artistic creations, and most of all in communities of artists. Have you ever wondered why it is especially artists who seem to take greater license in life, have more affairs, more divorces, a less restricted attitude?

But perhaps Plato opposed experiential truth even though his own story included a great part of experience. Art Plato believed, was three times removed from the truth, a copy of a copy. Ultimately it was Aristotle who completed the task of developing a totally deductive kind of truth. He, in turn, gave artists back their reputation and turned over to them the important task of helping to spread the truth.

This just about concludes our discussion of Plato, one of the greatest philosophers of all time. If my description at times sounded a little disrespectful, no harm was intended. A little disrespect sometimes helps us to realize that our great heroes were only human. They, too, were human and made mistakes; and even though in many things they were ahead of their times, in others they were deeply involved in and bear the signs of their own age in their writings and in their ideas.

Plato founded a school that was called **The Academy**. It lasted for over 800 years. Athens, famous at its height and well known, had long lost its political clout and had ceased to exert any more political influence in the Western world.

Don't forget to go to your ACTIVITY BOOK and complete the Activities on Plato. It will help you to see whether you really understood the material.

◼ 4. ARISTOTLE (384-322 BCE)

◼ A. MAN AND STATE, ARISTOTLE'S THEORY OF HAPPINESS

ARISTOTLE
(384 - 322 BCE)
© 2006 JupiterImages Corporation

Aristotle was a student in Plato's school for over twenty years and became one of the most prolific writers in the ancient world. Aristotle wrote about many different subjects, from cosmology to physics and morality. He also wrote on biology, psychology, politics, and rhetoric. Finally, in his book on poetics, Aristotle set a standard for artistic works that has influenced all Western writing well into the Twentieth Century. This is especially true for dramatic works.

Again I will focus only on those of Aristotle's ideas that have had a major influence on our theme of compassion, cooperation and partnership. The concept of **happiness** must be among the most important ideas any philosophy can deal with. So let's begin there.

Before continuing to read, turn to your ACTIVITIES BOOK and follow the instructions. In particular, you should write a short essay on your own ideas about happiness.

Now watch the short film *Man and State: Aristotle's Theory of Happiness,* available in any library. The film is produced by Encyclopedia Britannica and features one of the best known Aristotelian experts and modern philosophers, Mortimer Adler. If you would rather read an original text or can't find the film, you can of course also read Aristotle's book The *Nicomachean Ethics.*

After watching the film and before you continue reading go to your ACTIVITIES BOOK and write short answers to the questions raised about the film.

◼ B. DON'T WORRY, BE HAPPY

Aristotle was not an idealist. He rejected outright Plato's *Theory of Forms.* He could rather be characterized as empirical in his thought, though we don't want to call him an empiricist either. **Empiricism** as a philosophy was developed many centuries later in England, at the beginning of the scientific age. Instead of looking for answers in another world, Aristotle searched this world and found what he was looking for here.

Aristotle had learned from his father, who was a medical doctor in the Northern Greek town of Stagira, to observe nature very carefully. In those days, a doctor of medicine was not so much involved in writing prescriptions and dispensing chemicals as he was in very carefully investigating and analyzing natural plants and minerals in order to discover their medicinal uses. From this activity, the young Aristotle might have learned to analyze and to classify. And this became a major preoccupation in his professional life as a philosopher.

From watching the short film on Aristotle's *Theory of Happiness* and listening to Professor Adler's explanations, you get a good idea of how Aristotle's systematic and logical mind worked. Aristotle applied the rigor of **logic** to everything he investigated. Ultimately he believed that with the tools of a logical mind one could understand the whole world and everything in it.

Aristotle applies this same rigor of logic to the idea of happiness. He begins by asking what kind of "goods" we try to acquire during one's life time. There are, of course, a great many of them, but some of them stick out. Aristotle believes there are exactly five "goods" that we could all agree on as being most important: health, wealth, knowledge, friendship and virtue. These five, as well as all other goods that come to mind, Aristotle calls instrumental because you achieve them in order to reach some other good. Even those five important goods pale before one good that is supreme. That supreme good is happiness. Happiness alone is an intrinsic good, because you achieve it for its own sake. Everything a living organism does is done ultimately to achieve happiness.

Would you agree? Is happiness such an ultimate, **universal** good? Aristotle thinks so, and with him many Aristotelians, such as Professor Adler, who has followed Aristotle's ideas throughout history.

C. TELEOLOGY

A perfect example of a principle that Aristotle developed is that happiness is an ultimate good. This principle, called teleology, has deeply influenced all of Western thinking. You might still today, in a modern biology book, read that insects, for instance, exhibit teleological behavior. That simply means that when they are building their hives and their communities, they seem to have a purpose, a purpose that is larger even than their own, individual lives. Teleology means that and more.

Teleology – Do We Ever Reach Perfection?

HEY! WHERE DO YOU WANT ME TO PUT THIS THING?

FINISH LINE

Aristotle believed that everything in this world is created with purpose in mind. Everything has purpose. The first question that comes to mind is of course who put it there? Aristotle's answer is simple: God, the ultimate craftsman, the most powerful creator, put purpose into all things when he created them.

You can see why Christians, when they came in contact with Aristotle, liked some of the things he said. But since he said other things that they didn't like, Christian philosophers initially turned to Plato. Had it not been for Muslim scholars, who preserved and translated Aristotle's works during the European dark ages, Aristotle's writings might have been lost for ever. But we are getting ahead of ourselves.

The second question you should ask is this: how do we know that this is so, that everything has a purpose? This is closely related to the question of whether everything has intention. Aristotle answered these questions with a resounding affirmation. Everything has intention and purpose, at least everything that is alive.

But how do we know? Aristotle found the answer to be bound up with the question of change. Even earlier philosophers had asked the question: "Why do things change?" Looking around, it may be hard to ignore the fact that everything is in a constant state of change. In fact so much so that one philosopher made this the principle of everything by declaring: **panta rei** – everything changes.

Another one said: "You can't step into the same river twice." True enough, isn't it? We call it a river, but what you step into has certainly changed. It's different water every day, every minute. Even we human beings exchange every cell in our body every seven years.

Aristotle has an elegant answer: Things change because they try to reach their final destination. And that final destination is, you guessed it, perfection. **Teleology** means everything is striving toward perfection.

So here you are. Aristotle did not have to leave the cave, enter an ideal world of forms, or use some obscure type of memory to know the perfect form. It was built right smack into the middle of things. Things have perfection built into them, but they are not quite there yet; that is why there is change in the world.

Is that how it really is, you might ask? You can easily think of a million things that change, and not always for the better. Just think for a moment: Did my tooth break in order to reach *perfection*? What about my hair? Baldness certainly isn't a sign of perfection, is it? But wait. Aristotle made a distinction between instrumental "stuff" and intrinsic causes. Your teeth and your hair are only instrumentally you. It's nice, of course, if you have them. But an implant is maybe just as good and a nice hair piece goes a long way. The point is that you have many characteristics that can be taken away from you without really changing who you are. Perfection lies in what you are essentially, in what you are by nature.

So what am I *essentially*? What is my nature? Aristotle is not shy when it comes to using his analytical method. Try making a list of all the characteristics you can think of that constitute you as a person, sort of a computer program in long hand or a code of who you are as a human being.

Are you finished with the list? Probably not, but lets stop here and cross off everything that you can cross off and still be you. Got it? Right off the bat you can take away everything external to you, things that you might consider yours: your car, your hiking boots, all your clothes in fact. Forget about your skin, too. Without your skin, you would be a pretty strange looking you, but you still would be you. Well, you ask, what is it then that Aristotle is after?

Maybe it would help to ask what makes you essentially you? 'Ah,' you say, 'the food I eat, the air I breath, the blood in my body take even one of these essentials away for any length and I am dead, right?' Well, yeah, but that only shows how far we modern people have moved away from this kind of Aristotelian thinking. His whole philosophy is actually often called **essentialism**.

'Now you really got me curious,' I hear you say. 'You mean air and food is still not the right answer?'

Actually, no! In our modern, scientific age we are influenced by materialistic thinking, whether we want to be or not. And essentialism is the opposite of **materialism**.

'That's great,' you squirm. 'If you can't explain one difficult concept, use another one and hope I get it. I am sure materialism is not what I think it is, either.' Give it a try.

'Well, a materialist is someone who is into material things, like the 'material girl' who is, or rather was, Madonna before she turned mystic.'

You were right, that's not what it is. Materialism is a philosophical belief that begins with the primacy of materia. Everything there is can be explained by referring back to materia. Materia is all there is.

So now, what is an essentialist? An essentialist believes that materia is only the shell and that what truly exists is the essence of each thing. The essence is eternal, unchangeable, and from god.

'Aha, so it's exactly like Plato's form or idea? Did I get it now?'

Not exactly. I told you Aristotle rejected the **Platonic** forms. But you are right, they are pretty similar. Only for Aristotle, essences are part of each thing rather than something existing in another world. When Aristotle was rediscovered after the Middle Ages by young scientists, they were happy to encounter an ancient philosopher who encouraged them to find what is important by doing research in this world rather than referring them to another, heavenly world to find out what is real and true. Hence, Aristotle became the favorite philosopher of the young scientists.

'And when did this belief in essentialism come to an end? You've said yourself that we modern people don't believe in it anymore.'

Plato's forms reside in the intelligible world. Aristotle's essences are part of each thing located in this world.

I could let you guess. It is the result of the work of one of the most influential scientists of the nineteenth century. Did you guess? No, it was not Einstein. This scientist was more of a biologist. Yes, now you've got it: Charles Darwin, of course. Darwin changed the way we look at nature forever. Essentialism was replaced by his **theory of evolution**, one of the concepts that survived to this day. This shows you both how influential Aristotle was, his theory surviving almost into the twentieth century, and how truly revolutionary Charles Darwin was. No wonder churches fought his influence tooth and nail, and in spite of overwhelming evidence to support his ideas, the fight continues to this day.

The concept of essentialism is so important that I would like to look at it yet from another angle. You can think of Aristotelian essentialism as a large box system with a little box for each species. This box system actually includes everything, not just animate things. But for our purposes let's consider just living things. There is a box for all frogs, a box for lizards, and a box for squirrels, and so on and so on. Why boxes? These boxes represent the essential features that make a population or, species, as we would say today.

When god creates a new individual, be it human being or goose, a box is ready for the new creature to fit into. The boxes were made before the individual appeared. Yes, you got it, just like Plato's forms preceded the existence of things, so Aristotle's essences precede the individual. Nature or essence precedes existence. While the ontological difference between the two great philosophers is kind of minimal, the epistemological difference is important and has huge consequences. Plato's forms reside in the intelligible world. Aristotle's essences are part of each thing located in this world. Ontologically both are ideal metaphysical concepts, real things for an idealist, mental constructions for a materialist.

Although this is quite different, you may say, "So what?" The real difference comes when we ask the question, "How do we know about each?" For Plato, it means going on a mystical journey. For Aristotle, it is a journey into the world, a scientific journey of discovery. For Aristotle, finding the essential nature of each thing is a matter of empirical and deductive thinking.

▨ D. A First Lesson on Logic

I once had a friend who was a great collector of things. He asked everybody he knew to turn over to him all kinds of objects that had outgrown their usefulness. You can imagine how quickly his inventory grew. Eventually he bought a huge, empty house with many rooms. On the top floor it had a great big ball room. Here he began storing his found objects. The room filled up quickly because he accepted everything, even our old Christmas tree. There was an old bicycle next to a manual typewriter next to a gas clothes dryer. Pretty soon the place was filled with junk. He never accepted the fact that when you collect things you must have some principle of grouping things together. He had none. Kim was not a garbage collector, but that is a different story.

And then there was George's Place. Everybody knew grumpy old George. He lived right outside of our small farming village in rural Michigan. George was a garbage collector. If you needed a replacement piece for your broken hay bailer, you would go to George's Place. He asked you what you needed or just looked at the piece in your hand and then took you down long isles of tractors, down the isle of old mowers, a sharp left into the water pump isle, and pretty soon he ended up in the hay bailer isle. Everything was neatly ordered. Everything was junk, but it was neatly organized junk. George was a real Aristotelian. And my friend Kim, well, he was an artist, a modern artist.

As I said at the beginning, as the son of a medical doctor Aristotle had learned early on to pay attention to detail. He collected many things from many different countries. He even asked friends who traveled a lot to bring him samples of objects, animals, and plants that he couldn't find back home. As he began to sort those objects, he realized that certain things had similarities and he grouped them together. Pretty soon he arrived at a whole system in which everything had its proper place. He believed that this is how god had made the world. Every individual object belonged to a large class of objects, just like George belongs to the larger group of garbage collectors and Kim belongs in the artist's box. If you now look back at Plato, you can see their similarities. What was the ideal cookie cutter form for Plato becomes this Aristotelian box in which everything had to fit. Aristotle called the boxes not forms, but universals. He believed that god had made the **universals** before each individual thing.

Just like the Forms in Plato's world, the **Universals of Aristotle** preceded the individual object. The only difference between the two philosophers is how they arrived at them, how they learned about each universal. Plato knew about the forms through inner vision; for Aristotle, it was the result of careful analysis.

Collecting things in Aristotle's world is called using **induction**. This is a little bit like collecting evidence in a murder trial. Once you have found the evidence, you can use deduction to identify further objects. Through induction you have found the universals. Once a universal is established you use it as a pattern for further identifications.

Since these universals were created by god, Aristotle believed, of course, that everybody who searched correctly and did the necessary research and comparison would come up with the same conclusion. Hence, he believed that universals are universal – true everywhere for everybody.

That is of course the problem. We all know today that, even with the best of intention and research, we sometimes come up with different conclusions. Just observe how two people having witnessed the same accident can end up with two completely different stories.

Well, you say, they just didn't observe carefully, or one didn't have her glasses on so she didn't see things right.

That's just it; today we know that we all have our unique perspectives. But even today not everyone can agree on that. Some still believe we all should see things the same. And those who believe, like Plato and Aristotle, that we all should see things the same way, often conclude that everyone else who sees things differently must, of course, be wrong. Later I will develop the argument as to why everyone today should understand that we see things differently;

that argument has a lot to do with science. But first let's go back to Aristotle and his ideas about logic.

Through induction you gain knowledge of the universals; and through deduction you apply your knowledge to individual objects.

This simple formula provides the structure for every prejudice in the world. To be fair, though, we must also say that without this formula, science would simply not be possible. Some even believe that long before Aristotle developed these ideas, people used them to sort out the world by using language. Think about what it means to see a tree.

Some even believe that long before Aristotle developed these ideas, people used them to sort out the world by using language.

■ E. ON LANGUAGE

I once traveled by train in the former country of Yugoslavia, from Sarajevo to the Mediterranean coast. The train goes high up into the mountains. On the way, I looked out the window and saw this great, majestic cliff seemingly extending straight up into the blue sky. Way high up, there was a little ledge and on this ledge there was a little tree, hardly holding on to the rock. I actually greeted the little tree, crossing somehow the distance between us. I will never know whether the tree heard my greeting. I had encountered this little tree as an individual, and I had made a spiritual connection with it.

This must have been how ancient people developed special relationships with objects in their environment. They believed, however, that those objects talked back to them. So they gave them special names, attributing sounds, character, and gender to the objects with which they communicated. That was, perhaps, the beginning of language. Language is the representation of the natural world through mental constructs – audible or visible signs. Once a community begins to accept a certain sign for a certain object, language is only a small step away. Ancient people were now able to name an object and make a visual representation in their minds without the object being present. Maybe those mysterious cave paintings were a representation of past events for an audience in the present, just like we modern people tell stories and take photos or make movies.

The next step in the development of language would have been the generalization of a certain sound that initially only meant one specific tree, to all trees. You can imagine what a giant step that must have been. Since ancient peoples did not differentiate between a tree as a material object and a tree as a living spirit. It was all one and the same for them, and they might have thought that the same tree spirit inhabited all trees. So when they encountered a new tree that they had never had seen before, as I did in the Yugoslavian mountains, they could use the same sound or word to address that new tree.

Language, as we know from ancient accounts, was a very spiritual affair. Ancient texts were revered as sacred, because the ancient people believed that they were a medium of communication with gods and with spirits.

Language evolved further when people, over time, forgot about the original spirituality that once inhabited each word. Today we use words without ever thinking about what they originally meant or signified. By the time the Greek philosophers wrote their treatises, language had become a practical means of communication, like a vessel that carries a liquid but by itself is worth nothing.

Today we would say words and sentences are like plastic cups: you use them, and after their use, you can toss them in the garbage. Because of the great abuse of language by modern politicians, a contemporary poet experienced the use of words as being like poisoned mushrooms in his mouth. Just as Greek poets bemoaned the loss of spirituality in language, so modern poets have described the ultimate decay of language, especially in the political arena of manipulation and double speak. The art forms of surrealism and Dadaism were grounded in this realization, the recognition of the decay of language. Poets tried, in vain, to respiritualize language by breaking it down to its simplest phonemes.

Within the dominator paradigm, words exert violence on the objects they signify and language is used for domination alone. There is, however, an entirely different way to account for the origin of language that predates the violent way of naming things. I learned about this not through academic instruction but while working on a play. I was assisting a Latvian friend in directing a play, from her homeland, that was about three hundred years old. The story was set in a transitional period from old pagan animistic customs to Christian religious beliefs. This happened quite late in Latvia, where pagan beliefs were practiced well into modern times. To find this in mainstream European culture, you would have to go back several thousand years to the times when Homer wrote *The Iliad* and *The Odyssey*.

What I learned from this play was that ancient people may have named things in nature not to dominate but to communicate. Language does not necessarily need to impose violence on the signified **Other**, but on the contrary may be a friendly tool for establishing relationships. In this light, the interpretation of words and language as an expression of violence is clearly dated. It is a production of the dominator mind, which still prevails today.

F. SOME MORE ON LOGIC

Aristotle developed a formal approach to verify that people have made true statements about the world when they speak. Through the application of rigorous logical rules, he hoped to develop a language that would increasingly and better represent the world the way it really is. To verify the integrity and consistency of statements, Aristotle invented what became known as a syllogism.

You probably came across syllogisms in math class. There you learned that if a equals b and b equals c, then a also by necessity equals c. This is the basic model of how a syllogism combines two unrelated terms, a and c.

We can apply the same systematic approach to language. Here Aristotle used the famous statement: All men are mortal (a), Socrates is a man (b), hence the conclusion, Socrates is mortal (c). You see that the first statement gives a characteristic of a general kind, the second

61

applies that general term to an individual case, and the third draws the conclusion, which if **a** and **b** are true is believed to be also true. This was Aristotle's attempt to make true statements about the real world. The first term is called the Major Premise, the second is the Minor Premise because it relates to an individual case, and the third is for obvious reasons called the Conclusion.

> Try a **syllogism** yourself. Can you construct similar models that help you make true statements? What are the conditions that make a syllogism true?

Aristotle was aware that the outcome of his syllogism would depend on the truth of the major premise. If the first statement were not completely true (e.g., all albinos have red skin) or were the result of some prejudice, your outcome would of course also be false. Similarly if the first term contained a contradiction, the outcome would not be true.

Aristotle was aware of these problems. He said that all major premises have to be based on true **archai**. An **archai** in Greek is a first thing, or true thing. Can you think of modern words that are related to archai? Therein, of course, lays the major problem with Aristotelian logic. The question of truth has only moved one level deeper. Over fifteen hundred years later, during the European Enlightenment, the philosopher Immanuel Kant proved that one will never be able to find those true archai and most of Aristotle's logic went straight out the window.

Well, not quite. There are still philosophers today who defend Aristotelian logic and think it is correct and helpful. But logic today is hardly ever used to verify the consistency of language with the real world, mostly because this has become the job of science. Philosophers still use logic to check and verify the consistency of verbal statements. You can analyze a political speech for consistency. You will also be able to use some of the other figures of logic that Aristotle developed to analyze language. You can expect to learn these special features in a logic class. Computer science students are the students who are still most likely to need logic. Our computer programs are most often written using Aristotelian logic.

What we have learned is that the real world hardly ever behaves with the consistency of a logical machine. Modern critiques have found that one of the main problems with Aristotelian logic is that it does violence to the real world. You might really wonder now how that can be. How can a logical statement, which is after all just more words, do violence to the world?

Some philosophers have said that, any time we use a word, we actually freeze an object in time and prevent it from developing any further. You might consider the following true story and figure out how it relates to logic and violence.

A Caucasian female schoolteacher in Oklahoma planned an "ethnic minority appreciation day" for her sixth-grade class. The class had a large number of American Indian students; therefore, part of the day was devoted to a unit on Native American heritage. An American Indian student had designed a bonnet and dress of her tribe. Her fellow students expressed appreciation and admiration for her costume and demonstration of a tribal dance. However, the teacher remained silent. Several days later the student received a low grade for her participation in the activities. The teacher praised the student's dance technique and beautiful costume, but stated critically that the costume was not typical for her tribe, that her dance was not traditional, and that the assignment was graded on "authenticity, not fantasy." The parents of the child demanded a meeting with the teacher and the principal. During the meeting the father expressed anger at "White folks always telling Indians who we are."

The teacher's only response was to show the parents an anthropology book with what she claimed to be the typical headgear and costume of the family's tribe. The photos and drawings were from an earlier time, some fifty years ago. The tribe had undergone changes which were expressed in changed regalia.

(From *Compassion, A New Philosophy of the Other* by Werner Krieglstein. Copyright © 2002 by Rodopi. Reprinted by permission.)

This story shows how the obvious lack of empathy with and ignorance of, a living tradition can end in total misunderstanding and insult. The teacher lacked sensitivity for the still developing tradition of an active tribe. The French philosopher Derrida pointed out how much harm we do to living things by freezing their development in concepts and in language. As this story emphasizes, this is especially true for living traditions, after anthropologists or other academic disciplines catalog them. The feedback loop created by such a system and by a teacher who reinforces the "academic truth" is remarkably powerful and, at times, nothing short of genocide.

Let's look at how Aristotle's logic could be applied to the story. The child uses inductive reasoning to assemble her exhibit. She observes what her tribe wears and how they dance and shows this in class. The teacher however uses only deductive reasoning. She takes the material she found in the anthropology book as the rule to be followed, and it becomes her Major Premise. Then she compares it to the child's costume, which she uses as the Minor Premise. Since she finds the two different and assumes that her Major Premise is correct, she comes to the conclusion that b is wrong and the child's costume is not authentic. You can see now how a syllogism can be used wrongly to develop wrong conclusions and prejudices. It all depends on the "truth value" of the Major Premise. If it is not right, nothing derived from it can be right.

The problem then is with the Major Premise. We will learn later, when we introduce the philosophy of the German philosopher Immanuel Kant, that we can never be one hundred percent sure about the absolute truth value of anything. Kant believed that this inability to know anything the way it really is was only a problem of our perception, a problem of how we see things.

The thing itself (das Ding an Sich) can never really be known. I will show that this is a problem inherent in the observed thing itself. Nothing in this world is a dead object. Everything is capable of change over time. Capturing something as a concept is like taking a freeze-frame picture of that thing and then assuming that it will always be the same. It does violence to the object in not allowing it to change.

Aristotle applied the concept of teleology to human history as well. You probably have no doubt in your mind when asked to think of history as something that goes like an arrow always into the future. You probably also have hardly any doubt in believing that history is always progressing,

63

which means that tomorrow will be better than today. You were taught this. It is the essence of the American dream, but it is also deeply rooted in Aristotelian thinking.

Together with his belief in the ultimate rationality of the universe, Aristotle's belief in the linear advance of history may well be his strongest and most lasting contribution to the development of Western civilization. You may even doubt that anybody thinks differently.

Yet there are many cultures and important civilizations that believe history goes in circles, or perhaps cycles. Some believe that things and events return in short succession; most often, you find the belief that history returns and recycles in great time spans of perhaps millions of years. This is the belief of the Hindus, a religion which has millions and million of followers and is perhaps the oldest surviving belief system originating in the ancient world. You can see that this idea that everything comes back encourages a belief in the transmigration of souls. Ancient people believed that after a person died, the body would go back into the earth, which was believed to be a goddess. From there a person's soul was reborn into a new body in order to start life all over again. Often people believed that misfortune or fortune in the current life was the result of good or bad actions in a previous life. In **Pagan** religions this was known as the **Law of Karma**.

▨ G. THE FOUR CAUSES AND THE ROLE OF ART

Aristotle's linear concept of history changed the ancient view of cyclical history. He might have gotten this idea from his concept of change and perfection. Remember that Aristotle believed that all things change in order to reach perfection. In this process, Aristotle said that

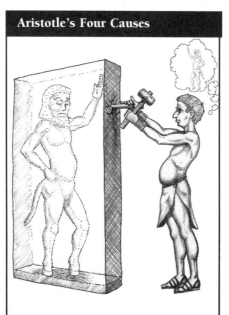

Aristotle's Four Causes

everything goes through four phases or 'causes.' The first phase is the efficient cause. This is the author of an event or object. Aristotle used the image of an artist, who makes a piece of art to illustrate his point. The artist, as the maker of the art work, is the **efficient cause**. The **material cause** is the stuff from which the art work is made. In the case of our example, it is the raw marble. The **final cause** is the purpose for which an art work is made, or its final destination. This could be the decoration of a temple or a home. Now there is one more cause left, which is the **formal cause**. This is the most complex of the four causes because it has a dual interpretation. It can either be the form or shape that artist sees in her head or it can be understood as the shape somehow already indicated within the material itself. Ideally, it is a combination of both. In her creative work, the artist enters into a dialog with the material and lets the material participate in the creative process. This latter view was often realized by artists during the Renaissance who rediscovered Aristotle's aesthetic views. They felt that his ideas encouraged a renewed interest and appreciation of the natural world.

You see, contrary to Plato, Aristotle had a very high expectation from the artist. You remember that for Plato, the artist's work was three times removed from the truth, a bad copy of the ideal. Artists were shunned from his ideal state. Aristotle, having himself reflected and formulated many rules for good art, put the artist back up on an important pedestal. For Plato the philosopher alone was privileged to find the truth; for Aristotle, the artist actually became the helper of the philosopher in the process of finding truth, because the artist's mission was to establish universals.

This high responsibility that Aristotle bestowed on an artist eventually became problematic. Modern artists found this to be less an honor than a shackle. What if they didn't see the world as whole and as beautiful as Aristotle (or the Church) saw it? What if the world didn't appear to them to be rational at all, but rather a playground of irrational ideas, or even mean gods, who were out to "get" innocent human beings? Artists who lived and worked in the Nineteenth Century, and even more so during the Twentieth Century, found that the world had a rather irrational quality.

Modern artists began calling Aristotle's aesthetic ideological: a rather forceful imposition of an optimistic view of the world, which they often could not share. Much of modern art can be understood as a direct opposition to the Aristotelian view of art as collaboration aiming for perfection.

In a similar way, modern philosophers also challenged Aristotle's view of history as a continuous march toward progress. European historians in particular declined to see history in this positive light as a march toward a better tomorrow. They even reinterpreted the ancient view of historical cycles as a pessimistic return of eternal suffering and misery. Foremost in spreading this kind of pessimism in their interpretation of the cyclical return of history were the German philosophers Wilhelm Schopenhauer and Friedrich Nietzsche.

One final thought. Aristotle's teleological concept of history survives still today in two important areas. The first area is in the distinct character of European science. Scientists have followed Aristotle's optimism and belief in the ultimate rationality of the whole universe. This means that, at least in principle, everything in the universe is knowable and can be understood by the human mind. Of course, no one has ever checked everything. That is impossible. Scientists also generally believe in the continuous progress of our knowledge of the world.

The second important influence of Aristotle's view of history, enshrined in the very fiber of American life, is what we call the American Dream. This involves precisely the idea of continuous progress: every new generation will be better off than the previous one. This belief, in its completely material interpretation, is the bottom line of the modern consumer society. It is behind the seemingly unstoppable drive of multinational commerce on its way toward global domination.

▨ H. A FEMINIST CRITIQUE OF ARISTOTLE

As you can already imagine, Aristotle's ideas had a tremendous influence on Western philosophy and civilization. His views affected science, technology, art, and culture. For over two thousand years the philosophical program Aristotle began was also the backbone of all Western philosophy. His insistence on universality, objectivity, and essential truth remained, even in their denial the focus of philosophical writings.

wow !

Modern feminists have rightfully emphasized the **misogynist** view of almost all philosophers of the Western **canon**. Aristotle's misogynist view is exemplary. Feminists pointed out that Aristotle firmly believed that the female is somehow an incomplete and deformed male. Males, Aristotle said, are meant to command, while women are meant to obey. They quote him as saying: "matter yearns for form, as the female for the male and the ugly for the beautiful." In the same vain, Aristotle believed that in the creation of a new child, the mother only contributed the matter, while the father contributed the form.

While one could excuse some of these ideas by pointing at the limited knowledge these Greeks had of biology, the more important question is how deeply these erroneous views influenced his whole philosophy. This is indeed the critique brought fourth by feminist philosophy. Could it be that all of Aristotle's philosophy, especially his construction of logic, objectivity, and universality infected by gender bias?

Aristotle promoted, after all, a clear distinction between matter and form. These two were never considered equal partners, but form was always superior to matter. When he then identified form with maleness and matter with femaleness he made a clear distinction of unbridled male superiority that ultimately infected all his thinking.

We will see that as a consequence, Western philosophy continued to promote a hierarchical model of mind over matter, defending male superiority as being ordained by God and the nature of things.

CHAPTER III: MEDIEVAL PHILOSOPHY

▮ 1. Augustine (354 - 430 BCE)

Let us fast forward through the next six hundred years. Keep in mind that both Plato's and Aristotle's schools in Athens were still in operation, but the influence of Greece as a political power had all but disappeared. Not so its influence on culture and philosophy.

The political focus had long ago shifted to Rome and the Roman Empire, though it, too, was in decline. It became the playground where the young Christian religion began to gain influence and to flourish. Greek philosophy had its major effect through a replay of Plato's philosophy known as Neo-Platonism.

To get a broader grasp of the historical background I suggest again consulting your ACTIVITIES BOOK. Watch the short film *The Medieval Mind* produced by Encyclopedia Britannica. While watching the film keep in mind that it covers a tremendously long and varied period. It starts with St. Augustine already archbishop of the North African town of Hippo, with the fall of the Roman Empire, and ends at the height of the Middle Ages. While the first few hundred years right after the fall of the Roman empire are considered the Dark Ages , because of the lack of any central authority, the second part is a period of high economic activity and cultural development, as well as architectural innovation.

**Augustine
(354 - 430 BCE)**
© 2006 JupiterImages Corporation

This first part of the film deals with perhaps the darkest time in European history – the Dark Ages. Dark because all central authority had vanished, people had to live in small groups without protection, marauding groups were vandalizing the country side, and huge masses of people moved over the continent in search of new opportunities and a more secure life. It was also the time when the young Christian faith spread throughout Europe, converting the pagan tribes they encountered, often by cunning and manipulation rather than by making them familiar with the message of the gospels and the doctrine of the faith. The Bible was not yet translated from Latin, the language used by church people. The church service itself was held in Latin as well. For common people, this was an incomprehensible language.

Inspired by the Neo-Platonic philosophy of the young Church, Platonic dualism ruled the medieval mind. You can clearly recognize this in the movie. Heaven or hell, salvation versus damnation, following the call of the flesh or the vocation of the Church, those were some of the dualistic tensions present in the medieval mind. These same tensions can be found in the very life of the first great church leader and philosopher Augustine, who with his philosophy inspired people in the centuries to come and with his contributions to Christian doctrine deeply influenced the development of the young Church.

Augustine was born in Northern Africa in a small town named Stagira. His father was a pagan and his mother a Christian. As a young man who was searching, Augustine became involved with a small sect of religious believers who followed the prophet Mani. Therefore they were called Manicheists. They believed in the equal power of good and evil forces in the universe. These forces were always battling with each other, sort of like an early Star Wars scenario, except that their battle ground was not some galaxy far, far away, but right here on earth, inside the human soul.

You can imagine how young Augustine, who liked to party and had several affairs, took to this religion. He liked the idea that being unfaithful, getting drunk, and altogether living an uncontrolled and passionate life was all part of a divine plan. When you believe that cosmic forces are fighting inside of you for superiority and the outcome is not your own responsibility, you are able to free your conscience from accountability and guilt. These questions of responsibility, free will, and influence of God's grace and faith became problems Augustine struggled with all his life. He wrote major works on this topic, the most famous of which was a book called *Confessions*.

In spite of his lascivious life style, young Augustine was a good student and a deep thinker. He had what one could call a passion for the truth, which brought him initially to join the Manicheans. He had read the Bible and found many things in it that were contradictory and incomprehensible. Among the Manicheans, having a critical mind was encouraged. As a Manicheist he was free to criticize the Bible, much to the dismay of his mother. He also fathered a child without being married to the woman and later was betrothed to another woman of a good family who was still too young to marry. While he waited for her to mature, Augustine even had a few other concubines on the side. One of his favorite prayers was: "God, let me be chaste and well tempered, but not quite yet." Thus was the early life of someone who was destined to become one of the great pillars of the young Christian Church.

The big change in Augustine's life came at the age of 31. He became attracted to the philosophy of Plato, which offered him an outlet for his rational and critical mind. Augustine became one of the leading representatives of what has become known as Neo-Platonism. Neo-Platonism is the adjustment and reinterpretation of Platonic ideas to fit the new religion of Christianity. It is relevant in the context of this book because many followers of Christianity are simply unaware that many of the concepts that they believe to be biblical actually originated with Greek philosophers. Some supposedly Christian concepts are in reality a synthesis of Greek philosophy with Judeo-Christian beliefs.

The lasting turn in Augustine's life came from what is often seen as a sign from God, or at least Augustine saw it that way. One day he argued with a friend in a garden about some philosophical problem. His friend left in anger. Augustine threw himself down under a tree and cried, frustrated that he could not find a satisfying answer to the problem they had pondered. At that moment he heard a child's voice say: "Take it and read." Augustine went into the house and opened the Bible. He had been reading the letters of St. Paul who himself allegedly had been converted to Christianity by a bolt of lightening coming down from heaven.

In the letter to the Romans, Augustine now read the words: "Let us walk honestly as in the day; not in rioting and drunkenness, not in chambering and wantonness" (Romans XIII). In this instance Augustine decided to change and devote his life to God.

Augustine's conversion was, figuratively speaking, like a personal call to walk out of the cave. It was a calling he could not resist. Augustine now realized that Plato's true ideas and forms

Augustine:
SAPIENTA > SCIENTIA

were hidden in the images and parables of the Bible. From now on he tried to reconcile Plato's rational and idealistic approach with the messages he found in the Bible. What Plato saw in the heaven of ideas and forms, Augustine believed to be located in the mind of God. God's mind, in turn, is revealed to us in the Bible. Augustine began identifying God's mind and the revelation in the Bible as interpreted by his Church as sapientia, the ancient idea of wisdom. In contrast, the world was represented inside the cave, the world of passion and fleshly desires. This world he called scientia, from which the word science was later developed. Sapientia, in Augustine's mind, was always superior to scientia. Even when your senses tell you differently, you have to follow the rules laid down in sapientia, the wisdom of God as revealed to us in the Scriptures. Can you see how this insight prepared the ground for the great conflicts between the young scientists and the church at the end of the Middle Ages? Augustine also defined love and gave a Platonic reason for love. In ourselves, we are incomplete. Because we are not complete in and of ourselves, we need to find completion through our love of God. Other loves, such as the love of fellow human beings and the love of things, are also important in this process, but always secondary to the love of God.

Augustine struggled deeply with the problem of human freedom. This of course is closely connected with the question of how evil came into this world, and this leads to the even more important problem: why did God, if he is all powerful, create a world in which there is so much suffering and evil? This last problem became known as the question of theodicy, the defense of God in the face of overwhelming evil.

Can you remember how Plato dealt with the problem of evil? Generally, for the Greeks, evil was not a real power. It was simply the absence of knowledge. Augustine might have been tempted to adopt this view, but there was one big problem. Christians did not believe in the preexistence of the human soul. The soul was created by God together with the body. So Plato's explanation that evil came into this world as a result of the lower gods tampering with the soul on its way down from heaven could not be adopted. Of course, assuming the existence of lower gods would have been equally unacceptable. So Augustine utilized an event in the Old Testament that had found little attention so far to address the problem of evil. The Old Testament was really part of the Hebrew Scriptures, but since Christianity added the New Testament, which contained the life and the teachings of the Christ, those Hebrew books became known as the Old Testament for Christianity.

In the creation story of the Bible, it is reported that Adam and Eve had lived peacefully in the Garden of Eden in harmony with God and their environment. This is strongly reminiscent of the Greek idea of the Golden Age when men and women were equally able to communicate with the gods. People treated each other with respect and lived in peace with each other and their environment. The Hebrew myth contains a test God gave to the first human beings. There was a tree in the Garden from which they were not allowed to eat. No reason was given, just: "Don't eat from this tree."

Can you hear your mother say when you asked why: "Why can't I do this?" – "Because I told you so." You remember how tempted you were as a child to do exactly that which you were forbidden to do. So it was with our so-called first parents. They were tempted by no one less than God. Eve succumbed to the temptation first. You can see how already, here in this early phase, the seeds of male domination were planted. At the same time the snake, once considered a holy animal by many pagan religions because of her awesome power and healing poisons, was turned into the incarnation of evil.

Evil Humans:

Hebrew

Augustine

According to Hebrew tradition, God's temptation of Adam and Eve was to prove their maturity by allowing them to have free will and make their own decisions. In other words, their choice to eat from the tree was proof of their independent mind and freedom. Augustine took the story to mean exactly the opposite. He interpreted the bite in the apple that Eve offered to Adam as a sinful act that tainted all of Adam and Eve's ancestors from now on. Hence this act became known as Original Sin. This was Augustine's interpretation of how evil came into this world, or better, how human evil entered into the world.

There was still the problem of why there are so many natural disasters that cause all kinds of misery. If human beings were endowed with free will and, tainted by original sin, more often choose evil over good, then what about nature? Augustine found another explanation that was buried in the old Biblical stories. Before the world was even created, God had surrounded himself with angels, which he created. Being a good God, he created them all good, but he gave them the power of free will. So even before human beings were created, there was a great uproar in Heaven; part of the angels rebelled against God because they wanted to gain the same powers as God. So God exiled them from Heaven and from then on they represented the forces of evil.

Evil in Nature:

For Augustine these fallen angels were spearheaded by Lucifer, which literally means carrier of light. Lucifer now also became known as Satan. From now on these evil angels were the forces behind the destructive powers in nature. In this way Augustine solved the problem of Evil. In the writings of St. Paul, Augustine found ample affirmation for the idea that humanity is inherently evil and weak. Humanity, according to this belief, is incapable of salvation without the intervention of God. No human action can lead in the direction of salvation, only God's all powerful grace.

Augustine & The Power of Interpretation

Perhaps the most important lesson we must take with us from our studies of Augustine is contained in the one sentence: Credo ut intelligam. In English that means: I believe in order to understand. It always puts God's sapientia, contained in the Bible, first. Even if your senses tell you differently, it is the instruction by God, as expressed in the Bible that contains the truth. Keep that in mind as we move on and enter the age of scientific discoveries.

Young scientists, by and large, followed the philosophy of Aristotle. They relied increasingly more on their senses, which they believed gave them an objective report of the world and the way things are. Scientists eventually developed powerful instruments to prove to the authorities that there senses gave them an accurate account of the world, more objective than what was said in the Bible. So strong was the scientists' trust in their senses, and even more in their instruments, that Galileo invited the Pope to look through the telescope and find for himself what he refused to believe: that the earth was not the center of the universe. Galileo was able to prove that there were other heavenly bodies that moved in circles, not around the earth, but around yet other bodies in the sky. He was punished with house arrest for his disbelief that the sun moved around the earth. It took the Vatican until the last decade of the Twentieth Century to admit that the Holy See was wrong and Galileo was right.

GALILEO + SCIENCE

■ 2. THE END OF THE MIDDLE AGES AND THE RISE OF SCIENCE

We have arrived at the height of the Middle Ages. Having gone through the lawlessness of the Dark Ages, a new era has emerged. Architecture shows this perhaps more than anything else. During the Dark Ages the few churches that people were able to build served not only as houses of worship but also for protection of the faithful. You can see this by the thick walls and small windows. The doors could be shut to keep intruders outside. There was no police power that people could turn to and no military force to protect them.

This all changed at the end of this dark era. As so often, the change was brought about by economic developments and commerce. During medieval times most people lived in rural areas and supported themselves through agriculture. This was an agriculture that produced just enough to feed its owners. So from generation to generation, farms were passed on from father to oldest son. Other children, and there were usually many as is common in such agricultural societies, often ended up in monasteries, either as brothers or as monks. Here they joined a readymade community that offered them lifelong sustenance and support.

In the lands north of the Alps there were some cities, left over from the time of the Roman occupation, to which cultural and political activities had shifted away from Italy, after the fall of the Roman Empire. But there was little use for cities during most of that time and no one wanted to live in them. So for centuries they mostly fell into ruins.

At the end of the Middle Ages or at its height, all this began slowly to change. As I said before, that change was driven by commerce. Peasants in those days began using their ingenuity and made a number of inventions that changed the way they were using their animals and the land. They invented the shoulder harness for the horse so that it was able to pull a heavy load. For its hoofs they invented horseshoes, which were unknown to even the Romans. Once a horse's hoof was worn out, usually long before a horse had aged, the Romans had to discard the horse. The invention of the horseshoe enabled those farmers to make use of a horse for many more years.

For their fields, they invented crop rotation. They learned that planting different types of crops on the same land would make the land much more fertile. As a result of all these inventions, late medieval peasants began producing more and more surplus from their land. Can you figure out what they did with that surplus and how this began changing the whole society?

Let me tell you the story of a young peasant son, Meier Helmbrecht, whose father had produced quite a bit more than the family could use for themselves. The story is reported in one of the oldest novels written in the German language. He took the surplus and went to the next city where others like him from other areas of the country had come to trade goods with each other; and so a new use for the cities slowly developed.

Young Helmbrecht made a good profit with his merchandise. When he came home, all the peasants were happy and grateful and threw him a big party. He had more profit than farming itself would have brought for many generations. So he went out again, was successful again, and came back to be celebrated. But the next time he went to the city, perhaps he had gotten too sure of himself or perhaps the competition was growing, because he lost everything and then some. Helmbrecht came back to his village a poor and broken man. And instead of remembering his former success, the peasants now kicked him out and blamed him for straying away from the right path. Needless to say he ended in misery. The moral of the story, of course, was to put out a conservative warning sign to all those young men who were tempted to go out into the world and make a quick fortune. The author wants to tell them to stay at home, make an honest living just like Dad did, and not get lost and warped in the cities. It goes well a few times, but eventually it will catch up with you. Sound familiar?

Nevertheless, progress was inevitable. More and more often, young peasant men heard the call and turned to trading to make a living. Cities grew rapidly, and with growing commerce there was a new need for a centralized government which could maintain a military force for the protection of the land and its citizenry.

One big problem was the Church. The Church, and especially the more or less independently organized monasteries, had accumulated an incredible amount of land. In fact, at the end of the Middle Ages the Church had become the biggest land owner in Europe.

How did the Church acquire all this wealth? I told you about the children of peasants who were not used on the farm because there were too many of them. Often the younger ones joined a monastery. Well, the church or the monastery generally asked for a hefty endowment to be paid in order to take in a young peasant son. This was often given in the form of land. The land was leased out again to the peasant, except now he had to lease the land from the church and pay a hefty rent, often more than half of the crop. In this way the church got richer and richer and the peasantry, well, they got poorer and poorer, even though they were the ones who had made all those inventions. As a result of these problems the peasants got increasingly angry and eventually rose up against the religious authorities, using their pitchforks and other tools as weapons. These so-called peasant wars lasted for several hundred years and cost hundreds of thousands of lives. It was the beginning of a long series of uprisings against undue domination. The Reformation, the French Revolution, the American Revolution, and the Marxist revolutions, events that span many hundreds of years were all steps in the march toward freedom, equality, and democracy that continues on today.

But toward the end of the Middle Ages, the Church and Europe had different problems. Islam was a relative new comer on the scene. Compared to the thousand-year history of Christianity, Islam was only four hundred years old, and was a fast-developing energetic religion, uncomplicated in its appeal to simple people. Islam made big advances into the heart of Europe. After its start in the deserts of Saudi Arabia, it had spread rapidly into Northern Africa and was now moving into Spanish territory. Soon it occupied large territories of Southern Spain, bringing with it a new culture and new administrative rules. As a religion, from the onset Islam had a very strong focus on family and community. Religious commentary tried to regulate the smallest details of community life, including giving legal instructions concerning almost every aspect of social life, while in theological respects remaining extremely simple. During times of unrest and insecurity of the late Middle Ages, this new religion had a great influence. It quickly spread its message without having to rely on military power.

Christian Europe prepared to fight back in three distinctly different ways:

A. The military response: The Christian church, in connection with Christian rulers, assembled huge armies who as crusaders went south to "liberate" the Holy Lands. What started as a territorial conquest ended in bloody battles for religious superiority? Muslim armies consolidated and fought back, advancing northward as far as the city walls of Vienna.

B. The love response: Christian missionaries, specifically the Franciscans, by showing the caring and loving side of Christianity, tried to prove to Muslims that Christianity was ultimately superior. They often worked in predominantly Muslim communities as social workers and helpers.

C. The intellectual response: Wherever Christian and Muslim intellectuals lived in close proximity, as they did in the Spanish cities, organized public debates concerning the deep questions of the Christian faith. While Aristotle's philosophy had been shunned in the Christian world of the Middle Ages, Muslim philosophers had preserved his text, which now spread through Christianity as well and found numerous followers. Aristotelian logic found a new appeal and was used as a promising tool to defend the dogmas of the Christian faith. This new merger of Christian dogmatism and Aristotelian logic produced a movement in the Christian world that became known as Scholastic or school philosophy. It was the enormous attempt to formulate a logical Christian theology. Our next philosopher, Thomas Aquinas, was as a young man thoroughly instructed in the rigorous discipline of Scholastic philosophy.

On Natural Law

You might recall that this became a problem during the confirmation hearings of one of the current Supreme Court judges, Clarence Thomas. This problem was later over shadowed by the Anita Hill affair. Judge Thomas, himself not a Catholic, nevertheless was educated in a Catholic school, where natural law is taught as a matter of course. This is in apparent conflict with the American tradition. Can you think why?

American law is based on the constitution. For a Supreme Court judge to depend in argumentation on natural law would be unconstitutional. He or she is obligated and sworn to refer to the Constitution as the ultimate authority.

An obvious example is the question of homosexuality. According to natural law, as interpreted by Thomas Aquinas and the Catholic Church as of today, homosexuality is against nature. Current science has nearly univocally concluded that homosexuality is not a choice. In this light it can not be against nature because a homosexuality is born with this sexual preference. Though hard to imagine for someone with a different preference it is not against nature. In this case, according to the American Constitution, which is silent about sexual preferences, a judge would have to decide with the best scientific evidence available, not according to some outdated natural law.

■ 3. THOMAS AQUINAS (1224-1274 AD)

**Thomas Aquinas
(1224-1274 AD)**

© 2006 JupiterImages Corporation

As a young man Thomas Aquinas, the son of an aristocratic family, joined the Dominican order. His family was quite opposed to his choice and supposedly tried to tempt him away from becoming a monk with a beautiful woman. As a monk he studied philosophy and theology at Naples. Later his education brought him to some of the greatest teachers of the time. He was thoroughly trained in what became known as the school or scholastic philosophy.

The goal of scholastic philosophy was to use Aristotelian logic in theology. You might wonder why theology is not taught in American public schools. It's because of the strict separation of church and state in the United States. Theology is the attempt to use scientific or logical means to prove the existence of God and to develop a natural foundation for the rightness of the teaching of the Catholic Church. This became known as the Natural Law theory, the idea that nature when investigated correctly gives us universal laws put there by God.

Aquinas' philosophy represents a departure from the Neo-Platonism and Augustinianism of the Middle Ages. This meant a turn away from revelation and a new emphasis on the value of the natural world. Like Aristotle, Aquinas trusted that God, having made nature, has imbedded in it eternal laws which we as human beings are able to recognize and understand. It was no longer necessary to learn about God through the Bible alone; Aquinas believed that by studying nature we find out about the nature of God. Just like Aristotle he believed that through careful observation of nature and rigorous application of logical rules it is possible to find the truth.

▇ 4. THE FIVE PROOFS OF GOD

This trust led to the famous five formulations proving the existence of God. His cosmological proof begins with an empirical observation. Everything you observe is continuously changing and moving. Every move has a cause, something that made it move, which again is moved by something else, and so on. You come to a seemingly endless line of things that make each other move. Of course, logically you have to admit that this cannot go on for ever. Or can it? Well, Aquinas, following Aristotle, concluded that somewhere the buck must stop. Someone one had to be the first mover, and that first mover, yes, did you guess it? That first mover was God. Therefore Aristotle called God the Unmoved Mover. God is the one who makes everything else move, but does not need to be moved himself.

The second and third proofs are quite similar to the first, all variants of the so called Cosmological argument. They all begin by referring to a certain order in the universe. The fourth is more a moral argument, referring to God as the guarantor of perfection and goodness.

The fifth argument is perhaps the most compelling argument and finds new defenders even today. It is called the Teleological Proof of God or also the intelligent design proof. Perhaps the simplest way to understand this argument is to give you an often used example. Imagine you are a kind of Robinson Crusoe walking on a deserted beach somewhere on a south sea island. You see only rocks, sea shells, dead fish, and water. Your hopes are down ever to find another human being. But suddenly you find a wrist watch. You pick it up and realize it is still ticking. Now your blood is pulsing, your heart is beating faster, and your adrenaline is pumping. Someone must have been here not too long ago, another human being. Your hopes of being rescued have gone up by a thousand times.

This is somewhere similar to the conclusion many people come to when they contemplate the world, our life, and the universe in all its vastness. Even today, modern science tells us that that the initial conditions for the universe to make intelligent human beings possible must have been so incredibly fine tuned that it is nearly inconceivable that it happened by accident. Somehow this world, so these people say, is only possible if it has been designed by an intelligent being. If the watch you have found on the beach makes you conclude that some intelligent creature was there before you, think about how much more compelling the argument is that some intelligence must be behind the creation of all this beauty and complexity in the universe. It is indeed hard to believe that it all came into being by accident. That is the essence of Aquinas' teleological argument. Later we will look at some modern alternatives to the intelligent design argument.

So what is the heritage of this great philosopher who supposedly wrote more than a million words? Very few people today have read much of his work, but his influence on the teachings of the Catholic Church and ultimately on Western Civilization is enormous. As described above, his most lasting impact is in relation to his natural law theory. The official teachings of the Catholic Church rely heavily on this Thomistic construction. From Aristotle, Thomas Aquinas had learned that God imbedded his eternal laws into nature.

By carefully observing and analyzing the natural world, we therefore get information about the divine plan. Aquinas hope was that this plan would not contradict the Bible but expand and build on it. With this turn away from Platonic philosophy, Aquinas spurned the development of science. Scientists were now allowed and encouraged to search into nature to find out about its inner making without having to feel that they were on the wrong path, away from God. Of course, when they started to find evidence that contradicted the Biblical stories, the Church reacted quite swiftly. That struggle continues on until today, concerning moral problems surrounding issues of human sexuality and abortion.

The second field Aquinas excelled in was his use of the rational mind to solve problems. With Aristotle, Aquinas believed firmly that the universe could by understood by we human beings and that even God was somehow understandable for the rational human mind. It has been pointed out, however, that toward the end of his rich and busy life Thomas Aquinas great mind fell into silence. Some have drawn the conclusion that the great thinker had realized that the secrets of the universe and specifically God were not transparent to the rational human mind. They could only be reached in silence and through contemplation. Thomas Aquinas had perhaps become a mystic.

The Catholic Church on the other hand remained firmly committed to natural law theory and against individual search for truth or mystic experimentation. As late as the 1990s the Vatican issued a statement condemning meditation and yoga exercises. In an authoritarian system there remains a fear of the flock finding their own way to God and the truth. Therefore the Church strives to continue to be the gatekeepers of eternal wisdom, even though human beings have matured to the point where they can better handle false magic and negative influences from spirits and ghosts.

CHAPTER IV: RENAISSANCE AND REFORMATION

◼ 1. THE RENAISSANCE

It is long known that history moves in cycles. Which forces drive those cycles is much debated. Karl Marx, the famous German philosopher, said that the historical forces for change are fundamentally economic. History is a continuous evolution of classes struggling against oppression. The oppressed people rise up against the oppressors and gain the upper hand for a while. Once they are in power, they begin oppressing others who in turn eventually rise up against them until they have gained freedom; and the cycle goes on until finally humanity consciously breaks this cycle and reaches the end of history.

Michelangelo: The Creation of Adam
© 2006 JupiterImages Corporation

How will this end of history be reached, according to Marx? Humans will realize that the cause for this ongoing struggle is a difference in economic wealth. Since the beginning of time this difference in the distribution of goods, has been the reason for continuous revolutions. Once the world's goods are distributed equally so that everyone receives according to his or her needs the struggle will finally be over; and the earth will reach a kind of paradise which Marx called a communistic society. This is the way Marx saw the history of Europe, moving on a global scale toward an enlightened society in which violent struggle for superiority can finally come to an end because universal justice has been achieved.

Renaissance, Reformation, and the European Enlightenment were stepping stones on this movement toward a global humanity united in peace and justice. We will see how this view of history, still containing Aristotle's teleological sensibility, was developed by European philosophers from Kant to Hegel and formulated most pointedly by Marx.

The Renaissance is generally known as a rebirth. That's what the word itself means. A rebirth of what? The Renaissance was a rebirth of the classical Greek spirit in philosophy, architecture, and social life. By the end of the Middle Ages, Christianity had spread over most of old Europe, pushing its frontiers far into Ireland and Eastern Europe. Originally these had been pagan countries with a strong pagan culture. What the Roman armies did not achieve, the new religion did. A silent revolution had swept the European lands. I say silent not because the introduction of the new religion was not at all connected with violence. It was, but compared with the violence used by the Roman armies, the spread of Christianity was much more subtle and benign and much more similar to the way American culture is spread around the world today by giant hamburger chains and global commerce (though of course violence is not excluded if we think of the recent war in Iraq).

Christianity expanded by the use of silent manipulation, which many would call conversion. As a philosopher, I believe that to convert someone honestly, the converted should be made aware of their options. Christianity, and most other religious movements, decisively tried to avoid this. Christian missionaries often incorporated pagan feast days and overlaid their own new messages. This was often not realized by the converted believers for centuries. During the church services, they even used a language completely unknown to the followers – Latin. This way the newly converted pagans saw familiar imagery, as in the feasts of Easter and Christmas, but the message had changed.

Today we often think of pagan religions as primitive, barbaric, and perhaps filled with violence. Nothing could be further from the historical truth. As I have pointed out when introducing the history of the ancient Minoans and the associated Golden Age, all old European societies had been remarkably peaceful; and, in regard to their social origination, quite sophisticated. They had as well a quite elaborate religious structure that guided their natural lives here on earth in cycles of birth and rebirth and encouraged a peaceful and considerate existence with a distinctive moral code.

Much of this had been destroyed in the struggle against the advancing Roman armies and because of the violence these armies brought with them. The Romans own goal was the enslavement of free people. But over time armed resistance creates a violent culture itself. Often the ancient ways are forgotten, as the example of Native American history so clearly shows. The violence of the conquerors finally becomes the way of life for the conquered.

So it was in old Europe before Christianity, supposedly a religion of peace, was spread. What was initially, and perhaps to this day, not fully understood was that Christianity and Islam as well are religions that ultimately do not promise peace in this world but in another more distant world called heaven. This may not necessarily even have been Christ's original message. But under the influence of Platonic dualism, which ruled Christianity during the Middle Ages, this world was identified with absolute evil and the other world, Plato's invisible world of ideas, and the Christian heaven, was understood as the ultimate good, the real home for humanity. In this light, the world was seen by medieval people as a valley of tears, a wayside inn that we use for a couple of years only to leave it behind to find our final destination in heaven.

On this journey through life there was little importance given to earthly things. Building on Plato's Republic, the body was seen as a brother donkey, a part of this hostile, strange world that drags our good soul down to earthly pleasures and away from our true destination. Continuing ancient pagan rituals of self flagellation, masses of people beat up their bodies in public displays. Even today in some remote Christian places, such as in the Philippines, on Easter young men are nailed to the cross; and during the religious festivals of Shia Muslims, groups of men beat their bodies until the blood flows. This became common place among medieval Christians, but compared to the old pagan rituals in which flagellation was a means to achieve ecstatic unity with the spirits, the meaning had changed.

The central focus of medieval Christianity was the image of the suffering Christ. Since artists were forbidden by the Church (some would say guided) to solely depict religious images in their art, the presentation of the suffering Christ was probably the most painted and sculpted image during the Middle Ages. In other areas, too, pagan imagery remained but the Christian meaning was substituted. Since major parts of the Christian message remained shrouded in a language that the common people could not understand, Christianity came not as enlightenment but as a sophisticated form of enslavement.

Looking from a cyclical perspective of history, the Renaissance represented a first major move away from medieval dualism and otherworldliness. With Marx, we can say that the historical epoch of the Renaissance was first of all economically driven. I outlined above how medieval peasants, at the height of medieval development, had made enormous advances in technology that drove a change of society from being primarily agricultural to a trading society that eventually built a strong middle class. This did not exist during the Middle Ages. The new merchants were proud of their economic achievements which in turn made them proud of themselves as human beings. This new found pride in humanity was the primary engine behind the growth of the movement we know as the Renaissance.

New found pride in humanity was the primary engine behind the growth of the movement we know as the Renaissance.

Merchants became popular everywhere, and they began populating cities from North to South and from East to West. The new found wealth allowed them to divide up work-related activities in the cities, something that had not existed prior to this time, at least not since Greek and Roman times. It allowed them to institute leisure time, an extravagance unknown to the peasants. Besides many new churches, theaters and concert halls were built to provide spaces for entertainment of the masses. Cities became independent first, protecting themselves against intruders and regulating life within. This new form of socialization soon spread to other regions and lands, eventually creating what we know today as the nation state.

Cities such as Venice, Florence, and Padua in Italy – but also Paris and Prague – became powerful centers of the new Renaissance. Central to the core of the Renaissance revival was the philosophy of Aristotle. So while economic forces made the new historical stage possible and could not be understood without them, there were many other factors involved. The philosophical and spiritual factors went far beyond the economic factors.

I do not believe that Christianity itself would have had the power of renewal represented by the Renaissance. The Renaissance rather represents a powerful influence of pagan forces that lay dormant in the underground of European societies for centuries. They now recognized in the philosophy of Aristotle a certain kinship, and combined, they broke free and revolutionized European society from the bottom up.

What specifically was the draw of Aristotle's philosophy? To illustrate this it is perhaps good to use one of our visual examples, Umberto Ecco's The Name of the Rose. Umberto Ecco is a well known professor of philosophy and linguistics in Italy. His novel was the result of years of historical research. When first published, it became an instant bestseller which was promptly put on the list of forbidden books by the Vatican. Again of course, I encourage you to read the book; but the movie is a good rendition of the novel.

At first sight you may think that it is Brother William's use of Aristotelian logic that is most reminiscence of the Aristotelian influence on the late medieval world which became the hallmark of the Renaissance. This is only partially true. Umberto Ecco created, in his character of Adsel, the servant and apprentice of Brother William, a more accurate image of the coming age. With his persistent use of the logical mind and his unbendable belief in the truth of the written word to set human beings free, Brother William is a perfect example of the scholastic scholar, represented by Aquinas and many others.

It is the young Adsel who represents the future, still a few centuries away. Why is this so? His importance for the history of the future plays out in the background of the role of the peasantry in the movie. At first the peasants are depicted as totally dependent on the Church. As was often the case at the end of the Middle Ages, peasants had to lease, from the church or monastery, the land that they worked and then turn in much of their earnings to the church or monastery. As their reward, they received promises of a glorious future life in Heaven. Don't you think our present government wishes sometimes that it had such an explanation for raising taxes? Social security was not an earthly safety net, but a heavenly one. No one could ever check whether the earthly powers had robbed the bank.

By the end of the movie with the tower burning, one of their own to be burned on the pyre, and the church authority in general upheaval and in retreat, the peasants pick up rocks and get their pitch forks ready to rise up against the unjust authority of the Church. The Church's life blood has waned due to excesses in its exercise of power and wealth. This movement of the peasants' revolutionary struggle began here and ended in the Reformation and splitting off of the protestant churches from the mother church in Rome.

Not Brother Williams, but Adsel has made a connection to that revolutionary element represented by the peasantry. This is why the explicit love scene in the film is so important. It points toward a new evaluation of earthly love, "the only earthly love" he ever new as he expresses at the end of the film, when the camera pans high up into the sky seemingly wanting to embrace the whole earth as the new love object of the coming Renaissance. At this point in history it is still an illegitimate love, at least from the perspective of the intellectuals of the time who were mostly committed to service to the Church. But the new Renaissance man took Aristotle's use of empiricism, combined it with Aquinas' suggestion that the divine was a feature of the natural world, and remembered their own pagan preference for earthly pleasure and earthly fulfillment. This he combined with a new found pride in his own achievements, producing the Renaissance, one of the most powerful movements in history.

Economically powerful, intellectually proud, and culturally sophisticated, the Renaissance man became the proverbial image of the highly educated and well rounded individual who is socially engaged in society, culturally active in the arts, and scientifically involved in a broad number of disciplines.

Unfortunately, this spiritual renewal, heralded by the new Renaissance, continued the misogyny that had dominated medieval society. Despite this, and even though they lived in the shadow of the Church some powerful women developed and promoted their own often heretical ideas. Hildegard of Bingen, a nun in the Eleventh Century who presided over an all woman monastery, wrote music and poetry, and at times refused to let men be present at all woman's Mass. This is only one example of such women.

It is often said that women had less access to philosophy because of their suppressed social status. I think this is only partially the reason for the lack of female contributors to the catalogue of Western philosophers. A deeper reason is found in the reality that Western philosophy had, from it's beginning, been distinctly defensive of male dominance; and, as such, had little attraction for women who saw themselves differently. While this could also be said of the Christian religion itself, there is the fact that many women became active within the Church and were devote religious believers. In addition, the point remains that religious symbolisms are so varied and religious imagery so rich that women could easily find points of identification even within a religion that was at least on the surface thoroughly male dominated, though, as Riane Eisler pointed out, throughout the ages there were many Christian women in the iconography of the Catholic Church. The veneration of Holy Mary was provided for women to identify with a Queen of Heaven, a distinctly pagan image that will be refuted by the Reformation, the next movement in history that we will deal with in some depth.

Medieval Altar Piece
© 2006 JupiterImages Corporation

Before we move on, one more word about the Renaissance artist. For artists, the Renaissance represented the removal of heavy, giant chains the Middle Ages had put around their necks. During the dark times of the Middle Ages, the Church was in complete control of the arts, allowing only the creation of images of Biblical stories. Any personification of pictures was strictly prohibited, as was the depiction of familiar scenes. Everything had to refer back to the Biblical land and depict the story of suffering and final salvation through the risen Christ.

Toward the end of the Middle Ages, artists allowed themselves increasingly more freedom as the grip of the Church loosened. Artists more often used to depict faces of people they knew in the midst of Biblical figures, painted the picture of their home city in the background while the foreground still showed the scene of the birth of Christ or the Renunciation in which Mary received the message from the angel to become the Mother of God.

One particular story demonstrates how worldly things slowly began influencing religious art. While this is, of course, easily still recognizable in visual arts of the times, I will give you an example of how this played out in a drama in, a play which the church authorities, probably the village priest, had arranged to commemorate and bring closer to the people the message of the risen Christ. We have three versions of the same story as it evolved over fifty years and was written down over approximately half a century by writers of the time.

As I said, the play is about the resurrection of Christ. In its center are the three women, three Mary's as reported in the Bible, who arrived early on Easter morning at the tomb where Christ had been buried only two days ago, only to find the heavy rock rolled away and the tomb empty. According to the Biblical story, an angel tells them not to worry, because Christ has risen from the dead. They tell this happy news to a group of apostles advancing toward the tomb. These men now go to the community of the apostles in hiding and tell them the happy news. Now at this point a pagan twist is introduced: in later versions this run to tell the good news to the other apostles becomes the central piece of the performance. In the last version, the run has turned into a competition between the young men of the village to show who the fastest runner is. The fastest runner was probably then the choice for the most desirable woman of the village. The whole performance had become so worldly that church authorities felt compelled to ban it from church property and from performance within the Church.

Medieval society was hierarchically structured following the three tiered social order laid out by Plato in the Republic. In this Feudal system the lowest tier was occupied by the peasants. These peasants at the base began pushing from the bottom up against their oppressors. The feudal system or feudalism is a societal structure best represented by a pyramid. The broad base is filled with average people, the middle by an elite class of soldiers, dukes, and landowners, and the top by the nobility headed by the king or the pope. The Church in this sense always understood itself as a shadow or spiritual pyramid behind the material, earthly pyramid of worldly powers. The pope claimed to have received his authority directly from God which he could transfer to the worldly power, the king. With the beginning of secularism the power structure changed and feudalism began to disintegrate. But in some countries, foremost of them Russia, feudalism lasted into modern times.

■ 2. THE RISE OF THE MIDDLE CLASS

At the end of the Middle Ages this feudal system, as it was called, began to disintegrate. It was challenged in a number of ways.

First there were the peasants, who occupied the base and were pushing from the bottom up against their oppressors. The second challenge came from the newly developing middle class that first began to replace the decadent class of vassals and lords. But as their power and influence grew, they made completely new demands on the crown. In the new merchant economy, exchange of land was swiftly replaced by exchange of money, the currency of the new middle class. The new middle class was also self-conscious and individualistic. Like the peasant son, Meier Helmbrecht, the whole class had broken away from the collectivistic life of agrarian society and had developed an individualism, which they found had been first developed among the Greeks. Proud and independent, their new philosophy was human centered. You can imagine that these new humanists were a bad fit for medieval feudalism. They soon lost trust in being protected by the king and began to equip their own armies to protect the merchant fleets and the cities. Whole cities declared themselves independent from the central authorities of the time.

■ 3. THE REFORMATION

The third challenge came from within the Church and eventually caused Christianity to split, a schism that lasts into the present. The secular and materialistic spirit of the Renaissance had not stopped in front of the gates of the Church itself, but swept through her like a brush fire. Religious leaders had become more secular, caught up in infighting aimed at the very heart of the Church, which at times was being run by three competing popes. Bishops dressed and lived more like worldly princes, and to support their habits they made money by selling indulgencies and other sacred services.

The discontented faithful had also adopted the independent and critical spirit of the new middle class. They ceased to be satisfied with being ruled from the top, even if this elite claimed to speak with the voice of God. They wanted to read the word of God themselves and make up their own minds. A powerful new technological invention, the printing press, came to their aid.

You probably have a difficult time imagining a world without books. The movie you watched in preparation for the last unit gave you a pretty good impression of the value of books before easy copying became available. Books had to be handwritten and since the parchment they were written on disintegrated every so often, those few handwritten books had to be treated very carefully; hence, they were copied over and over again. No books were available for the average Joe like you and me, and there was no public library to turn to either.

The printing press was invented in Germany in the 1450s and changed the situation immediately and profoundly. When the reformer Martin Luther decided to translate the word of God for the first time into his native language, German, the powerful new medium came to his aid. Believing that everyone had the right to read God's word and do independent investigation, he took away the privilege to interpret God's word from the hierarchy of the church and gave it to the people. Everyone, Martin Luther believed, was a priest and could interpret the Bible for herself.

This caused quite a revolution in the Church, whose leaders had naturally considered themselves to be the legitimate interpreters of the gospel. For the first time in the history of humanity, people believed that each person had an individual conscience that could guide them through life.

There are too many important aspects of the Reformation to mention them all here, but I would like you to consider those that became decisive for our theme of compassionate thinking and cooperation. Reformed churches in general purged Christianity of any remaining pagan elements. Focusing primarily on God's work, artistic expression in all forms but music was generally shunned from Protestant churches and their services. The focus of worship became God and his son, Jesus Christ, through whom God had acted in this world. Gone were all the Saints and gone was the extensive Maryolatry, or worship of Mary, that often gave, especially to the female half of Christianity, a sense of having a gender representative in heaven. Under the influence of the new spirituality, music as a spiritual expression reached new heights.

A generally more rational approach to questions of faith bears the signature of Aristotle. This new rationalism, combined with the trust and pride in the individual's power, heralded in another great movement that we shall consider when we discuss the Enlightenment.

CHAPTER V: THE AGE OF REASON

■ 1. RENÉ DESCARTES (1596-1650)

Although it is probable that not too many people know its real meaning, **René Descartes'** statement, "I think, therefore I am" could easily make it among the best known phrases in the world.

René Decartes (1596-1650)
© 2006 JupiterImages Corporation

Imagine that you are sitting in front of the fireplace in the evening. You have been sitting there for hours contemplating difficult philosophical questions. Among the most troubling of these questions for you is this one: What can we really know for sure? The fire in the fireplace is slowly burning down; only the embers are glowing, throwing an eerie light on the room around you, which slowly falls into darkness. You are dressed in a heavy winter coat, because the fireplace is the only source of heat and it is cold outside. You ask yourself: What do we really know for sure, I mean really? Many people have asserted many things, but these were all just assertions. Let's doubt everything that can possibly be doubted. This is Descartes' situation and this very doubting made him the father of modern philosophy.

After first asking skeptically what was this man thinking when he made such outlandish speculations, you will find out that he was quite a serious man. Descartes was a trained mathematician and scientist who nevertheless throughout his life maintained a healthy respect for the power of the Church. He did not want to upset anybody, really. So after doubting pretty much all the old rules and truths, he made a 180 degree turn and introduced a benevolent God who comes to the rescue of our doubting mind and saves the world from being doubted away.

He probably changed his mind the following day, when he had to rekindle the fire in the fireplace and could not figure out how to make ends meet. But that night of radical doubt everything, and I mean everything, pretty much disappeared into oblivion. The whole world around him had vanished into doubt. He even imagined that a mean and deceptive God might presently cheat him into believing that the glowing embers in the fireplace were really real and the toes in his house shoes really were freezing.

The one and only thing he was unable to doubt away was his doubting mind. So maybe he first formulated for himself, "I doubt, therefore I am", but then he generalized the idea uttering the famous phrase, "I think, therefore I am." Not even a deceptive and evil god could make him believe that he existed when in reality he didn't.

Descartes was not crazy or high on some drug. He was a clear-thinking mathematician. His goal was to apply the rigor of mathematics to all philosophical questions. Before he knew it, he had lost track of the real world. Nothing seemed to exist except his doubting self. By implication, he may have concluded that you too are similar to him in being another doubting self. But that was already a matter of contention for this radical doubter. An evil god could have tricked him into believing that even you exist. This of course raised the thorny issue for Descartes of why write all those books if all that's out there is a world full of deceptions.

Well, remember what I said, Descartes was not crazy; he did not want to have a run in with the powers of the Church. Just recently they put on trail and condemned Galileo for a lesser offense. Saying that the whole world was an illusion, talking about a deceptive God who makes you only believe the world is real, would be powerful stuff from which to construct a case of heresy against you.

So in order to enjoy a safe reality and on the way please the Church, Descartes quickly introduced an all loving God who guaranteed to the rest of us that the world was really real. But nevertheless the method of radical doubt he had introduced, stuck and became the hallmark of modern philosophy. We don't want to take anything for granted that some one assures us is true. In order to withstand philosophical scrutiny, every assertion from now on had to undergo the test of radical doubt.

To do the guy justice, Descartes mostly designed his radical doubt to debunk old scholastic assertions, like those proofs of the existence of God put together by Aquinas. Yet nevertheless, in the process of doubting, he had nearly lost the whole world, including your lunch packet, the Chicago Cubs, New York City, the Golden Gate Bridge, and everything else. Descartes and a Buddhist monk could have easily met half way and neither one would have known that the other one was there. (Who says philosophers can't master a joke?)

Incidentally, you may know Descartes from a whole other angle. Cartesian algebra, the coordinate system that the man invented, is still in use today. Pretty good for some one who is all into doubt!

Descartes is credited with another little tidbit that had great consequences. Animal rights activists, listen up! Descartes wrote a little but extremely consequential essay about the inability of animals to feel pain because they don't have a concept for pain. Would you believe this? He described animals as little machines that may squeak and scream when you hurt them, but all this is just mechanical expression of nothing meaningful at all. Animals just can't think, and thinking is what you need to express and therefore feel pain. Take that for a rational line of thinking! But scientists, who were ready to start animal experimentation on a full scale, swallowed Descartes' reasoning hook line and sinker, as they say. They even applied the same line of reasoning to the treatment of children who, until Freud came along, were operated upon without anesthesia since the same argument was applied to them as to animals.

Another important aspect in respect to Descartes' long lasting influence needs to be mentioned. Descartes divided the world into two, a thinking world and an extended world. I like the two Latin terms he used: res extensa for the extended thing and res cogitans for the thinking thing. This was another convenient arrangement that served both scientists and the Church. Descartes declared that scientists should be free to experiment with res extensa, the material world, while *res cogitans* was left for the Church to administer. This division, reminiscent of Platonic dualism, became the so-called Cartesian dualism that survives far into the modern world. One side effect of this division was finally dismantled by postmodern deconstruction. This was the effect Cartesian dualism had on consciousness research, or the study of the human mind. For many centuries such research was not considered to be a legitimate domain for science. After all, the mind was distinctly one of those res cogitans, a thinking thing, and that was the domain of the Church. Sigmund Freud finally came to the rescue!

So did Descartes' philosophy help to create more compassionate human beings? Most emphatically not. His achievements can be seen in making the human mind less gullible to false absolutes and false truths. His contributions toward mathematics stand beyond question. But his influence on the humaneness of humanity was dismal. For too long his dualism served as a pretense for not exploring the human mind and consciousness. His description of the natural world as automatons without emotions added to the whole concept of the universe as a machine, a lifeless construction.

■ 2. ISAAC NEWTON (1642 - 1727)

Isaac Newton's contribution to science became known as Newtonian Science. It gave birth to the philosophy of **Deism**, or the idea of a totally mechanical universe presided over by a disinterested deity, who had started the world like a giant clock but now left it alone to its own devices. This made the classical understanding of the universe as a machine possible.

Isaac Newton
(1642 - 1727)
© 2006 JupiterImages Corporation

We will not specifically treat Newton as a philosopher, but he nevertheless influenced the modern world view profoundly. The world of classical science is often depicted as a giant tinker toy, you know those pieces you played with as a child. Or, perhaps you were more the Lego type. That fits the bill, too. In fact, the guy who invented Lego, a Danish man, was a kind of philosopher. He was fascinated with the idea that one could take one small unit and build all kinds of things with it, perhaps even a whole universe. In his own way, Mr. Lego was an Atomist. If you ever make it to Denmark, I recommend checking out Legoland. You can sit in piles of Lego blocks and create your fantasy castle or whatever you want, all day long. You can even drive a Lego car and get a Lego drivers license.

The important thing in the Newtonian world was laws, those iron laws of nature. In this mechanical world, everything could be determined with precision, from now until doomsday, with nothing left to chance. Can you imagine the excitement? If you want to know what's in store for you at the next party, whether you will score with Mary this time or not, you visit a Newtonian scientist. She will tell you exactly what's in your deck of cards, I mean exactly: who you will end up marrying (no, it's not your Prom date). You will be told how many children you will have, what sex they will be, and the date and circumstances of your death. No, you will not be killed in a car accident, but something like it that is just as bad. And finally you will find out how your kids will die and how the world will come to an end.

Whoa, I hear you say, that's way too much information. And we all know that no science could ever make those predictions. That is, today we know it. Back then it was a different story. People really believed in this promise of science. Since everything was connected by cause and effect, and everything evolved according to eternal laws of nature, everything could be known with precision, if one just knew all the initial conditions.

No, scientists back then were not totally stupid or gullible. They actually were pretty smart. They knew that we would never be able to know all of the initial conditions, that is, every little detail that was the case in the beginning. But here is the beauty. They thought only big things mattered. It's sort of the same as when I give you a little kick, and it only hurts a little bit,

87

and you are likely to be able to ignore it; but if I kick you really hard, it hurts a lot, and you have to go into action. That is how they thought the universe was constructed. Little things in the beginning mattered little and could be ignored; only big things mattered. Therefore when Newton calculated the movement of the moon around the earth, he had no problem in ignoring the influence of the rest of the universe on the moon and the earth. All he needed to do was to calculate the earth as it related to the moon, just those two objects. He didn't even have to consider the mass of the two bodies; he treated them as if they were points. His calculations came out pretty darn near correct. But today, after we have learned from Chaos Theory that initially small conditions can have a decisive and unpredictable influence on the outcome of an event, through feedback loops, Newtonianism has lost much of its convincing power. So don't worry. If you want to know which sweetheart you will marry, you still had better look in a crystal ball or make a pilgrimage to the Oracle of Delphi.

■ 3. SPINOZA (1632-1677)

SPINOZA
(1632-1677)
© 2006 JupiterImages Corporation

Spinoza, born to a Jewish family in Amsterdam, was excommunicated as an atheist at the age of 24. He was the first philosopher who truly broke away from Platonic and Cartesian dualism by proclaiming that God was in everything. This view is called pantheism. Shunned by his community for his unorthodox views, Spinoza made a living as a simple lens grinder. He died early, probably because of all the glass particles he had inhaled. In his only work, called Ethics, he outlined his pantheistic view. This view reminds me remotely of Aristotle, but also has a mystical component probably taken from Spinoza's knowledge of Judaic Cabalism.

Cabalism, which first began in the Jewish Diaspora in Spain during the 11th Century, had multiple influences on European, but particularly German, philosophy. It's influences can be found from Hegel to Marx, Adorno, and Habermas, as well as in the French philosophers Foucault and Derrida.

The heart of Cabalism goes back to a revision of the original Biblical creation story by a Rabbi called Isaac Luria. Here is his story:

Gershom Scholem, a contemporary Jewish scholar, extensively researched into the history of Jewish mysticism, especially Cabalism. Scholem reports about the school of Isaac Luria, which arose in Palestine as a transplant of Spanish Cabalism after the exodus of the Jews from Spain at the end of the Middle Ages. Luria added a new version of the creation of primal humans to the existing symbolic creation stories of the Cabala that lent itself to a clearer and more vivid interpretation of mystical reality and underlined the need for mysticism and redemption. In a world of impermanence and insecurity, full of yearning for redemption and the coming of the Messiah, Luria's symbolic story provided a vehicle for active involvement of humans in the process of salvation.

According to Luria, when God created man, sparks of divine energy broke out of the first man's eyes. Clay vessels that were supposed to catch the sparks broke in the process. The fragments of the clay vessels, interspersed with sparks of the divine, tumbled through empty space. From the pieces of the clay vessels the things of this world came into being. The sparks of the divine scattered leaving divine goodness in the world. Divine spirit and soul was present in people and things. Thus, Lurianic Cabalism saw the sparks of the divine exiled from their true home and calling out for redemption. Shekhinah, the presence of God in the world, was the feminine side of God. Shekhinah was exiled and wandering in sorrow, crying for redemption. Redemption was known as Tikkun, or the restoration of the primordial harmony. By uniting oneself to God in Kawwanah, or mystical intentionality, and by uniting oneself to those sparks of the divine in people or things, one can lift those divine sparks out of their cramped imprisonment and free them to rejoin the divine.

We will soon see how Spinoza's pantheistic philosophy infused with Jewish Cabalism left its imprint on Western philosophy.

4. EMPIRICISM VERSUS RATIONALISM

You have probably never given much thought to whether you were born with some specific ideas, concepts, or notions. Although there are some distinct similarities, this is not the same question that is critically examined in the famous nature versus nurture debate.

Remember the last time you discussed your sexual preference with your friend? Your friend insisted that you were born with the tendency to love girls, but you sort of thought that it was a learned behavior. That is the part of the nature versus nurture debate. Most scientists today believe that a person is born with a sexual preference, which of course means that you would have to work against your own nature to change it. For a homosexual it would be unnatural to try to be heterosexual. There are many more characteristics that we are born with. These things are part of our genetic makeup.

JOHN LOCKE
© 2006 JupiterImages Corporation

That is not what the debate about **empiricism** versus **rationalism** is concerned with. To understand this set of questions we have to go back all the way to Plato. Remember how Plato argued that we know about those eternal ideas or forms? He believed that my soul, before it came into my body, had a prior existence. It knew from the time it had dwelt with God how things ought to be in perfection. How else, Plato asked, would we ever know what perfection looks like? We never have seen perfect things in this world, have we? I hear you say, the new BMW you got for your 21st birthday is pretty darn perfect, at least until you put the first dent into it before less than a week had passed, backing up in a parking lot at Blockbuster. Well, the car is pretty perfect, but you still need to have a good warranty and good insurance, just in case.

That is not the perfection Plato was after. Plato thought more of a perfect circle, a perfect boyfriend, perfect love. We have seen all kinds of near perfect things in this world, but even to know that something nears perfection, you have to have a sense of real perfection and that you never get by watching things in this world. That is the kind of thing you must be born with. In Plato's philosophy these ideas are called innate. An innate idea is an idea that you have at birth. You don't get it from experience.

Wait a minute, you say, my little brother has no clue what a perfect ice cream sundae looks like. He'll eat anything that comes in his reach. Plato said that those innate ideas are just slumbering inside of you until they are awakened by a relevant experience or a good teacher.

So, you say, next time I can't find a solution to a calculus problem, I'll just ask my little brother? You said it's already all inside of him, so he should easily give me the solution. Well, not quite. It is inside of him, but it needs to be awakened. Education, for Plato, is literally leading people out of the cave and making them aware of their own inner knowledge of perfection, the knowledge they already possess but are not quite aware of.

Now you say, that is really a bunch of... Not so fast. We are all children of our scientific age, which is thoroughly empirical. The empiricists made the famous statement, another one of the top ten: The mind at birth is a tabula rasa, an empty slate. Your mind is blank at birth, with no innate ideas. Everything you know, you know through experience. That is the empiricists' dogma. That is what they believe. You can see now that we are all brought up, more or less, with this empiricist credo.

In the Seventeenth and Eighteenth Centuries these questions caused a furious debate. By and large it was philosophers living in England, Frances Bacon, John Locke, and David Hume, who defended the empiricist view. Perhaps they had a more practical outlook on life. They were children of merchants, of business people, people who traveled a lot and had seen the world. Science and scientific methods were also much more accepted in England, and this promoted a thinking that was more informed by Aristotelian philosophy. If you remember, it was exactly the problem with innate ideas that made Aristotle depart from Plato.

Empiricist philosophy had a great influence on the way we educate our children. In Plato's world, the purpose of education was to wake up what is already in the mind. My grandparents' generation believed that a person had certain talents or gifts. A good teacher would spot those talents and build on them. Though one might disagree with Plato's premise of inborn ideas, the effect it had on teaching was just that: teachers were to watch children carefully and help them to develop to the best of their abilities. I kind of like that view of education.

Under the influence of empiricism, education changed. A teacher lost the expectation that the child had those talents. The mind was a blank slate; everything had to be filled in from the outside. Sometimes when I look at education today, at the way facts are dispensed, it makes me think of a child's brain that has been drilled open with a funnel attached to the hole, and facts are poured into it. Not a very empowering process, is it?

Let me briefly sum up the difference between the **two schools of thought:**

Empiricists believe that all our knowledge comes from experience. Knowledge, the Empiricists say, is a **posteriori**. While they admit that there are complex ideas that we can never really have experienced, they contend that these can all be traced back to experience. While the early empiricists, like John Locke, turned halfway rationalist when the question of God came up (we have not necessarily experienced God), the later modern day empiricists, also called logical positivists, claim that certain questions like the one about God should not even be asked. It is a nonsensical question.

Rationalists say that our mind can have certain ideas and know certain things that it cannot have experienced. The human mind is capable of what they call intuitive knowledge, from which it then can deduct other valid knowledge and can trust that it is true. The rationalist Descartes used this intuitive knowledge to reclaim the existence of the external world and of God. You remember that his skeptical mind had led him to put in doubt everything that could possibly be doubted.

Rationalists invoked intuition mostly in regard to knowledge about morality and beauty. How else would we know what's right and wrong and what is beautiful and ugly? When you ask yourself these two questions, you will probably come out squarely on the side of the empiricists who say again that it's all experience. If we hadn't experienced goodness, we would not know it, and beauty is obviously in the eye of the beholder.

Watch out when you argue that that's what you believe, because that's what is right and true. That would not take into account the power of education, upbringing, and yes, indoctrination. Wise men have discussed these questions at great length and have often agreed to disagree. They are difficult questions and simple answers are almost always wrong.

You need to know one more concept in this respect. The questions of rationalism and empiricism are all questions of epistemology, or epistemological questions. Philosophers know about a special area of philosophy they call epistemology. After ontology, ethics, and aesthetics, epistemology is the fourth large field of philosophical concern. It deals with all questions of knowledge. How do we know something? How can we be sure that what we know is really what is out there? We will see that precisely this question, the question of knowledge will become the key to understanding the philosophy of one of the most difficult philosophers, Immanuel Kant, who said of himself that he was ushering in a Copernican Revolution in philosophy. And that he did.

The Renaissance – "Oh, men and their priorities..."

I think therefore I am, but my **mind** thinks, & all I can see without doubt is my **body**... Therefore, the **mind** is the province of our unknowable God, and the **body** is the province of our **knowable SCIENCE** !

SACRED PHYSICAL / LOWLY MENTAL

DESCARTES

Order in the universe is like order in a well-built clock... Therefore, the universe **IS** a well-built clock. I'll revolutionize science & discover the universe's laws: I'll **BREAK** the clock to peek **INSIDE** it !

SACRED ORDER / LOWLY CHAOS

NEWTON

My eyes & my telescope do not lie - I believe what I **SEE** and will risk my freedom to challange dogmatic thought. Therefore, the evidence of our senses shall be the **RULER** and our own intro-spective minds shall be the **RULED** !

SACRED EXPERIMENT / LOWLY LOGIC

GALILEO

These men's logic is beyond my wit, and progress from their methods is inevitable... and men prefer progress. Therefore, the Church must loudly praise God for science, and scientists must quietly praise the Church for granting permission !

SACRED POWER / LOWLY POWER

THE CHURCH

How does the rationalism versus empiricism debate relate to our topics of compassionate thinking, cooperation, and partnership? We can pretty much say today that the case for rationalism is lost. You could convince no one that cooperation is the way to go by claiming that you just intuitively know so; not after Darwin demonstrated, empirically, that evolution of all life advances through competition and survival of the fittest. The case for cooperation and partnership will have to be made empirically. I will later give at least an outline of how I plan to do this.

Even to derive reasons for goodness from intuition or a priori arguments as Kant had proposed does not have many followers today. We are and will be children of a scientific and pragmatic age. We believe what we can test, what can be empirically verified, or at least what can be convincingly demonstrated that something once existed and was used with some success.

In this respect there is great hope that moral ideas, those that connect with cooperation and partnership, or living in community and selflessly helping each other, are not solely human achievements but can be found in great abundance in the natural world. This includes the world of animals and plants, even one-celled organisms, and possibly even the inorganic world.

■ 5. IMMANUEL KANT (1724-1804)

Immanuel Kant
(1724 - 1804)
© 2006 JupiterImages Corporation

Kant's greatest achievement is that he gave a central role to the observer in the way we experience the world. Classical science as initiated by Isaac Newton left the world as an objective construction following iron laws. There was no place for the observer. Science adopted this view and many scientists still today are convinced of it, even though Albert Einstein and Quantum Mechanics did the same thing from a scientific point of view that Kant had done from a philosophical perspective. Kant himself called this observer dependence involved in experience a Copernican Revolution. Like Copernicus, who had moved the Earth out of the center of the universe, Kant moved the subjective observer into the center. The way we see things, he argued, is forever influenced by our perception. We will never really know what things actually are in and of themselves. That recognition should have robbed scientists of their objective world, since making statements about the world, even scientific ones, is forever influenced by our perspective, by the way we see things.

One intellectual of the time, the well known German writer, **Heinrich von Kleist,** who knew Kant's work, was so shocked about the consequences of this insight that he said: It's like we were all born with pink eyeglasses fastened to our sight. We cannot take them off. We see the world and everything in it is pink. Now we have a hunch that things really are not all pink, but there is no way for us to know how they really are.

Here is a quick explanation of why I think scientists should have taken Kant a lot more seriously back then. It takes us into Twentieth Century physics. In his *General Theory of Relativity,* Albert Einstein showed that space and time are not objective, natural constants. Space and time are not a neutral background for physical things to evolve in front of. Einstein showed that time and space depend on the observer's position, that is, upon his or her perspective. If you travel fast, close to the speed of light, space warps and time slows down. This observer dependence was confirmed by quantum physics. Here it turned out that the objects of the quantum world, tiny quanta called electrons, photons, etc., behave differently when observed than when not observed. When not observed, they behave like a wave; when somebody checks them out, they collapse into a bullet-like point or particle. When Kant speculated that the objects of this world are probably not at all what we think they are and that our mind adds much to the way we perceive things, he had his finger on a very modern way of looking scientifically at the world.

If you think this is not a big deal, think again. The quantum world is not some strange creation you visit in Disneyland; it's what you and I are made out of. It's the world of the smallest units of nature we have found so far, and everything, really everything, is made up of it. Why don't I see it, you ask? Well, it's just so small. Consider this: seeing an atom from where we are is like spotting an orange on earth with your naked eyes while looking from the moon. It's that small. And the smallest particles are still several billion billion times smaller. If you think of it, you must admit that this is truly a marvelous, complex, and ridiculously fascinating world we live in.

So with these two discoveries, science should have caught up several centuries ago with where Kant had tried to guide us, but by and large scientists today are still steeped in mechanical, Newtonian thinking. They acknowledge Einstein's discoveries, but then go on ignoring spacetime as a real player in their theories , and they use quantum mechanics to build all kinds of consumer gadgets but refuse to take its implications seriously.

Kant should properly be called a rationalist, though he tried in his philosophy to find a synthesis between the rationalist and the empiricist position. The empiricists believed that all judgments were based on experience and therefore *a posteriori*. By combining two empirical judgments, we can reach a synthetic *a posteriori* judgment. These are conclusions we make that add something new to our knowledge base. But ultimately they can be traced back to experience. For the empiricists, intuition never entered into this picture. For them, ideas about God, freedom, and life after death had to remain either illusory or simply wrong, because none of these things could ever be experienced.

Now Kant added something new to this debate. In certain instances, he said, it is possible to make synthetic a priori judgments. In plain words, this means that one can have intuitive ideas that are not derived from experience. They add something important to our knowledge base and are true, mostly because we need them to be true. If you think that this kind of argument is a little twisted, you are not the only one, but Kant spent a lot of time and effort to prove his point. Anyone who wants to disprove him, probably will have to spend the rest of her life researching and writing. More than half of your life will be spent reading his work, the second half understanding it, and the third half refuting his ideas. You get my drift. Not only is his work difficult to read in the original German language – I can vouch that it is even more difficult to read in translation. In any case, but especially in the case of Kant whose sentences sometimes stretch over half a page, translation means interpretation. So when you read Kant in translation, always be aware that you are reading what the translator thought Kant's sentences meant. And the meaning is not always obvious.

Besides initiating the above mentioned Copernican revolution, let me focus on t**hree major contributions Kant made to humanity**:

- he made a major contribution to the idea of the European Enlightenment of which he was one of the strongest advocates;

- his work in ethics has revolutionized the way we think about morality in general; and

- he wrote an impassioned plea advocating world peace and cooperation among the nations, something very novel and revolutionary for his time.

I will treat each of those topics in some depth.

■ A. THE EUROPEAN ENLIGHTENMENT

You notice that I am making it a point to call the Enlightenment we are discussing here the European Enlightenment. This is because it is distinctly different from another Enlightenment which I call the Eastern Enlightenment. So not to be confused, let me briefly tell you what the Eastern Enlightenment is all about. You might have heard the story about when the Buddha sat under a Bodi tree. After living an ascetic life for many years searching for enlightenment, it came over him quite suddenly. In a flash of lightning, he realized the real truth. From then on, he was a changed man and began to teach this specific type of Eastern Enlightenment. No one really knows for sure what exactly the Buddha experienced, and you certainly get different answers depending on which sect of Buddhism you are asking. The only thing we know is that it came instantaneously, not after a long, logical search. In fact, logic is often in opposition to this kind of enlightenment. Eastern practice to reach enlightenment varies. For most, it has something to do with emptying out your mind and letting go of everything,

Immanuel Kant & The Role of the Observer

THE MIND ISN'T BORN **EMPTY** - IT CONTAINS BITS THAT HELP IT OPERATE FROM **BIRTH.** NUMBERS, SIZE, CAUSE... ALL PARTLY **MIND ?**

WELL THEN, IF MIND IS BORN WITH **FILTERS** IN IT **ALREADY,** HOW DO THESE FILTERS EFFECT THE WAY WE PERCIEVE **REALITY ?**

HMM... SOME OF MY WINDOW HAS **SPOTS** ON IT, BUT SOME OF IT IS **PERFECTLY CLEAR...** OK, **WHAT** WAS I THINKING ABOUT AGAIN ?

including your own sense of self, to which by nature you try to cling. Reality is often seen as an illusion, the cause of all suffering. To be free from suffering and reach enlightenment, you have to let go of reality and practice nonattachment. Then you may realize that all is connected and the way to achieve enlightenment is the middle way, not doing anything in the extreme because it will only lead to more attachments.

I have said that this type of Eastern enlightenment is diametrically opposed to the Western or European Enlightenment that we are concerned with here. Since I sincerely believe that today humanity is at the threshold of yet another enlightenment, a third enlightenment, which to some extent will combine and synthesize the two prior Enlightenments, it is good to spend some time with this idea.

"Enlightenment is the release of humanity from its self-conditioned dependency."

– Immanuel Kant

Compared to the sudden, intuitive method of the Eastern enlightenment, the European Enlightenment is based on reason and rationality in that it has its roots in Greek philosophy. Many philosophers say that the Enlightenment–from now on I will always mean the Western type actually started with the Greeks. They claim that Homer's Odysseus, by stepping out of the mythical crowd and making logical, individual decisions, became the first truly enlightened hero. From then on, the march of the Enlightenment, though taking twists and turns, never quite stopped until, during the European period we call the Age of Enlightenment, it came to full fruition. Like every great movement it soon tapered off, making way for new mythical, romantic, and some downright barbaric ideas and movements. The Enlightenment period brought the first truly global approach to human history, and was a time of great ideas, of the brotherhood of all humanity, of eternal peace and cooperation, and of tolerance that accepted difference. The centuries following this great advance were marked by mass murder, outright slavery, and genocide in a style never known before. Many call that period, which includes much of the Twentieth Century, the lost or forgotten Enlightenment (die verschüttete Aufklärung).

In a small essay, What is Enlightenment?, Kant laid down his ideas for humanity to advance to the next higher level. The whole essay reverberates with the great expectations that this self-proclaimed "citizen of the world" bestowed on humanity, even though in all his life he never left his hometown of Königsberg. The words he used to start the essay have become renowned for their noble call for autonomy, self reliance, and pride. From them, there could be made a straight connection to Martin Luther King's famous mountaintop speech.

"Enlightenment is the release of humanity from its self-conditioned dependency."

With this plea, Kant put the idea of autonomy in the center of political activism and set the stage for the great revolutions of human liberation and individual independence that swept the world during coming centuries. As you can imagine the intent of the enlightenment to set all human beings free from dependence on others, self-caused or not, is by no means finished. Nor will it perhaps ever be, not at least until the female half of humanity has been included, all around the world, in the ideals of equality and liberation.

It is a noble goal for which much human blood has been spilled. The German poet, Friedrich

Schiller, a friend and admirer of Kant, put these noble ideas into many of his famous plays. One of his poems has become world famous and was set to music. You probably have heard the "Ode to Joy" many times played at Olympic events and other gatherings of world union. It is a powerful plea for universal brotherhood that is watched over by the eternal spark of the divine.

I would like to conclude this brief introduction to the European Enlightenment by retelling a story of tolerance and truth that reportedly originated among Jewish rabbis. It became the center piece of a German Enlightenment play written by Gotthold Ephraim Lessing.

This play takes place in the ancient city of Jerusalem and centers on the combined wisdom of tolerance found in the three major religions. In searching for truth, Nathan, a wise old Jew, tells the Parable of the Rings. In olden times the story goes, a father possessed a very precious ring that had the power to make the wearer liked by everyone. From generation to generation this ring was passed on to the first born son. But during one generation a father had three sons and loved them equally. Shortly before his death he called a goldsmith and had two more rings made. Then he summoned his sons, each separately, to pass out the rings. Each son believed he had the authentic ring.

After the father died, the sons discovered the fraud. They started fighting over who possessed the real ring and ended up before a judge. The judge told them that their father might have lost the original ring and that they may all have fake rings. But regardless of who possessed the real ring, that ring had the power to make its owner beloved by all people. The judge advised the three sons to go out into the world and pretend that each had the right ring. The one loved most would certainly be recognizable, and the truth would be known. From time to time the brothers returned to the judge to see if the truth had been found, but none was loved by the rest of the world more than the others. The judge, representing human reason, sent them away again, telling each to do his best.

▨ B. KANT'S ETHICS: A CATEGORICAL IMPERATIVE

Kant made a major contribution to ethical thinking. He had to. His critical philosophy had taken the basis out from underneath all ethical consideration in philosophy prior to himself. He also wanted to make ethical thinking agreeable with the tolerant ideas of the Enlightenment. In other words, it had to be an ethics that all people could agree on, a universal ethics. By his time it had become abundantly clear that not all people would ever agree on the Ten Commandments, the cornerstone of Christian ethics. These commandments were also not acceptable, because they helped little in regard to human autonomy. They were given by God who was, from the perspective of the Enlightenment, an autocratic ruler who simply demanded obedience. From Greek philosophy, the Enlightenment adopted the idea that everything including ethics had to be reasonable. A mature and autonomous human being would not follow a commandment unless he or she thoroughly understood why it made sense to do so.

So Kant used reason and formulated his Categorical Imperative. An imperative is a must, a rule or a lawcategorical means definite, uncompromising, and unconditional. He wanted to make the reason for being good stick, just like the Ten Commandments. He wanted to create another deontological ethics, but this one based on reason, not because it was ordered by a law. Deontological ethics literally means an ethics based on doing your duty, doing something just because it's the right thing to do. You feel compelled or it is your duty to act this way or that. Another deontological ethics would be the Judaic/Christian one based on God's command or natural law (remember Thomas Aquinas?). According to that theory the laws of nature command us to act moral in a certain way. Kant's deontological ethics is based solely on reason, or on the reasonable universability of an action.

Kant's deontological ethics was different from the Greeks explanation for Goodness. In arguing what is good the Greeks made reference to nature and the universal rules that could be found in nature similar to Thomas Aquinas. The Greek search for goodness was an ontological one; Kant's ethics is rational, and only rational. Here is the way he formulated his categorical imperative:

'Act always so that the principle of your action (Kant calls this a Maxim) can become the universal rule in a universally good world." Or another formulation: "Act only according to that maxim whereby you can, at the same time, will that it should become a universal law."

What does this mean? Well, whenever you do something important, stop to consider whether it's the right thing or not, before you do it, and think about what would happen if everyone in the world did the same thing. Would the world be a nice place to live in? Would you want to live in such a world?

Take our example from the very beginning in the film *So this is Philosophy*. The factory owner is faced with the decision of whether to use a certain type of plastic bottle for his milk or go back to using glass bottles, even though he has just read the newest research that shows that those plastic bottles can cause cancer in the workers. Now apply Kant's imperative and see the result. What if he thinks in his mind, what if every factory owner in the world ignores this newest research and continues production of these plastic bottles, even though it's damn clear that the stuff is lethal? It would not be a nice world, would it? Workers would never again trust their working conditions. They would band together, get their own workers councils, do their own research, and then fight for better living and working conditions.

But wait a minute, you say. Isn't that exactly what happened? You are right, that is exactly what has happened during the past two hundred years. Workers have realized that they can't trust their bosses and that they better look out for their own rights; and they have made great progress in this struggle. But that is just it, it's all a gigantic struggle, a continuous conflict between the have and havenots, or to use the terminology of Karl Marx who figured all this out, a class struggle between the owners of the means of production and the proletariat, those who have nothing but their own labor to sell. Oh, if the world had just listened to good old Immanuel, the school master from Königsberg as they call him in Germany, much violence and bloodshed and revolution could have been prevented.

So while Kant's imperative is certainly a good attempt to formulate a universal ethics, it is hopelessly idealistic. People simply don't reason this way. Perhaps someday they will, when we have reached another Golden Age. Marx dreamed of this as the perfect communist society. Maybe this goal will be reached when everybody has been convinced that being good creates a win-win situation for everyone involved. Maybe, it's still worth thinking about and hoping for. Isn't it?

▓ C. KANT'S PLEA FOR WORLD PEACE

Kant's final contribution that we want to consider is his thoughts on global cooperation and world peace. He spelled this out in a small pamphlet titled, *Zum ewigen Frieden* or *On Perpetual Peace*. The idea of globalization, you see, was not invented in the Twentieth Century at all, nor the concept of a world body to secure peace, such as the United Nations. Kant had already proposed to create political stability and security among nations by uniting the world in a loose federation of autonomous republics who all guarantee mutual non interference and cooperation. They would all reduce their military spending by a huge amount, because, since all could trust each other, there would be no need for a large military. They would, of course, all have to agree to a universal set of principles that would govern their conduct.

I challenge you to quickly name ten reasons why this idea of Kant could not work, neither back then or now. I would bet that religion and religious ideologies are among those reasons. If only people everywhere would listen to the parable that I told you in the last chapter about the rings. When you think you are the only one who has the truth and everyone is else is wrong, think again. It isn't that I want to take your truth away. You are entitled to it, just like everyone else. But the true test for the value of your truth will be when your actions are judged by the love and understanding your truth has created, not by the converts you have made.

We will still deal with the philosophy of Karl Marx in more depth, but I can already tell you that he was wrong in one important issue. He looked at the whole world as a battlefield. Everything was focused on conflict. Gandhi was much more balanced in his approach. He once said that following Marx we would have to kill all the rich people, but that would be down right foolish, because it would be like killing the goose that lays the golden egg. Gandhi instead proposed to convince the wealthy people that a more equitable distribution of wealth is ultimately in their best interest. Kant would have probably agreed.

Gandhi is reported to have given additional advice that is much in the spirit of the European Enlightenment. One of his dedicated followers, a Hindu man whose young son had been murdered by Muslims, asked the master what he could do to end the emotional pain and how he could ever learn to forgive. Gandhi told the man that he should go out and adopt one of the many Muslim orphans and raise him as his child, not as a Hindu, but as a Muslim.

Before you continue I would like you to turn again to your ACTIVITIES BOOK. Watch the movie "The Mission." Believe me, if you haven't seen it before, you will like it. It plays around the time when European nations began to turn to capitalism as their economic system. They exploited other countries and used slavery to maximize their profits. The Church, the official church that is, often did nothing and even stood by and condoned those actions. There were plenty of movements within religious groups who opposed slavery and tried to help the oppressed. In The Mission, a group of Jesuit priests tried to do exactly that. They tried to save the native population from slavery by helping them built viable profitable communities for themselves.

These communities practiced profit sharing, a principle they say was used by early Christian communities. The head monk of one of the missions refers to a group in Paris, which had practiced the same type of profit sharing about a hundred years before Marx wrote his anticapitalistic philosophy. Guess who inspired Marx in these ideas? You are right. He was himself raised by Jesuits and was well informed about those Paris communities or communes as they were called. The only further step Marx added was to ban religious influences in his future society. He had too often experienced the Church's siding with the wealthy and not assisting the poor, even though of course this is totally against the spirit of the Christian gospel, especially as it is expressed in the Sermon on the Mount.

CHAPTER VI: THE POST KANTIAN ERA AND MODERNITY

■ 1. GEORG WILHELM FRIEDRICH HEGEL (1770-1831)

We will shortly consider the three major philosophies that arose in response to the Kantian dilemma, as Kant's recognition about the impossibilities of ever knowing the true thing in and of itself or, in short, not knowing any independent truth. But before we do this, I would like to introduce you to my favorite philosopher, also of course a post Kantian. His response remained unique and is very difficult to fully understand. In response to the futile effort to ever find absolute truth, **Georg Wilhelm Friedrich Hegel** proposed dialectics as a new kind of logic distinctly different form Aristotle's linear logic.

Georg Wilhelm
Friedrich Hegel
(1770-1831)
© 2006 JupiterImages Corporation

Hegel is hard to understand, because there is a lot of confusion surrounding the understanding of dialectical thinking, in the way Hegel had it in mind. Part of this was Hegel's own fault. As is so often the case with philosophers, who are after all only human beings, they change the way they look at things and interpret things. So there is often a big difference between the ways a philosopher sees the world as a young person compared to when he gets older. Actually often in hindsight the views of the younger person are more appealing than the maturing views of the older sage. (I don't say always, just often, because that would not speak very highly of my own case.)

Hegel's philosophical heritage is split right down the middle into left Hegelians and yes, you guessed it right, **Hegelians**. I don't know if that is the reason why still today we think of the more conservative politics as right and the more liberal or radical as left. It certainly would fit the pattern and it hinges on the interpretation of Hegel's system of **dialectics**. Let's begin from there.

The concept of **dialectics** actually goes back to our favorite philosopher Socrates, and therefore implicitly to Plato, because Plato wrote everything we know about Socrates. In Plato's dialogues, dialectics is a rhetorical device. It was used to make an effective speech. The idea goes back to the sophists who, if you remember, did not believe that truth could ever be fully attained. So in a speech you would make an argument, then construct the exact opposite, and then see where the investigation would lead you. The argument was called a thesis, the counterargument of course the antithesis, and the result, which often was kind of a compromise, would of course then be called a synthesis.

Hegel begins the **Aesthetics** by stating that Being and Nothing, which on the surface seem to be diametrically opposed, are exactly the same when emptied of all content. This was a slap against all metaphysical speculations that identified God with the Absolute Being. Absolute Being is not more and not less than Absolute Nothingness. What really is something, and makes everything something, is the process of becoming. So when Absolute Being recognizes its own Nothingness, it has recognized itself as something. But that something is nothing by itself, except this act of recognition. So if you want to build a metaphysical creation story from this, you could say, 'God is everything who recognizes him/her/it self to be really nothing, but in that recognition becomes something, and that something becomes the world with me and you in it.'

We, too, recognize our own nothingness. In that recognition, the mind recognizing its dwelling place in the body as the totally Other, we create or establish our own existence. The material world is thus totally Other, alien to the mind, but without it the mind is nothing; and vice versa, the mind is the totally Other, alien to the body, but without it the material world, too, is nothing. This later insight might be a bit harder to grasp, but we will come back to it soon.

Now you can perhaps understand why so few people really grasp the depth of Hegelian dialectic. I will spend the rest of this book, and probably the rest of my life, trying to understand its deep meaning and most of all trying to spread its importance.

Hegel begins the Aesthetics by stating that Being and Nothing, which on the surface seem to be diametrically opposed, are when emptied of all content exactly the same. This was a slap against all metaphysical speculations that identified God with the Absolute Being. Absolute Being is not more and not less than Absolute Nothingness. What really is something and makes everything something is the process of becoming. So when Absolute Being recognizes its own Nothingness it has itself recognized as something. But that something is nothing by itself except this act of recognition. So if you want to build a metaphysical creation story from this you could say: God is everything who recognizes to be really nothing, but in that recognition becomes something, and that something becomes the world with me and you in it. We, too, recognize our own nothingness. In that recognition our mind recognizes its dwelling place in the body as the totally Other, but without it, mind is nothing.

This recognition creates and establishes our own existence every moment. The material world is thus the totally Other, the alien to the mind, but without it the mind is nothing, and vice versa, the mind is the totally other, the alien to the body, but without it the material world, too, is nothing. This later insight might be a bit harder to grasp, but we will come back to it soon.

Now you can perhaps understand why so few people really grasp the depth of Hegelian dialectic. I will spend the rest of this book, and probably the rest of my life trying to understand its deep meaning and most of all trying to spread its importance.

I told you that Hegel and many other philosophers were influenced by Jewish mysticism, especially Judaic Cabalism. As you might recall, this specific branch of Judaism suggested a strong search for God and the divine by submersing yourself into the material world of things. This was acceptable because the world of things was not just evil, the way Medieval philosophy had seen it, but the spark of the divine had been exiled into this world as the feminine part of the masculine God. Now, by submersing your mind into the materiality of things you are able to find and rescue the divine spirit and in doing so reunite it with God. This is how meditation, mystical practices, and involvement with the material world of things had found a new avenue.

In many ways, this reemergence into the material world was very much a return to the ancient past, the world of Dionysus and pagan practices. Except now the search for the divine had become more specific. Its focus was the God of Abraham for Jews or the Savior sent by that God for Christians, Jesus Christ. Christian mysticism had never quite subsided, but found new heights under this pietistic movement.

Hegel's philosophy, especially his dialectical scheme, encouraged this kind of spiritual search. On one hand it was community oriented, by suggesting that the truly evolved spirit was represented by the best in each community and eventually by the best, represented by a global federation of communities in the spirit of Kant. On the other hand, his philosophy encouraged a private meditative and aesthetic approach in the search for the divine, which will again be found in Nietzsche's aesthetics and in the Neo-Marxist interpretation of Marx's philosophy. In all fairness, in an all-around evaluation of Hegel, I must admit that he probably favored the more cultured and evenhanded communal approach to spirit that is expressed in his philosophy of history. Hegel, like all of Western philosophy except Marx, was committed to order as expressed by an orderly conduct of society. He favored laws over revolution, just like Socrates and the many philosophers after him. The law was often seen as the rightful expression of the divine in this world.

Western philosophy before Marx feared the Dionysian spirit of upheaval and Chaos, and Hegel was no exception. He once called the revolt of the people Bacchantic riots, a distasteful expression of lawlessness and disorder even if in the name of God. Hegel was no revolutionary. This was the mission of his most dedicated reader, Karl Marx. Marx turned Hegel's philosophy upside down, and the world would never be the same again.

Before turning to Karl Marx and his peculiar use of Hegelian dialectics, I would like to introduce two other philosophies that represent a major response to Kant's challenge: Existentialism and Pragmatism. Both of these philosophies bear on our topic of liberation, cooperation and partnership, one in a negative way and the other, pragmatism, in a positive way as a still valid approach to the world.

■ 2. EXISTENTIALISM

Existentialism, the philosophy of my youth, is in many ways a dead end of the Western philosophical search for an absolute answer. While its absolute is found in each individual's ability to choose, the best these philosophers could come up with was the sad realization that the ultimate choice we can make is to take our own lives. And while we can't argue that this is so, it simply pushes to the extreme the logic of death that started with Aristotle, who chose the argument as an example of the validity of logic, using Socrates' mortality as an illustration.

Existentialism focuses on existence, rather than on the Aristotelian universals or essences, as these ultimate true descriptions were called. You may recall that Aristotle said that if we take everything accidental away from a particular object. What is left is its essential substance: that which, when you take it away, makes the thing disappear. In short, if you take a person's soul or life away remember the two were the same for the Greeks then a person will cease to be a whole person and turn into a corpse. So it is the same with everything else. Just as Plato's ideas were the essential part of each object, so for Aristotle these were called universals, the inseparable part of each object.

103

Since Kant had proven (or claimed to have proven) that those universals will never be found and that they are simply unattainable and unknowable to us, the search for what to replace them with was on. Of course, one option was not to replace them at all. For the existentialists, the answer was found in the very existence of things. What you are is what you are; the important thing is that you exist. Now it's up to you to make something of yourself. No one is there to help you along.

▪ A. SÖREN KIERKEGAARD (1813-1855)

Abraham sacrifices Isaac
© 2006 JupiterImages Corporation

Sören Kierkegaard was not a happy man. I think his greatest unhappiness came from his strict religious upbringing and his bad experience with women. As you might imagine, the cards life deals you often enter into the philosophy you construct. Kierkegaard was the son of a fairly stern protestant minister in Denmark. During all his life he struggled with his faith in God. How does that make him an existentialist, you might ask? Well, Kierkegaard was what is called a Christian existentialist, and as such he still has quite a respectable number of followers. To some extent, I also believe in the basic experience of his life, an experience of deep despair, of being forsaken by God, and yet, in spite of that experience of existential loneliness, finding it worthwhile to make something out of yourself.

For Kierkegaard, ultimately it was a deep belief in God. He chose to believe in spite of his logical mind telling him, over and over again that there was no sense in believing. He believed that the universe is empty and unresponsive. There is no God to console or to rescue you. You see in relation to faith, reason and belief are in ultimate opposition, irreconcilable forever. God is dead and yet we must believe, otherwise there is no meaning for us. So let there be no meaning, your logical mind tells you. And your whole self screams in return: there must be meaning; even though it is absurd, I need meaning. It is as if, in the deepest night of despair, you have to create God in order to make sense of your life. That is the depth of Kierkegaard's Christian existentialism.

Kierkegaard's philosophy struck a deep cord over a hundred years later, after Europe had gone through two devastating world wars and lay in shambles. Not only were its cities in ruin, everything people had put their beliefs in had come to a grinding halt. Armies were defeated, millions had died, and nations had fallen into oblivion. Sartre looked to existentialist philosophy for something to hold onto. He also liked the focus on existence rather than essence that this little known philosophy promoted. Under his influence existentialism became one of the best known philosophical trends of the twentieth century. Many young intellectuals, who, like the young Sartre, had survived WWII, often, in resistance to the Teutonic invaders, followed Sartre's call.

Sartre's existentialism, however, with its emphasis on suicide as the ultimate means to demonstrate human freedom, continued the direction of Western philosophy of being morbidly focused on death rather than celebrating life as a great gift. This is why I call existentialism the dead end of Western philosophy.

▓ B. Jean Paul Sartre (1905 - 1980)

Sartre could not follow Kierkegaard's turning to God for rescue. The idea that there was a God, anywhere, who could have let the horrors of the past war happen, was perhaps too much for anybody to conceive. So Sartre drew the ultimate conclusion: There is no God. Another German philosopher of the Nineteenth Century had shown the way. Friedrich Nietzsche's proclamation that God is dead suddenly became more important than his proclamation of the Übermensch, Nietzsche's superman concept that had helped support German fascist ideology and nationalist hypocrisy.

So Sartre proclaimed himself to be an atheist existentialist. Nothing essential in this world existed prior to your existence; if anything existed previously, it is of little consequence in any absolute sense. You are thrown into this world, you find yourself in it, and now you are faced with making decisions. It is the decisions that you make that shape who you are, neither an ultimate purpose nor a design, as Aristotle assumed. The only thing you know for sure is that you can leave this life at any time. The possibility to commit suicide is the ultimate guarantee of human freedom.

Sartre wrote a number of stage plays, and his best friend, Albert Camus, a gifted young playwright, wrote a number of world famous plays revealing their deeply existentialist philosophy. Existentialists, since Kierkegaard, had lost the belief that philosophical ideas are spread through rational, organized discourse. Can you figure out why they resorted to story telling and playwriting rather than writing in the tradition of Western philosophy? Camus died young, in a car accident, which many thought of as the tragic fulfillment of existentialist freedom.

As a young resistance fighter, Sartre had no problem knowing which side he was on. This became less obvious during the more peaceful times of the post World War II era. Young intellectuals, wearing black turtleneck pullovers, sat around in Parisian cafes and philosophized about the world. Their movement and their philosophy spread around the world and became the prime movement of the young generation in the Western industrialized world. In America, it gave birth to free-spirited flower power generation and hippies of the Sixties and Seventies.

When Sartre, aging and maturing in his philosophy, began losing his revolutionary spirit, he asked himself how the heroes in his plays would know which of their actions were right and which were wrong. In the developing consumer society of the West, his existentialist philosophy gave him no direction. Relying only on the power of your personal will, without any other guidance, leaves a person quite rudderless. What really was the difference whether you turned out to be a Hitler or a saint? Both required the power and conviction of a strong will. Was that, then, all that there was? Was the difference between a criminal and a savior only in the different path you took, by chance? Ultimately, Sartre could not believe this. His friend Camus had written a play about one of the cruelest Roman dictators, Caligula. In a quite nonjudgmental way, he showed this despicable person's powerful will, but there was nothing in Sartre's existentialism to condemn such actions. Another of Sartre's artist friends, whom he called the Holy Genet (Saint Genet), even turned Kant's categorical imperative on its head and proclaimed: Act always so that the maxim of your action can become the law in every criminal's den.

In his old age, unhappy with this development of existentialism, Sartre turned to Marxism for answers. After we introduce the most American of all philosophies, Pragmatism, we will deal in depth with the philosophical intricacies of Marxism. More perhaps than any other philosophy, the philosophy of Marxism shaped and continues to shape the modern world. This is true even long after its official representative, the Soviet Union, has joined the vanished historical movements of the past.

■ 3. PRAGMATISM

WILLIAM JAMES
© 2006 JupiterImages Corporation

Pragmatism is the philosophy most thoroughly influenced by science and commerce. If, so far, many philosophical ideas have often sounded strange to you, it will be different with pragmatism. It is the philosophy most familiar to you, and therefore you might not even have recognized it as a specific philosophy. In scientific jargon, we would say it is part of your

paradigm. Its ideas are so familiar to you that often you can't even imagine that anyone could think differently. This, on the other hand, is the deep purpose of philosophy. It is to make you aware of your own hidden assumptions, those ideas that you don't even think to question. It is to make you recognize your own paradigm, so that when a paradigm shift might be in the making or might be necessary for humanity to survive, you are not left out. You might be left behind if you were overly committed to your old paradigm, your old beliefs and values, even against all odds of your own personal survival.

This, too, is a pragmatic consideration, that life is always superior to death, whether this is your own or someone else's. Nothing is worth losing your life for, not your country, not an idea, not a world view. When I say nothing, I like to immediately modify this. Risking and losing one's life for others who are in immediate danger is noble, and nothing can be more worthy. So if my family is threatened or attacked, I would be the last to sit passively and not come to help. When you come to the help of others who are helpless themselves, it is an even nobler act.

At the core of pragmatic philosophy is this practical question: but does it work? No matter how rational some idea sounds, what good does it do if you can't make it work? I believe deeply that this question is ultimately the one by which everything will be judged in the end.

Of course, the problem with this approach is the question of how long one should wait to see if something works. Could one say that the equal status of men and women in society, which we believe existed in ancient civilizations, ultimately disappeared because it did not work? Should we believe that male domination is a success story, because it survived some two thousand years of an admittedly pretty bloody history? If the result of all these dominator models which now prevail all around the globe is eventually the smoke of a mushroom cloud, domination will have failed, but there will be no evening news left to tell us about it.

As in science, under pragmatism everything became open for experimentation. This had a tremendous effect on education and religion, an effect that has not always been positive.

When it comes to choosing a religion, American society is probably the most consumer oriented society in the world. American religious choices are often likened to a Scandinavian smorgasbord. All the religions are presented in front of the customers who are free to choose. And often they take a bite here and a bite there, depending on their present taste. I often compared the small village that we lived in, while running a farm in Michigan, with the rural villages where I grew up in Germany. German villages have ten pubs and one church;, in the United States, it's the other way around.

This free choosing of religious affiliation is in large part the result of pragmatic philosophy. William James, the founder of American pragmatism who was himself not a religious person, saw no harm in religion as long as you could find a personal use for it in your life. Pragmatic sociologists in turn made sure that religion had a proper place in the social order, not because they were particularly religious, but because they thought of religion as a moderating factor in social life, something that kept people from becoming rebellious and over-demanding.

Pragmatic educators, most famous among them John Dewey, were well aware of the awesome importance of education in a child's life. They wanted schools to get away from "book learning" and immerse children in an active learning schedule filled with outdoor activities and hands-on projects. As a result, American education is much more practically oriented than any other in the world; but the pragmatic approach has a strong downside. A child's mind is not a computer that can be filled with information. Important questions in life often do not have a yes or no answer, either. Following this scientific approach, American education often treats difficult questions in a black and white, binary fashion. Who is the "good guy" and who is the "bad guy" shows the oversimplification of this approach. Such a simplified method, rather than teaching differentiation and critical thinking, ends up treating every problem in the world as a Scantron test.

The result is that American children are overtested but learn to little. They often fail to acquire a critical mind capable of critical thinking. Pragmatists introduced a new idea of truth. They despised the traditional concept of truth, which they derogatively called "a copy idea of truth." You have an ideal copy of what you believe is true in your mind; and when some event occurs or some new object appears you simply compare this with what you have stored in you memory banks as the true copy of that occasion. If it fits, you call it truth. Pragmatists replaced this with a pragmatic test for truth which is closely modeled on the scientific method. You set up an experiment with what ever you want to test and see if it works. If it does, you call it true as long as it works.

So what did pragmatism do for compassion, cooperation, and community? Most of all, I think it provided a method for testing the value of an idea. There simply does not seem to be a better way to find out the truth than by testing it. If healthy communities produce more compassionate children and finally more compassionate adults, then healthy communities should be promoted. This can be tested and thus become scientific. If cooperation yields better results than competition, in terms of the happiness of human beings, then cooperation should be made the number one health concern in a society. If creating compassionate human beings reduces the crime rate and increases the all over well-being of individuals should be declared a public health issue. Whatever diminishes it should be officially regulated.

So what did pragmatism do for compassion, cooperation, and community? Most of all, I think it provided a method for testing the value of an idea. There simply does not seem to be a better way to find out the truth than by testing it.

Does this mean that I propose to create a totally regulated society? Not at all. The mere fact of over-regulation often reduces all the positive impacts of cooperation, compassion, and partnership. I believe that in general, people live happier lives if they are in charge of their own affairs. But this, too, cannot be shoved down the throat of any individual or country; rather, it must grow from within. If the marketplace in one country is extremely anxious for another country to open up its borders to free trade, it seems highly hypocritical to pretend that spreading democracy is the real reason for an invasion and overthrow of a foreign government.

■ 4. MARXISM

In our discussion we have finally arrived at the last of the three major philosophies that were developed as a response to the Kantian dilemma of not being able to frame the truth in an absolute way. While pragmatism was invented and evolved in America, Marxism like existentialism was distinctly European. These two contemporary philosophies are therefore considered continental philosophies. Even though Marxism contains many pragmatic elements, it is essentially an idealistic philosophy. It is not idealistic in the same way Platonism was called idealistic. Marxism does not begin by assuming that in the beginning there was an idea, which could be God, a spirit, or some other mental construction. Marxism rather assumes that mind and matter are like the two sides of the same coin. They cannot be separated but mind and matter are linked to each other by being forever opposite of each other. This is why true Marxism believes in a dialectical origin. Marxist philosophy is therefore called dialectical Materialism.

Karl Marx
(1818 - 1883)
© 2006 JupiterImages Corporation

Let's face it right from the outset. Marxism today is no longer a popular philosophy. It's not even a philosophy that many philosophers would openly confess to, at least not in most parts of the world. There are still three major countries and a few minor ones that openly confess to Marxism as being their philosophical ideology. Among these, only China is a fully industrialized country and a world power. Marxism, many would contend, has lost its importance in a world dictated by the freewheeling laws of the marketplace. Ever since the Soviet Empire, the first power that had fully embraced Marxist ideology, came to a screeching stop and basically disintegrated as a world power right before the eyes of history, Marxism as a moving force seemed to have lost its steam.

And yet, as you will see, many of Marx's ideas might sound strangely familiar to you. This is partially because Marx made some extremely important contributions to the way sociologists and other scientists still view the world today. This is also because some of the major ideas we attribute to Marx are not solely Marxist, but have been developed in other theories as well. So when, for instance, you come across Marxist elements in American feminism, it could be that those who developed the theories were instructed, as young students, in Marxist ideology. Then, growing older, they evolved, changed, and dropped some of their youthful convictions while adhering to other. It could also be that they arrived at these new convictions independently, which would show that Marx's basic analysis of the way things operate was not so far off the mark. In any case, many of Marx's analytical projects, especially his analysis of the forces in history, have become quite common tools in academic disciplines, most recognizably in sociology.

At the Frankfurt School during the Sixties, I received instruction in a kind of Marxism that was distinctly different from the orthodox Marxism generally taught in Eastern European schools. It is what became know as a Neo-Marxist interpretation of Marxism, mostly referring back to the young Marx, who then was heavily influenced by another German philosopher, Ludwig Feuerbach.

Feuerbach was known for his interpretation of religion as a mere projection of human needs and hopes into an imaginary heaven. People living in basic misery on earth had to invent a heaven and a merciful God to create hope for themselves. Religious institutions ultimately constructed a powerful and absolute system of justice that eventually would bring down the powerful and reward the misery of the oppressed here on earth by projecting eternal salvation into the after life. Perhaps you can recognize the promise of Jesus Christ in the Sermon of the Mount in these ideas. He, too, promised that the murderers will ultimately not triumph over their victim. God is a god of justice, for Christians, Jews, and Muslims alike. However, Feuerbach declared the whole religious underpinning to be an illusion.

Marx was also influenced by Hegel, as I said earlier. He took Hegel's dialectic and turned it upside down. For Hegel, history was the movement of spirit, becoming its opposite in the material world, and then moving through history in a spiral-like advance toward spirit. In this view, history is an evolution of materia toward spirit. You can see the Hebrew/Christian conception of history hidden in this Hegelian scheme, except that the spirit was not seen as the spirit of a particular God, but a general, more abstract philosophical idea. It also has roots in Aristotle's teleological views.

As I said, Marx turned this scheme upside down. In the Neo-Marxist interpretation, he used the left understanding of Hegel taken from his Aesthetics, rather than the right interpretation taken from Hegel's philosophy of history and his philosophy of right. In Hegel's aesthetics, spirit is hidden within. As Adorno would have said, spirit is hidden in the "micrology of things." As in Isaac Luria's creation story and as practiced in Jewish Cabalism, spirit can be approached and perhaps made visible in the aesthetic act of turning materia into a piece of art. Any real work, in this Neo-Marxian world view, is creative work. The worker is an artist; the greatest artist is the revolutionary who realizes the ideals of humanity by creatively transforming history.

Any work that is not involved in this beautification process of turning materia into art is alienating work, not worthy for human beings to perform. Most work performed by the masses of workers in Nineteenth Century factories was of course utterly alienating work, because it was work for hire. Its main purpose was to fill the coffers of the capitalists, and ultimately helped to prolong the misery of the exploited masses. When the same work was produced in the steel mills of the young Soviet Union, its artists celebrated it as high-minded works of liberation, because now the result of the work was no longer seen as supporting oppression. During the first few decades of the Soviet experiment in Marxism, people from around the world joined the young movement in hopes of working toward true human liberation. Many more, in America and elsewhere, watched with hope this development that promised to bring about a paradise on earth. Workers would finally get the true rewards for their sweat, not in some distant heaven, but right here on earth. They felt greatly empowered by the idea that they, rather than some distant capitalist, were now the owners of the means of production.

Of course history turned out differently. The masses of workers under Soviet communism ultimately performed they same kind of alienated work, the fruits of which they were never really able to enjoy. Instead of capitalists owning the means of production, the communist power elite fulfilled the same cruel mission. When workers, disappointed by the meager results of their work, turned against their new oppressors, these same so-called representatives of the people used military force to stop any uprising or revolt against the establishment. Power indeed seems to have a way to corrupt people. The question is whether this is part of human nature. If so, hope for humanity is indeed dim.

Deep within Marx's philosophy was the promise that Marxism could change the nature of human beings. What Christianity had failed to accomplish, to create a loving, caring, compassionate human being, Marx said could be accomplished by correctly understanding and manipulating the forces of history. History, he said, moved in dialectical steps toward fulfillment. These steps were the result of economic conditions. Unequal distribution of goods resulted in a continuous struggle between those who have and those who have not, between the capitalists and the exploited masses who have nothing but their labor to sell. If we could find a more equitable distribution of goods, Marx reasoned, this class struggle would subside. People would then be happy to go about their work, feeding their families, and supporting life. Human nature would have changed from being greedy, selfish and compassionless into a nature that is compassionate, caring and creatively involved in the community. Can you see the parallels between these original Marxist ideas and the earlier introduced Partnership model? We will see how modern feminism also continued many of these ideas, but with a distinctly different focus.

You remember that toward end of his life, the major philosopher of existentialism, Jean Paul Sartre turned to Marxism. What did Sartre, the aging rebel and existentialist, find so attractive about Marxism? In contrast to Existentialism, Sartre saw in Marxist philosophy a clear proposal for ethics, a practical request to live a moral life. This he saw in the Marxist unconditional identification with the oppressed. Again we might recognize here a direct reference to the Christian Sermon of the Mount, in which Christ proclaimed a number of beatitudes. One was to call blessed those who identify with the poor, hungry and oppressed. In fact, if you ever take the time to work through one of recent Catholicism's most important documents, an encyclical called Laborem exercens, you will find many of Marx's social ideas cloaked in the language of the Catholic Church. After all, Marx was trained by Jesuits and was perhaps one of their most astute scholars. The main thing that Marx added to his social proposals was a clear critique of power. This, of course, was less agreeable to the power elite of the church who had mostly sided with those in power, claiming that doing so would help them do their important work for the poor. But as Marx well knew, power corrupts and, perhaps, absolute power corrupts absolutely. Incidentally this is what Christ knew as well.

You might recall from the movie, *The Name of the Rose,* that the question of wealth and power is not a new one for the Church elite. At the end of the Middle Ages, the Church had become immensely powerful and rich. Movements within the church, such as the Franciscans, reminded their superiors that Christ himself was poor and had blessed those who followed him in poverty. The Church hierarchy had little interest in giving up its status and wealth and reacted by isolating the movement into an order where poverty was sanctioned for its members but only with their promise to leave the Church at large alone.

A shock wave went through the camp of International Socialism when, during the Fifties, the extent of Stalin's genocidal cruelties against his own people became clear and could no longer be denied. Communism had started out as a hope for humanity. These revelations were perhaps the most devastating blow that this first truly international movement encountered, before its final demise almost half a century later, which was probably mostly the result of internal mis-management, both socially and economically. Stalin, as it turned out, had committed crimes equal to those of his arch enemy, the German fascist leader Adolf Hitler, whom this communist dictator now appeared to resemble in more than one way. Just like Hitler, in the name of an idea and national interest, Stalin had put millions to death and had sent millions more away to work under horrible conditions in the labor camps, called Gulags, that Stalin had established all over Siberia.

Perhaps the beginning of the end of Marxism's role in world history was when, at the beginning of the Twentieth Century, the young revolution did not take off in the well-developed liberal society of England, as Marx and his friend Engels had hoped that it would. They knew that their humanitarian ideas would work best in a society in which the rights of the individual were already well established and could no longer be completely squelched as happened in post Czarist Russia.

Russia, you see, at the time of the Socialist/Marxist revolution, was still a feudal society. You might remember that during the Middle Ages feudalism was the popular type of social order all over Europe. The king, with the help of vassals, soldiers, dukes and landowners, ran the country from the top down. Russia, at the time of the Revolution, did not have a king,

but for all practical purposes, the Czar was a despotic ruler just like a king. He ran the country with an iron fist, giving no individual freedoms to his people, who were mostly powerless workers on the land.

When the revolution happened in Russia, it was first greeted with enthusiasm as liberation from hundreds of years of subjugation. But the masses of people who, under the Czars, had never enjoyed the chance to exercise participatory power, failed to do so under the new regime as well. Marxism tried at first to institutionalize a system of permanent power sharing, much more radical than even most democratic systems of the West. It is important to understand that the first Marxists were federalists, and they were anarchists. They wanted to create small local units of power sharing cooperatives who would then join together in a rather loose federation to form a larger national unit. But the real power would reside with the communes.

When this system of independent communes failed to produce political unity fast enough, power struggles between the parties was resolved by installing a centralized party with absolute control, something Russians had been used to from the times of the Czars. The loosely organized communes offered little resistance to the power grab. Those who resisted were swiftly eliminated. The new leaders, Lenin and Stalin, consolidated power and eliminated everyone who was in their way. Gone were the dreams of a radical, democratic restructuring of society that would assign power from the bottom up. Just like in the old Czarist system, power was no longer held at the base but consolidated at the top. Czarist feudalism had turned into a Stalinist feudalism with the Supreme Soviet Assembly exercising power at will. This is not what Marx had in mind.

After the bloodshed of the Second World War, as the cruelties of the Stalinist regime became known around the world, some of those intellectuals who refused to give up the humanist ideals of true Marxism, began silently, and often in the underground of the Soviet occupied territories, to reinvent Marxism along the lines of what they believed expressed true Marxist ideals. This philosophy became known as Neo-Marxism.

■ 5. NEO-MARXISM

In traditional Marxism, the world is changed through the power struggle between the oppressors and the oppressed. Class struggle is the engine of history. This model relies on conflict and revolution to change history toward the better. **Neo-Marxism** found a new focus for historical change; it begins with Marx's analysis of human labor. Not only revolutionary forces but creative human work can permanently change the world and bring about better conditions for humanity. In traditional Marxism, most human work was seen as alienating for the worker. Workers, who were the oppressed tools of the capitalists, could change the situation only by withholding their labor. Strike as a legitimate vehicle for social and economic change, was invented. By massively withholding labor power, in a general strike of united workers, the capitalist system would come to a halt and the revolution could begin, which would eventually bring power to the oppressed masses. As a result of the revolution workers would take over the means of production. But instead of allowing this to happen on a local level, communist societies, declaring themselves the workers' paradise, allowed a new power elite to retool the cycle of oppression.

Neo-Marxism interpreted human work fundamentally differently, in a positive way. Not only strikes and revolutions but work itself had the capacity to creatively change the world. It included artists and intellectuals as creative workers for change. Listen to what Pope John Paul said in his famous encyclical on human work, "...man's life is built up every day from work, from work it derives its specific dignity, but at the same time work contains the unceasing measure of human toil and suffering, and also of the harm and injustice which penetrate deeply into social life within individual nations and on the international level."

There is a minute difference only between this and the Neo-Marxist interpretation of human work. There was no longer a need for masses of people to rise up against oppression; each individual had the power in his or her hand to change the course of history. Creative work or art became the motor for that change. This also included intellectual work. The emphasis had switched from manual work performed by the exploited proletariat to the intellectual work done by artists, philosophers and students. While solidarity of those involved in the struggle for liberation was of course still seen as a historical necessity, the new emphasis was on the importance of the individual in this process of change.

In the late Sixties, I was director of the Socialist Student Theater Die neue bühne at the Goethe University in Frankfurt, Germany. We had rehearsed a play of German workers speaking out during a general strike against unfair labor practice and for a shorter working week. Whenever possible we performed the play in front of factories and in public places. At the end of the short play we invited those who had stopped to watch us to join our teaching at the University in lecture hall VI. Here, our idol Adorno, had taught us that the real revolution would happen in an interchange between action and reflection. Action was the performance in the streets which was often combined with a mass demonstration. Reflection then followed when we met in the lecture hall listening to speeches of student leaders such as Rudi Dutschke and Cohen Bendit. Everyone met again at Adorno's lecture at 11 am to listen to his philosophical and sociological speeches.

Our declared goal was to have workers join us during those teachings, which hardly ever happened. We were convinced that a true change in society would only come when manual workers and intellectual workers joined forces and worked for the same goals. We wanted to understand our intellectual work as real work, compensated by society. We dreamt of power sharing and student participation in the administration of our university. At the end, when several female students bared their breasts during Adorno's lecture, this gentle professor who knew most classical music pieces in his mind gave up because he believed that the powerful dialectic of action and reflection had come to an end. Just like his great model Hegel he could not allow the "carnival of the people" the riots and the disrespect enter his own lecture hall, which he had always guarded with aristocratic command. Surrounded always by a dozen assistants this "Professor of the People" had never really been a people's professor. In his brilliance he kept himself unapproachable to the average student, and kept his distance to every one but the selected few. Soon after the incidence in his lecture hall the famous professor retired, and shortly thereafter he passed away.

This philosophical reinterpretation was behind the student revolts that took place around the world during the Sixties. Professors such as Herbert Marcuse in the United States and Theodore Adorno in Germany called upon students everywhere to use their intellectual powers in the service of social change and to end an unjust war that the United States was waging against the people of North and South Vietnam. Left wing revolutionary ideology had merged with the more peaceful goals of the hippie movement and of flower power, but the clear motor of the world wide movement remained a Neo-Marxist analysis of oppression and power.

MODERN RESPONSES TO THE KANTIAN DILEMMA	
HEGAL	DIALECTIC
NIETZSCHE	AESTHETICS
KIERKEGAARD (SARTRE)	EXISTENTIALISM
MARX	MARXISM
WILLIAM JAMES	PRAGMATISM

Adorno's Neo-Marxist philosophy built on Marxist aesthetics, an aesthetics that Marx himself never had written. In artistic work, the mind would truly find its other by submersion into the material world but not be satisfied there, not finding rest, but be turned back onto and into itself. Mind then finds that a rest of its own had been left in the very piece of art, like a spark of the divine. Art was forever the estranged home of the mind, not being pure but being affected by the material world, and necessarily part of it. In this sense, it was the work of the creative mind that would slowly affect the whole world, animals and all, until, as Adorno put it, all of creation would slowly awake to the kind of freedom that only mind can bring. "Dann wird die Natur ihre Augen aufschlagen" – "Nature will then open her eyes," Adorno was fond of saying, proclaiming a new dawn.

This powerful message of the important position of the creative mind was first formulated by another German philosopher, Friedrich Nietzsche. Nietzsche had pointed the way to Dionysian immediacy in the creation of art. Do you remember the God Dionysus in whose honor the Dionysian mysteries were celebrated in ancient Greece? In union with that god, ancient peoples experienced a special closeness to the divine and to divine truth. It was a truth that could only be experienced, the opposite of the Pythagorean truth of linear logic. While any mythical union with the divine seemed unattainable to the modern mind, these philosophers of immediacy, foremost of them Nietzsche, did not remain content with the philosophical results after Kant.

This powerful message of the important position of the creative mind was first formulated by another German philosopher Friedrich Nietzsche. Nietzsche had pointed the way to Dionysian immediacy in the creation of art. You remember the God Dionysus in whose honor in ancient Greece the Dionysian mysteries were celebrated. In the union with this God ancient people experienced a special closeness to the divine and to divine truth. It was a truth that could only be experienced, the opposite of the Pythagorean truth of linear logic. While to the modern mind, any mythical union with the divine seemed unattainable, these philosophers of immediacy did not remain content with the philosophical results after Kant.

For Nietzsche, Kantian philosophical speculations appeared schoolmasterly and pedantic. If the old god of metaphysics was dead, so be it. But one can not rest there. Only that despised herd mentality of the masses was inclined to despair. The visionary philosopher Nietzsche, in the darkest night of despair, conjured up superhuman strength to create god anew, out of the ashes of creative intention. Those progressive minds who understood the depths of the Nietzschean truth and were prepared to follow it, committed their lives to art and artistic creation. Adorno's negative dialectic provided the intellectual frame.

Two thousand years of the logical search for truth had suddenly come to an end. There was no more hope for the linear logical mind to attain truth. A new way offered itself in the Hegelian dialectical model when applied to the artistic process. Moving away from itself, the artistic mind found its temporary place in the material world by becoming one with it in the work of art. But it could not remain there. It had to find its way back to mind in the consciousness of the art consumer who could appreciate the residue of art (the mine) in the transformed artwork.

This circular process, applied to the whole of society, would ultimately purify and beautify society and bring about the final paradise on earth that Marx had dreamt about. For Marx, it would be the result of the taking over of power by the proletariat and the elimination of class difference. For the Neo-Marxist, it would be the result of creative human work that would ultimately turn the whole society into art. This dream of aesthetic renewal that would lead to a humanistic socialism was probably most diligently followed by the solidarity movement in Poland. Here many artists had worked for years to prepare society for an aesthetic and bloodless revolution that would change society forever and make it more sensitive and more humane. Andrzej Wajda's films were among the most outstanding examples that lead Polish society toward this kind of aesthetic renewal. I was personally privileged to take part in a series of theater festivals that were held in the Polish city of Wroclaw all through the Seventies and Eighties. At these festivals, the experienced organizers developed an aesthetic, dialectical performance model that was continuously refined over the years. In one of my earlier books I gave this report about dialectical communication.

The German author Heinrich von Kleist once said, "For it is not we who know, but it is a certain condition in us that knows." For this condition to develop, the right preparation is needed.

The last two festivals in Wroclaw had been very carefully planned and organized by the directors of the festival to comply, on an experimental basis, with a dialectical communication model. The festival was divided into three parts: presentation, integration, and cooperation. These were clearly separated by time and location. During the 1979 festival the order was: first integration, second presentation, and third cooperation. To give all 300 participants from Poland and around the world the chance to get to know each other, integration was developed. All participants were housed at a resort in the country. Without the pressure of imminent performance they could meet, get to know each other, and plan joint projects beyond the borders of race, religion, nationality and social systems. At the beginning of the festival the organizers announced that the international artist community was expected to produce a collaborative event at the end of the festival. Committees were formed and smaller groups initiated the process. That so many creative people with such diverse backgrounds had been brought together to speak, dance, and create, brought forth an incredible atmosphere of solidarity and excitement. After one week the groups moved from the small country town to the city for presentation. For one week they showed their individually produced plays brought to the festival from their home countries.

At the end of presentation, during two days labeled cooperation, the groups presented a collective piece of theatre created during integration and composed of multiple contributions. The performance was a kind of a tribal event in which, shortly before final extinction, the diverse members of the tribe tell their stories.

For the next festival, three years later, the structure had been rearranged. In response to analysis and criticism by participants, the organizers readjusted the format to reflect past experience. Analysis had shown that placing integration at the beginning of the festival posed problems. Groups that had traveled long distances and invested money and time to bring their plays to the festival remained apprehensive and preoccupied with rehearsing and technical arrangements, which caused many internal problems. This would ease up only after the main festival perform-ances were over and each group was able to present their show to the public. This made early integration difficult. Artists were also more inclined to contact others, once they had seen each other's work. Another factor for changing the order was the alienation created by moving into the large industrial city of Wroclaw. During the first week, everybody had been living in the same place, eating in common dining halls, and gathering in an easy and casual way. The small town's park, the friendly environment, and the curious country people all contributed to an intimate atmosphere. Once in the city, the groups were placed in different hotels, often miles apart. They had to make great efforts to meet, and generally individuals were left to themselves and their separate artistic work.

For the 1982 festival the order of events was reversed. It started with presentation in Wroclaw. For one week, over thirty groups performed in eight or ten different spaces throughout the city. Each play was performed about three to four times to allow festival participants and a large number of local people to see the plays. For integration all artists were transported to a ski resort in the Silesian Mountains on top of Snow Mountain near the Czechoslovakian border. Then, for the cooperative event, everybody returned to the city. During integration, which lasted four days, the festival organizers remained in the background. No general meetings were scheduled and no agenda was posted. Though all of us knew, a cooperative event was planned for the finale, nobody took charge of organizing it. A lot of time was spent socializ-ing, discussing and mountain climbing. A birthday was celebrated with cake carried up from the valley and Russian vodka. The night was spent in happy celebration; people from many different countries had come together. Among those present were Americans, Japanese, groups from Portugal, Hungary, the Soviet Union and both Germanys, Israelis next to a group from Palestine, Argentineans and Polish artists from all parts of the country. Poland was an ideal meeting place for international groups. A great hope was in the air, but also a desperate feeling of the end. With an obvious lack of leadership, intended by the organizers, small groups came together spontaneously to work on the task. From these grass root cells a general meeting was organized. At this meeting the organizers were present and gave a description of the different locations in the city that could be used for the event, though they made it clear that nothing had been prearranged. The possibility of having no conclusion would be an acceptable option resulting from the group process. They expressed their trust in the creativity of the participating artists to produce a suitable collective piece of theatre.

The artists, left to themselves, went to work and within two days managed to create an interesting and impressive piece of theatre, which was performed in a busy street in the center of Wroclaw on a Sunday afternoon.

In dialectical language such withdrawal of leadership is the creation of a negative frame. It is similar to putting a frame around an empty space or clean canvas and entitling it: Art Piece 22. The viewer is faced with creative emptiness, and the mind begins to create the content. Much visual art of the avant-garde followed this dialectical aesthetics. But the Polish festival is the only social event I know of in which a dialectical communication model was experimentally developed and successfully implemented.

The dialectical communication model, experimentally developed in Poland, shows:

- how to remain open to the unknown, to remain critical and creative at the same instance.

- that rationality is not an absolute, but the products of thousands of years of intellectual development.

- that this model represents a new step in the development of rationality to understand and realize both it's strength and limits.

In contrast to traditional rationality shaped by Aristotle, dialectical reason allows contradiction to develop and exist. It requires us to rethink our old theories of justified wars and conflict, and to replace them with a theory of individual and collective creativity. Perhaps we will have to relearn the Socratic truth: none of us understands the divine law well enough to be justified taking one's brother into court and accuse him of impiety, as Euthyphro did. Rational judgment without love may often be such an act of impiety.

■ 6. NIETZSCHE – MY FEAR, MY TREMBLING AND MY EXALTATION

I have left the best for the end, and quite fittingly, the best is also the most difficult. I am the first to admit, I am intimidated by Nietzsche. As a philosopher he is a giant, far ahead of his time. As a human being he deserves pity – pity for his miserable life, pity for his abusive upbringing, pity for his hate for women, pity for never reaping the fruits of his writings. In spite of all of this, he is a shining light in the dark. Long before Chaos Theory became scientific, this perhaps greatest of all philosophers spoke its essence when he exclaimed, "You must have chaos in your heart to give birth to a dancing star."

Friedrich Nietzsche
© 2006 JupiterImages Corporation

Socrates took the bull by his horns and shook him, trying to squeeze whatever is in it out of it, dissatisfied with whatever it yielded, nevertheless. Subsequent philosophers squeezed so hard that the bull gave up his life. They cut and analyzed until nothing was left but dead meat. Nietzsche was the philosopher to recognize this, declaring even the pitiable God of the

117

deists as nothing but dead meat. God is dead, but humans must revive God. Herein lays Nietzsche's mission and vision. Courageously he revived the bull, and instead of taking him by the horns he swung on top of it and asked his fellow humans to come along and enjoy the ride. And what a ride it was! No, what a ride it is!

Nietzsche knew that to take this bull for a ride, we need to be the very best we can be, have all the strength we can muster. We cannot allow ourselves to be timidly guided by rules made up by others. We must take on superhuman qualities; in short we must have power. Far from promoting a fascist power grab Nietzsche rather auspiciously foreshadowed the Human Empowerment Movement that has swept through America and Western societies ever since the end of the Sixties. Be the best you can be! It never made much sense to me when Allen Blum in *The Closing of the American Mind*, blamed Nietzsche for all the ills that had befallen American post-war society. If anything, Nietzsche was too little known and what was known was largely misunderstood.

Nietzsche also knew that the only way to have access again to the Other was not through the back door, but by facing it squarely, that means not intellectually, but existentially. The Apollonian focus with its emphasis on logic and reflection will always only reveal separation from the Other, a more or less dead skeleton. To reclaim life we must return to the Dionysian, to the pre-Platonic, pre-Socratian, even pre-Pythagorean. If we truly want to merge again into the arms of the Other we have to revive the god of altered states of mind.

Today we have much safer technologies to undertake this journey of discovery. But in order to avoid mass riots, this Dionysian emersion can only occur as an aesthetic act, limited by form and guarded by a caring community. It can never again be a public spectacle, mass hysteria, chaos as the limitless, or as Hegel called it, Bacchantic riots.

Nietzsche sensed that the depth of the Dionysian was forever beyond good and evil, each experience again an uncharted territory, even and especially as far as morality is concerned. In that it was and is the playground of the gods, but only a superhuman being is capable of going there and allowed to enter. Nietzsche boldly envisioned that the doors of perception can be opened again. Art and in aesthetic encounter are the pathway, and the divine may be found right underneath your skin, not in books, not in a distant heaven, and not in an earthly paradise.

What this takes is a giant leap of trust, trust that the universe is ultimately not mean and abrasive, and life is a freak cosmic accident, but that the universe is hospitable to life, filled with positive communication, and yes, even full of love. If that message is not easy to find in Nietzsche, it may not be so much his fault or the fault of his philosophical ruminations. As a philosopher he faced the gigantic task to even have to invent a new language. The old language of philosophy, as he saw it, was filled with false ideals and fake gods. For most of his life he felt misunderstood and isolated. Few of his contemporaries comprehended or even cared for his message, so that at the end even his own brilliant mind turned against him and threw him into the ultimate isolation.

His life, short of any caring or loving relationship that could have softened the impact of the Social Darwinism surrounding him, kept Nietzsche from envisioning anything but violence to bring forth the strength of the superman. As so often happens, Nietzsche's violent solution, mirroring Marx' solution for social problems by revolution and conflict, was thoroughly exploited by subsequent political movements. While fascism exploited the philosopher Nietzsche, Stalinism equally exploited the philosopher Marx. Today different solutions are on the horizon. The Partnership Movement and the Human Empowerment Movement are some of the main trends for advocating a more peaceful, harmonious, and creative future, both for the individual human child and for humanity as a whole.

As Nietzsche's call for a revival of the Dionysian spirit became more popular many young artists followed this siren song of complete liberation in chaos, but only few could successfully cope. The aesthetic highways are littered with the bodies of Dionysian heroes, from Jim Morrison to Janice Joplin and Kurt Cobain, to name a few. Fed up with the mediocrity of our social environment, the Dionysian call offers a strong alternative. Humanity can no longer afford to neglect it. This is Nietzsche's real heritage. But we have to prepare ourselves first by becoming the best we can be. We must offer the human child the best education and upbringing imaginable, so that experimentation into the Dionysian unknown does no longer have to be a running away from broken family, abuse and mistreatment, from useless education and enforced mediocrity that so often prevails in our public schools. The human child must be prepared, through positive family upbringing and creative education that includes yoga mediation and non-competitive physical education to a fulfilling unification with the source of all being, which can be found right underneath our skin.

For this we need functioning and healthy communities, some of which I have witnessed, but mostly only at the fringes of so-called organized society. We need healthy and whole families, not limited by conventional norms of monogamy and heterosexuality, but defined by the amount of caring and love that can spread to the next generation. We need social organizations on the large scale of nations and continents, even on the global level, that exert a minimal amount of interference in the individual lives of people, but rationally organize those things that cannot be organized on a local level. National defense is not what comes to mind here, because in a world organized by principles of partnership global violence would no longer be needed to preserve the currently prevailing dominator status quo. On the global scale justice, equality, and rational transparency must be the overriding values that provide a level field on the local plain for healthy communities to grow who in turn are the nurturing ground of healthy individuals.

Finally we need a philosophy that gives equal rights to the needs and demands of the body – something I claim to be the Third Enlightenment. This new awareness of the physical world recaptures the deep and universal belief of the ancient people that our universe is a living organism and a dead meaningless assembly of atomistic particles floating around in meaningless space to accidentally create life and us. A future science is ready to tell and confirm a different story.

As individuals become stronger and ever more empowered, they could safely leave Aristotelian equanimity behind. For short periods of time an individual, for him or herself, but sanctioned by the surrounding community, could submerse into the Dionysian fountain, only to safely return into a welcoming group of friends who witness and sanction the empowerment and provide safe return. The resulting empowerment of the individual, propelled by the experience of connectedness with the universe, would no longer be used just for selfish advancement but for the betterment of the community. Herein lays the true dialectic, extended into an existential experience. While reason and rationality must rule the life of the community, this same reasonability must allow for individual experiences of altered states, set within the limits not of artificial rules and restrictions, but only within temporal limits of sanctioned experimentation, allowing for safe return.

Shamanic practices at all times of history and at virtually every place of the globe have pointed into the direction of the Dionysian experience. This experience when undertaken with mature guidance has the power to reveal the Other, make it experientially available, and heal the rift. As Hegel predicted, the mind finds it total other in the material world. But aesthetic submersion, which ultimately is sacred immersion, can bridge the rift. Mind and body can experience Wholeness and Oneness, the ultimate gift of the gods. This experience assures the immense wisdom that was and is inherent in the natural world. Materia, said the French philosopher Merleau Ponti, is the bridge over the abyss that extends to the other side. In creative encounter we are allowed to experience it as vibrating, living, and breathing spirit everywhere.

■ 7. LESSONS LEARNED AT THE FRANKFURT SCHOOL

Let me summarize here what I learned from my education at the Frankfurt School as it relates to our topic of cooperation and partnership.

1. It is not violent revolution and conflict alone that can ultimately bring change and turn society toward more humanity and justice, but it is creative work that can create a win-win situation. This creative work is not limited to the artist alone but includes all creative work from the manual worker to the professor of philosophy.

2. The spark of the divine can be discovered and encountered within the material world. This happens whenever we relate to the world in this aesthetic, artistic sense. We need to be on guard not to let the mind dwell in this experience. If we do so, we run the danger of turning our unique experience into ideology, as Plato had done with the experience of the exterior of the cave. Once we have formed a philosophical or religious system out of our own experience, we have turned the individual moment into an ideological world view that is in need of ideology critique. This is quite similar to the process that was later called deconstruction in the postmodern context. Ideology formation is a continuous temptation of the mind, therefore ideology critique is its permanent companion.

3. The dialectical model, or the living dialectic as I prefer to call it, instills a trust in the goodness of the natural world. This is perhaps the most controversial and most insightful lesson I took away from Hegelian dialectic and Neo-Marxism. In order for the mind to willingly give up its role as a leader, which is what happens

in the aesthetic encounter, there has to be a certain trust in the goodness of that which one will encounter in the darkness of the Other. This will easily turn into what the German philosopher Ernst Bloch, a friend of Adorno's, had called The Principle Hope. It is a hope that in the end all will be good, and perhaps even a hope that the murderer ultimately will not triumph over the slaughtered victim. It is a hope in the ultimate justice of the universe. This hope, when you try to rationalize it, can only be understood as based in metaphysics and even faith. But the point of negative dialectics is that you only practice, but never ever formulate, this hope as a metaphysical scheme. If you do the latter, ideology critique is there to dismantle your certainty. Philosophy has hereby come full circle, ending up back where Socrates started. The philosopher is the watch dog who reminds everyone not to forget the search for truth; and when you claim you have found truth, the philosopher will be the first to limit your experience to you personally. Thus philosophy prevents you from permanently committing the mistake of most religions, telling everyone how to live their lives according to the rules of someone else's truth.

◼ 8. THE FEMINIST VOICE?

The history of our world, at least that of the past two-thousand years, is filled with the oppression of women and with violence perpetrated against women. For many this has almost become a law of nature, or the way things are. As Marx pointed out, for those in power this reference to the natural way of things provides a convenient justification. It has now become evident, however, that this has not always been the case. Today we have proof that ancient civilizations existed where women, as the givers of life, were revered, treated with dignity, and had an equal opportunity to advance and to gain leadership roles.

The bloody fact remains that the more recent history of humanity, wherever you look, is filled with violence perpetrated by one half of humanity against the other half. In antiquity, wife beating, female infanticide, and the treatment of women as slaves and chattel was quite common. Ancient philosophers, far from protesting this treatment, supported such **misogynist** practices by supplying philosophical foundations for it. In the case of Aristotle, this is well documented. However, there were some earlier exceptions. Pythagoras admitted women in equal numbers into his community and Plato supposedly allowed women to sign up for his famous school. But the beginning of philosophy marks the transition of humanity away from egalitarian social systems toward those of violent domination. This fact itself, and the progressive decline of female participation in society, may be brought forward as proof that in earlier times women were equally involved in the search for truth. In addition to this, there is today an over-abundance of archeological evidence that proves the existence of early, egalitarian societies. However one fact is clear – by the time Aristotle wrote his famous works, the status of women had markedly declined.

A woman, for Aristotle, was not considered a rational animal, as one modern feminist philosopher put it. In his Aesthetics, Aristotle remarked that a female character, when portrayed as too brave or too clever, is inappropriate in a tragedy. In other places, the great philosopher considered women as incomplete males, and in yet another place he says that, "as matter yearns for form so the female yearns for the male." When it comes to the acquisition of happiness, Aristotle was quite clear that he was concerned only with the happiness of boys, since happiness was probably never quite achievable for women. This depends, of course, on Aristotle's view of happiness as connected with rational awareness and his view that men alone are capable of reason.

During the Christian Middle Ages this oppressive attitude toward women, far from being criticized or eliminated, was actually intensified. With the Augustinian reinterpretation of the original story of the Garden of Eden, a woman was now the culprit for tempting Adam and for causing original sin. Showing her clear inferiority, woman was identified as having been created from a rib of Adam. Almost as an afterthought, God had suddenly realized that his supreme creation, man, was actually lonely and needed companionship.

By the Third Century, many positive references to women in the Christian Bible had either been eliminated or successfully altered to express the misogynistic philosophy of Church fathers. This occurred in spite of some powerful female images in the Catholic Church, such as the image of Mary, the Queen of Heaven, who was supposedly able to squash the power of a snake with her heal, and in spite of the important role women played in the ministry of Jesus. Woman was now seen as the temptress, whom the devil used to instill impure thoughts in man. Worse yet, woman permanently affected man's mind and diverted male thinking away from God and toward worldly things – the kingdom of Satan.

Even though Aristotle's writings were considered heretical during the Middle Ages, his views on women had already prevailed. Aristotle's identification of God as the principle of reason and man as the rational animal set the stage for a relentless oppression of women that reached its height possibly during the witch burnings of the 12th to the 16th centuries. Hundreds of thousands of women were accused, falsely of course, and tried by largely male courts as witches. When found guilty, the outcome in virtually all cases, these women were mutilated, tortured, and burned at the stake.

The influx of scientific thinking did in no way alter or end this oppression and exploitation of women. This was particularly telling on the treatment of women as healers by the newly developing science of medicine taught at the universities. From the beginning, women had only limited access to newly opened universities. Women who were traditionally known as healers were often knowledgeable in herbal medicine and especially in the mechanics of childbirth. As more and more restrictions were placed on the practice of medicine and as university certificates became the norm, women were shut out and often persecuted for maintaining their traditional roles.

This hostile climate against women lasted from the beginnings of philosophy well into the Twentieth Century. It can hardly come as a surprise that women, who in early antiquity were revered as the bearers of wisdom and the divine, had little chance to express their philosophical voices in any meaningful way. While in the history of Twentieth Century philosophy there are a number of women philosophers well worth mentioning, it is certainly somewhat shameful to have to admit that even in this critical assessment of Western philosophy I have not succeeded in discussing even one female philosopher among the canon of established white males. I set out to write an account from my own perspective, an account of those philosophers who informed, influenced, and guided my way of thinking. And here they are: established white males, all of them.

While it appears to me that the mainstream of Western, male-dominated philosophy has arrived at a dead end, feminism – as a new beginning – points into the future. My own philosophical instruction, beginning at the Frankfurt School with Adorno during the Sixties and ending at the University of Chicago, put me firmly onto a transitional path. First of all, I was made significantly aware of the need for a critical reexamination of the Western canon, even before I was influenced by feminist ideas. Today I see that many of Adorno's main philosophical concepts, influenced by Hegelian thought and a neo-Marxist interpretation of philosophy in general, already pointed to the future and prepared the field for feminist theories. Adorno's negative dialectic, especially as he expressed it in his Aesthetic Theory, already decisively pointed away from a purely rational approach that was still generally required by most socialist writers such as Bertold Brecht. The acceptance of the unknown Other was a major vehicle of his aesthetic theory. Adorno's and Horkheimer's concept of ideological critique foreshadowed the coming deconstruction that entered from postmodernism into feminism. When I finally encountered feminist theory, I was already well acquainted with several other main concepts, because of the neo-Marxist instruction I had received at the Frankfurt School. Feminist theory, which by all accounts, is of course quite diverse and far from unified, owes much of its program to Hegelianism, Marxist humanism, and neo-Marxist schools of thought.

In conclusion I would like to mention three teachers of feminist practice and theory that have influenced my philosophical development. I left the Frankfurt School in 1968 to study at the University of Chicago. I have to admit that little of what I heard there philosophically had any great influence on my development. Among mostly positivistic philosophers, I felt like a fish out of water and found temporary refuge in literature and through active involvement in theater. This was where I met my life's companion, already a feminist then, and a social worker. Her immense practicality counteracted my intellectual escapades quite effectively. From her I learned the principles of sharing and cooperating as part of the new family we began to create. We ultimately moved to a farm and lived off the land. As an organic farmer, I learned the humility of dialogue in harmony with nature, as opposed to rape of the land with chemicals and over-harvesting. We learned the value of crop rotation and companion planting. From other organic growers and from Native American friends, I learned the interconnectedness of all natural things of which we, as human beings, are an intrinsic part. We prepared all of our own food, nothing was wasted, and everything was recycled – "we lived with the beasts as beast" as the wise witch, Goethe's creation, demands from Faust when he requests eternal youth. Goethe's renaissance Faust was unable to follow the witch's demand. For us, there was a different renaissance in the making, practicing eco-philosophy long before it became a household word.

From my intimate connection with the birth of our five children, I learned about the strength of the female character. Ultimately, I learned about the wisdom of nature that had been obscured by the dominator detour affecting our sciences. I learned about the values of communal living and the values of caring and sharing. I learned this from the professionalism of my wife and partner who, as a social worker, always became intimately involved in every community that we lived in, changing it always for the better. From her deep involvement with the plight of minorities and her activism on behalf of the socially subjugated, I learned to understand the practical aspect of the Christian command to love thy enemy, as well as of the socialist ethical concept of being on the side of the oppressed. I learned to practice standpoint theory, long before feminist philosophy made this part of its program. This practical experience of perspectivism in action, more than Nietzsche's theoretical ruminations on perspectivism, ultimately influenced my formulation, many years later, of Transcendental Perspectivism as a new philosophy,

While actively working on our farm, I also practiced holistic aesthetic expression in a little theater company, the Whole Art Theater, that I had created in our village, Here I worked closely together with a visionary woman who worked in our little company of five as actress, writer, stage designer, and all-around assistant. A native of Latvia, this woman was part ancient priestess, part healer, part pagan witch – all this and more. I learned from her about the sacredness of objects and a spiritual relationship to others and things. Her Latvian people had perhaps not yet forgotten ancient pagan ways as the rest of Europe had during over two thousand years of Christianization. Christianity had arrived late in Latvia, and I imagine that pagan animistic practices are still quite alive in the countryside. This sensitivity entered into our creation of art when we prepared fairytales for children and experimental plays for adults. Never before had I experienced this kind of natural holiness that carried into daily life.

I made a profound discovery that changed the way I understood fundamental domination, when this Latvian woman prepared an old Latvian play for the stage, For Adorno, the need for domination seemed always to be a direct result of the awakening mind conceiving of itself as Self. The price for becoming self-aware appeared to be domination of the rational mind over the Other. Philosophically, the Other appeared to include everything unknown and unknowable. The Other included animals, my body, everything mysterious, night, chaos, and woman. The rational mind was to dominate over all of this by merely being. Human dialogue with nature was always a dialogue of conquering, domineering, and enslavement. Language itself became the expression of the domineering rational mind. If one wants language, one must dominate.

The Latvian play opened my eyes to a different reality. Long before the male dominated view of self, language, and communication was born, there was communication with nature that was non-domineering, gentle, non-possessive, and driven by love. It was the ancient exchange of human beings, under the influence of the Goddess that can still be found at the cradle of Western philosophy, but then was swiftly lost. It was prevalent at the time when the main philosophical emotion was still wonder, not dominance; when our dialogue with nature was still cooperative, not competitive; when human beings believed that their death was a rebirth into the womb of mother earth and that their main cause for being was celebration of life, not a preoccupation with sickness, suffering and death.

When I finally returned to the academic world in the late Eighties, I came across the writings of Riane Eisler, an eminent feminist scholar who had done extensive research into the origins of domination and had also proposed an activist program for the development of partnership models everywhere – in schools, child rearing, families, companies, and even on the international scale of nations. Her message was that people everywhere could again live in peace with each other, cooperating creatively and getting along without warfare and without violence. Eisler, who later became a personal mentor of mine, planted the seeds for a worldwide partnership movement, based on the principles of cooperation, non-violent conflict resolution, and the development of win/win situations, as I have outlined earlier.

While feminism itself is by no means congruent, or speaking with just one voice, there are a number of feminist principles that stick out and could be called a feminist program. I would like to conclude this chapter with at least a partial list of these principles.

Feminism proposes:

- give equal value to women and men

- ensure equal participation of women and men in decision-making, in families, economics, religion, politics, education, and other social institutions.

- create narratives and stories instead of treaties and discourse

- contextualize and co-create

- deconstruct and reconstruct

- engage in dialogue and negotiate meaning

- value local meaning

- learn to become comfortable with ambiguities, contradictions, and shifts of meaning

- understand knowledge as a process rather than as a result

- connect and network

- value holism rather than separatism

- work toward interdependence to achieve a balance between independence and interdependence

- create caring communities. The goal is to establish a balance between the rights of the individual and the needs of the community, (not to return to coerced submergence of the individual into the community)

- develop concerned and caring attitudes

- celebrate diversity and difference

- hear the voices of the silenced, creatively envision a better future, and work together to create an equitable and just world.

125

CHAPTER VII: TRANSCENDENTAL PERSPECTIVISM

I have taken you to the end of the road where Western philosophy can take you, and a little beyond. Western philosophy's road is a road in search for a certain kind of truth, which we may call absolute or universal. This search began with the Greek philosophers and lasted for two thousand years until Immanuel Kant proved it to be a fruitless search. Ever since, philosophers have been on the lookout trying to find another goal or focus. Some of those answers we found in the philosophies of pragmatism, existentialism and Marxism. There were, of course, other attempts, but none of them were any more successful.

■ 1. TRANSCENDENTAL PERSPECTIVISM

This leads us to my own philosophy, which I have called **Transcendental Perspectivism**. Transcendental Perspectivism begins with **Nietzsche's** recognition that the Other is real, though we can never really prove this. We can only experience it. The experience of the real Other in aesthetic encounter is then the basic act of establishing a world with its own boundaries outside of my own self. These boundaries are set by the realization of Transcendent Perspectives. My mind realizes its own structure producing capability first as a separation. If it was not for this activity of the mind to produce separation, all would truly be one and nothing would ultimately matter. Individual existence with all its joys, happiness and suffering could simply disappear. This is the goal of Eastern (Hindu and Buddhist) philosophy, to make the separation disappear by denying the existence of Self.

Transcendental Perspectivism accepts the existence of my own Self as real. By humanistic implication it accepts the reality of others who claim to have self as just as real. The creative encounter brings home this realization of self. In its own denial, in creative immediacy, the self disappears momentarily only to reappear again in the created Other, the work of art. Here, as if frozen in the materiality of things, the mind recognizes its own structures and its own presence, but in a state of alienation from its own source of selfness. The goal of Transcendental Perspectivism is to overcome this alienation through communication. This, it claims, is the essence of creative co-creation and spirituality.

■ 2. A PERSPECTIVIST MANIFESTO

1. Transcendental Perspectivism recognizes truth as experiential and personal, but not as objective and universal. Therefore all religious beliefs including agnosticism and atheism are respected equally, as long as they do not impose their values on others.

2. Transcendental Perspectivism prefers diversity and difference over singularity. These are assumed to be more natural and beneficial in evolutionary terms.

3. Transcendental Perspectivism rejects domination in all its forms. It especially rejects domination of men over women. For this reason Transcendental Perspectivism embraces a reevaluation of the philosophical canon from a feminist perspective.

4. Transcendental Perspectivism aims for cooperation and connectedness over competition and survival of the fittest. This, too, is seen to be more natural and adaptive.

5. Transcendental Perspectivism assumes that there is a unique perspective, an insideout view for everything that exists, including Nothingness. This puts consciousness at the center.

Transcendental Perspectivism accepts the existence of my own Self as real. By humanistic implication it accepts the reality of others who claim to have self as just as real.

6. Central to Transcendental Perspectivism is the search for the Other. Since all is consciousness we can communicate with all. This makes Transcendental Perspectivism a shamanistic philosophy.

7. Transcendental Perspectivism assumes a holistic view of the human body. Mind and body are one. Healing the body can never be seen in isolation and viceversa, a sickness of the mind affects the body.

8. As a shamanistic philosophy Transcendental Perspectivism provides the basis for a reanimation of the natural (material or inanimate) world. This will not result in a new superstition, but will be complemented by mathematical structure and empirical verification.

9. Transcendental Perspectivism bridges the gap between the sciences and the humanities. It reunites the various fields of the cognitive enterprise of humanity by providing a new and in depth understanding of the physical world on which all human knowledge is based.

10. By providing a full and indepth understanding of the physical nature of the human being, Transcendental Perspectivism initiates a renaissance of the body. It invites a physical celebration of the human being within a physical world. This reevaluation of the human body will lead to a third enlightenment, the Enlightenment of the Body.

11. By reconnecting humanity with the rest of the physical world Transcendental Perspectivism will initiate a new spirituality. This has been called a cosmic spiritually. It is cosmic consciousness because these new individuals will be fully aware of being members of a larger whole, as they themselves are the composite symphony of numerous smaller wholes.

■ 3. TOWARD A UNIVERSALIST FUTURE?

Looking back over this program of Transcendental Perspectivism, I must admit that it is rather a collection of suggestions, a call for practical implementation of certain ideas, and in many ways a strategizing for change. Does this program amount to a new philosophy? Transcendental Perspectivism certainly does not offer the kind of grand system to explain everything in the universe, as did the old philosophical systems of Kant, Hegel and Marx.

At the beginning of the Twentieth Century, most philosophers were convinced that the time of grand systems in philosophy was over. I tend to agree. There will never again be one universal way to explain the world, one model that fits all. That is precisely the message of Transcendental Perspectivism. It rests on the recognition that our different lives, our different interests, and our personal histories create in all of us different perspectives and different narratives, as the postmodern feminists would say, which we must all hold more or less to be true. Transcendental Perspectivism recognizes the reality of these existential positions, or standpoints, that often dominate and direct our lives and those of others. We can come closer to each other in reasonable dialogue, trying to understand the Other through communication. I believe that every future philosophy must be dialogical. The dialogical aspect of a philosophy makes it human-istic, open to others, not so much in order to convince them of my own truth, but to better understand where they are coming from. But this embrace of the other's standpoint must go far beyond mere logical and rational communication. It must extend to emotional and some-times even existential identification. My own truth must manifest itself in the way I live my life. In this, I can establish my true authenticity. In the same way, I must allow and encourage others to live their truth and establish their authenticity. Transcendental Perspectivism, by transcending one's own boundaries and respecting authenticity in others, can help establishing a global network of mutual respect.

OPPOSING WORLD VIEWS	
DIONYSIAN	PYTHAGOREAN
CHAOS	ORDER
EMOTIONS	REASON
CONNECTIVITY	ISOLATION
ART	SCIENCE
SUBJECTIVE TRUTH	OBJECTIVE TRUTH

So what is the prospect that this search for authentic selves will eventually lead to a universally accepted philosophy, boldly called universalism, by the founder of the global philosophical society now known as the International Society for Universal Dialogue? I have been part of this society since its beginning in 1988. Under the wise guidance of its founding father, Polish philosopher Janusz Kuczynki, this society of some four hundred philosophers from around the world has been exploring the possibility of creating such a new, global meta-philosophy. I believe that Transcendental Perspectivism is a necessary milestone on the way to such a new world view. Whether it should, or will, ever come into existence, only time can tell. I believe with Socrates that our deepest purpose here on Earth is to pursue the truth, while remaining intensely aware that a found truth is probably not the full story. In our postmodern times, it has even become questionable whether such a thing as the full story has ever and will ever exist. The universe is a continuously evolving organism, alive at every stage, self organizing, selecting and choosing our future. This is not done according to a pre-destined master plan, but is the result of continuous experimentation.

In this book I have tried to work out some of the main ingredients that would have to be contained in any future, universalizing philosophy. Let's review them here:

Universalism as a future philosophy will:

- be inherently dialogical.

- create a dialogue that must go beyond so-called rational communication to include conversations with animals, plants, crystals, and the rest of the so often 'silent' world.

- accept diversity in all its rainbow colors and shades;

Transcendental Perspectivism recognizes truth as experiential and personal, but not as objective and universal. Therefore all religious beliefs including agnosticism and atheism are respected equally, as long as they do not impose their values on others.

- treat all human beings, especially women, and sexual and other minorities as full equals, both socially and economically; Thus universalism will embrace the noblest principles of partnership and cooperative existence;

- put the highest priority on education of everybody, regardless of race, ethnic and cultural background, and gender. This alone can guarantee the true autonomy of every individual.

- develop the frame work for a sensible educational program that can be used everywhere. Such a program must take into account the diversity of people, the different learning styles, and must especially include time-proven educational practices from Eastern cultures, such as Yoga and meditation. The classroom must become the practice ground for the new partnership world. It must teach and practice principles of cooperation and non-violent conflict resolution, which are most readily conceived by all participants as having win-win outcomes.

- include a new covenant with the natural world. As Eco-philosophy in all its multiple voices has stressed, this new philosophy must sensitize all human children to the needs and demands of our natural habitant, globally conceived as mother earth. While traditional science served to de-spiritualize the world, a universalistic meta-philosophy must search for a new science that not only recognizes, but invites, a spiritual contact with the natural world. The time for dualistic separation of mind and body, that ruled much of Western philosophy, has come to an end.

- develop a new ethics of core values that are deeply entrenched in a scientific understanding of the universe. This will require nothing less than a revolution in science.

Thus, in the end, in spite of all the failures and shortcomings of Western philosophy, universalism will have to return to the search that was started by the ancient Greeks. The Greek philosophers believed deeply that by fully understanding and living in accordance with the laws inherent in the natural world, we would ultimately be able to live a better, harmonious, fulfilled, and happy lives. That, I believe, should still be the goal and is ultimately our only chance of survival. Ancient Hindu scriptures speak about the gods sending avatars down to earth. They are like saints or prophets. They are sent down because each epoch creates its own merely peripheral laws or dharmic values. These must be replaced and humanity must return to a set of dharmic values or cosmic core values. Today, I believe these must be based on science. But with its false sense of objectivity, current science is not capably of discovering dharma and value. Only when science begins treating the whole universe as a living and evolving organism, as did the ancient peoples, will value theory become a conceivable part of the equation. I deeply believe that dynamic cooperation and community creation will once again be scientifically established as universal core values. These concepts must become part of any future universal philosophy.

Even though much of current science is still far too strongly influenced by false mechanistic thinking, we have a tremendous advantage today over those ancient thinkers. Our knowledge of the natural world has increased a thousand fold, probably immensely more than that. But as I pointed out in the introduction, scientific knowledge also led us astray. As science was influenced by and partnered up with dominator thinking, it led us down dark alleys of misjudgments, exploitation, and at times downright evil. The scientific enterprise, while maintaining its careful and skeptical stance, must be liberated from dominator thinking and false biases that are its result. A dose of perspectivism can help here to realize that most probably in every so-called objective scientific law there is a little bit of the producer's perspective at work. This insight helps science to remain humble, open to change, and to avoid new absolutes.

My own truth must manifest itself in the way I live my life. In this I can establish my true authenticity. In the same way I must allow and encourage others to live their truth and establish their authenticity.

Any new universal philosophy must ultimately be based on science, rather than ideology. Nature has a way of guiding us in the right direction, when our instincts have led us astray.

CHAPTER VIII: APPENDIX

■ 1. IS THE UNEXAMINED LIFE REALLY NOT WORTH LIVING?

The birth of Western philosophy is marked by two prominent statements, quotations by two of the most influential philosophers of all times: Socrates and Aristotle. The first one by Socrates boldly claims that "The unexamined life is not worth living.," The second statement by Aristotle was used to illustrate syllogism, or a deductive inference of truth, the backbone of formal logic: "Major premise: All men are mortal. Minor premise: Socrates is a man. Conclusion: Socrates is mortal." For philosophers both of these statements are almost as hewn in stone as the Ten Commandments are for Christians and Jews; but both have always left me with a sense of discomfort, with an air of lingering doubt. In this paper I will explore how these two so-called philosophical "truisms" at the cradle of Western civilization may have contributed to a sense of alienation and to an increase in suffering among those who were subsequently affected by Western philosophy, religion and culture.

My grandmother's son, whom I never got to know personally, was an ordained Roman Catholic priest. He left the priesthood when he fell in love with a woman. This all happened during the turbulent years of World War II in the Sudetenland – a part of former Czechoslovakia, which at that time had been "liberated" by Hitler's army. Thrown out of his home in shame, my uncle joined the German army and disappeared somewhere in Siberia.

Until her death, my grandmother could not forgive her son for the unspeakable act of leaving the priesthood. For a devout Catholic of that time, this was one of the most horrendous acts a man could commit, as well as one of the most terrible things that could happen to a mother. Day in and day out, this tragedy haunted my grandmother to the end of her life. Throughout all of it, it seemed less tragic for her to have lost a son who was her flesh and blood than for him to have lost his soul to eternal hell fire. Thus is the power of religious indoctrination.

Human history is filled with such stories of immense suffering, some of it brought about by our own doing and some of it by the whims of natural events. When a powerful earthquake shook Lisbon in the 1800s and brought down a mighty cathedral filled with Easter Sunday worshippers, philosophers of that time asked the question (of course by no means for the first time) 'how can an all-powerful and all-loving God allow such misery? If God is in charge of earthly events, could He not have influenced them and delayed the earthquake for only a few minutes until the worship had finished and the church had emptied out?'

At that time, the deists had won the day. God had created a world that now ran according to iron laws. But in accordance with the optimistic spirit of the Enlightenment, philosophers generally took natural disasters neither as a mark of God's impotence nor even as an expression of his wrath, but as a sign of nature's overabundance and wealth. Accordingly, the young Immanuel Kant was bold enough to proclaim:

> The horrific effects of an infected air, earthquakes, and floods can erase whole popula-
> tions from the face of the earth; however, it does not appear that Nature suffers from

[1] *http:/www.tobisas-bott.de/Aufklarung. Pg 16.*

this. The immensity of creation is so great that comparing one earth or even one whole milky-way with it is like comparing one little insect with the whole earth.[1]

The mature Kant, looking again at the inexplicable horrors caused by natural disasters, saw them as a reason to affirm man's moral dignity and the ultimate freedom of his will. Expressing the spirit of the time, Kant was bent on seeing the best in the worst. For human beings, the depth of suffering has a lot to do with how we see the world. Suffering is deeply connected to interpretation.

Less than 100 years later in a universe now dominated by science, no loving God ruled from above and influenced events here on earth. Philosophers no longer could muster enough optimism to take life-sustaining meaning out of destruction. The laws of nature suddenly appeared no longer an affirmation of God's greatness, but rather the expression of cold destiny and of iron fate.

Georg Büchner, a German playwright of the 19th century, depicted God in one of his plays as a cruel and cynical tyrant who watches over us like over a fishbowl, pulling us on strings like marionettes. Descartes' hypothetical God as a deceiving tyrant suddenly had become reality. Defending the deaths of tens of thousands as a result of the French Revolution, Saint-Just, one of its main engineers, proclaimed:

> Nature follows its laws quietly and unresistingly. Man is destroyed when he comes in conflict with them. An alteration in the composition of the air, a flare-up of the tellurian fires, a fluctuation in the balance of bodies of water, and an epidemic, a volcanic eruption, a flood – each of these can bury thousands. What is the result? An insignificant, and on the whole scarcely noticeable, alteration of physical Nature, which might almost have passed without a trace, were it not for the bodies in its path.[2]

With a scientific eye the materialist Büchner concludes that within a mechanical universe, a compassionless God has become all but irrelevant. From the butchers of the French Revolution to Stalin's death camps, the new absolute rulers use nature to justify their own cruelties by referring to the merciless mechanism of evolution. Saint-Just shouts out:

> Shall the moral universe take more consideration in its revolutions than the physical universe? Shall an idea not have equal rights with the laws of physics in regard to annihilating that which opposes it?[3]

Once the mechanical universe was complete, the rest of the idea of a personal God that had survived the enlightened and deistic onslaught, was murdered by the new nihilism of the 19th century lead by Nietzsche's battle cry of a Dying God. What might have still survived this philosophical massacre was finally incinerated in the ovens of Auschwitz, Treblinka and Bergen-Belsen. In the wake of the slaughterhouses of the 20th century, the new cry for theodicy – the defense of God in the light of human suffering – found few if any defenders. The lost trust in divine help is perhaps best exemplified today by the power and size, as well as by the daily activities, of the State of Israel. The so-called "chosen people" who have built their historical reputation with their unfailing trust in the guidance of their almighty God, today

[2] *Georg Büchner: Complete Plays, Danton's Death (New York: Hill and Wang, 1963) pg 40.*
[3] *Ibid.*

trust their almighty army equipped with hellfire missiles, patriot defense systems and armored tanks to help them secure their place in the history of tomorrow.

If on the one hand much of what we make out of suffering is interpretation, and on the other hand it is suffering nevertheless, an intrinsic part of the human condition is it specific to human beings or is suffering even part of the existential condition of the whole universe? Is suffering the only thing that lies between us and a merciless universe, the only reality that reminds us of our divine origins?

We human beings are subject to myriad ways of suffering. Advanced consumer societies have developed a thousand pills and treatments to alleviate pain. In fact, we have become nearly obsessed with the elimination of pain. But will our preoccupation with the elimination of pain also eliminate suffering or will suffering always be with us? Perhaps we should first ask whether suffering has always been part of our condition. At the dawn of time, when human beings were in their infancy, was suffering also part of their daily experience? To investigate this we will need to look for answers in history, evolutionary biology and in mythological stories and art.

Should we start by investigating the sense of suffering that animal's experience? Few would now take seriously any Descartes' statement that animals don't suffer. The great philosopher believed this because he rationalized that animals cannot conceptualize suffering as human beings do. Recent books such as J. M. Masson and S. McCarthy's *When Elephants Weep* are well-researched testaments to the rich emotional lives of animals, filled with suffering and pain, but also with happiness and joy.

The realization that animals suffer is, at least among Western scientists, a relatively new one. For many centuries, scientists believed that animals didn't suffer. They might feel temporary pain, but since they more or less lived in the 'here and now' and did not have a temporal consciousness, their pain was nothing as compared to the suffering of human beings. Their screams of pain were nothing more than mechanical reflex. In a similar way, these scientists believed that children were quite incapable of suffering. As late as the beginning of the 20th century, operations on children were performed without anesthesia because doctors believed that children's pain and suffering was inconsequential since they could not conceptualize their pain.

Pain, we know today, is the flipside of feeling good; an emotional state that is found in all creatures we consider alive. Pain is the signal for living things to move into action. Without some sense of discomfort, as well as some sense of well being, nothing in the universe would evolve. In my book *Compassion, A New Philosophy of the Other,* I have argued that the state of feeling well or feeling pain can be found in all ranks of the universe, even at the level of the so-called inanimate world – in molecules, protons, photons, electrons and perhaps even in the very fabric of space and time. This view of the world, reminiscent of the animistic view of primeval people, today experiences a revival among philosophers of science in what is alternately called vitalism, pan-psychism or quantum animism.

It seems only natural to assume that suffering increases as organisms become more complex.

But suffering is a very subjective experience and therefore hard, if not impossible, to quantify. Not unlike our sense of selfhood, suffering is one of those qualities that we really only know from our own, very personal experience. By implication, we extend the experience of suffering to other human beings. But even in that respect, our imagination is quite limited. When images of thousands of people who are dying of starvation or AIDS in Africa are brought into our living rooms on the evening news, our comprehension and our ability to have compassion is extraordinarily limited. When we contemplate the suffering of animals, we have even less understanding.

Perhaps this was the reason why, under the influence of the deistic and mechanistic world-view, the suffering of animals was disregarded as being mere instinct. This absolved people from having compassion for the millions of animals living in concentration camp like conditions on American farms in order to be ready to feed the stomachs of our mass society. When scientists used human terms to describe the pain of animals, it was generally dismissed as unjustified anthropomorphizing. Today this trend is reversing somewhat. Perhaps our contact with other less scientific cultures and civilizations has opened our eyes in a new way. In my book, *Compassion*, I have cited many examples of the recent re-introduction of anthropomorphic expressions in describing animal behavior, including animal suffering and pain. In what has been called an atmosphere of postmodern science, the idea that animals suffer much like we human beings has become much more acceptable. On the other hand, there seems to be a consensus among scientists that animal pain lacks the depth of human suffering. It has slowly become evident, however, that animals not only do not feel pain in a merely mechanical way, but they also mourn the loss of their partners. It has also been observed that animals show delayed suffering as well, just like humans do. At least in regard to primates, this scientific insight negates the assumption that suffering is particularly human.

In similar ways, the compassion of animals toward wounded or dying members of their pack has also been observed. One of the earliest accounts of compassion expressed by an animal for the suffering of its human master is reported in Homer's *Odysseus*. After Odysseus has poked out the eye of the one-eyed monster, Cyclops, Homer reports that the giant's sheep feel sadness for their master as he cries out in pain. Again, upon his return to Athens much later, the only one who recognizes Odysseus is his old dog who wags his tail in happiness. The so-called naïve poet Homer understood the importance of compassion, even between human beings and the natural world. It is perhaps the loss of that communication that later Greek poets meant when they mourned the lost connection to the world of the gods.

Even before philosophy, religions were developed as a response to the loss of unity and communication with nature. From the beginning religions included a strong tendency to want to eliminate human suffering, but their affect in history was often the opposite. The main myth of origin for Christians, Jews and Muslims talks about a condition of happiness and peace at the beginning of humanity. Paradise supposedly was lost as a result of the hubris of the first human couple who wanted to be like God. This action of our mythical first parents was later seen by Augustine as the beginning of human sin and the justification for the presence of human suffering.

The creation myth of Hinduism, in contrast, places creation and destruction as equally balancing forces at the beginning of time. During Vedic times, as the caste system was instituted in India and domination became all pervasive, suffering was seen as a natural part of life. In Hinduism, the real world with its suffering was called maya – a world of illusion. Holding on to maya was the cause of all suffering. Even death brings no solution because it is only the beginning of a new cycle of suffering through reincarnation. Moksha, the final liberation, comes when one has moved up through the castes and finally escapes in *samsara*.

On this fertile ground of suffering, Buddhism was founded on the premise of eliminating human suffering in overcoming desire by ultimately eliminating Selfhood. Suffering, according to Buddhism, is caused by ignorance. Therefore, when ignorance is removed, suffering does not arise. Once the Buddha had realized this, he was freed from desire, ignorance and rebirth. He acquired perfect wisdom and attained Enlightenment. Millions of Buddhist tried to follow their guru and attain enlightenment by escaping suffering and the Self.

While Buddhism, which is by all accounts a highly civilized worldview, proposed to escape suffering by eliminating selfhood, Western philosophy moved in the opposite direction. Not without some self-indulgence, Western philosophers stressed the high status of refined suffering over the brute suffering of so-called lesser developed cultures. Thus, the level of suffering one could perceive evolved into a racist tool for competitive advance. Eurocentric scientists believing that their culture was supreme, assumed for centuries that human suffering among lesser developed cultures was also less intense. This view lead to the racist conception that so-called "primitive" people, such as black Africans or Native Americans, could be guiltlessly treated with greater violence since their "brute" state did not allow them to experience refined suffering like the "higher civilized European." George Mivart, a devout Catholic who lived in the 19th century and was a critic of Darwinian evolution, believed that physical suffering, "depends greatly upon the mental condition of the sufferer. Only during consciousness does it exist, and only in the most highly organized men does it reach its acme."[4] To underscore his racist beliefs, Mivart bluntly states that he, the author,

> has been assured that lower races of men appear less keenly sensitive to physical suffering than do more cultivated and refined human beings. Thus only in man can there really be an intense degree of suffering, because only in him is there that intellectual recollection of past moments and that anticipation of future ones, which constitute in great parts the bitterness of suffering. The momentary pang, the present pain, which beasts endure, though real enough, is yet, doubtless, not to be compared as to its intensity with the suffering which is produced in man through high prerogative of self-consciousness.[5]

One of the most poignant examples for such refined suffering can be found in Tolstoy's *The Death of Ivan Ilych*. At the end of his life Ivan Ilych looks back at a life of success, full of devotion both to his work and to his family. He has busily filled his days with taking care of all the little things that need to be taken care of. Everyone around him looks up to him. He is an accomplished man who should truly be satisfied with his life. In Aristotelian terms, he is a man who might call himself happy. In a Kantian sense, he has done his duty throughout his whole life. But is this enough?

[4] *George Marvin, Genesis of Species, 1871 quoted from S. J. Gould: Hen's Teeth and Horse's Toes, (New York: Norton & Co., 1983)pg 40/41.*
[5] *Ibid.*

Plagued by physical pain, which he tries to douse with medication and opium, the question bursts into his mind and looms larger than his physical pain, suddenly and unmercifully: "What if my whole life was wrong?" This question for ultimate meaning is triggered by an existential reflection. In logic class Ivan once had learned that "All men are mortal, Socrates is a man, and hence Socrates is mortal." Applied to himself now, this simple truism did not seem to make any sense. Why should the cold logic of a syllogism uttered some two thousand years ago apply to him now?

> He suffered ever the same unceasing agonies and in his loneliness pondered always the same insoluble question: "What is this? Can it be that it is Death?" And the inner voice answered: "Yes, it is Death." – "Why these sufferings? And the voice answered, "For no reason – they just are so." Beyond and besides this there was nothing.[6]

In an ice-cold mechanical manner, Aristotelian logic reveals death to the mind as the only true absolute – the only persistent archai. There is a straight line from the Aristotelian universal that reveals death as the most trusted absolute to the existentialist's conclusion which sees in suicide the most trusted proof of the freedom to choose. How can a seemingly fulfilled life end in such utter absurdity? The face of this death, when felt existentially, causes the deepest agony, the deepest level of suffering. Ivan Ilich goes through it and sinks into a black hole. Even Holy Communion, brought to him by the Orthodox priest, cannot mercifully help to put meaning into his wasted life. Finally he has to descend into the underworld, like Faust before him, or like Christ, or like the cunning Sisyphus. He stays there for three long days. He will eventually find a solution to his metaphysical pain in the tears of compassion he sheds for those he leaves behind.

> For three whole days, during which time did not exist for him, he struggled in that black sack into which he was being thrust by an invisible, resistless force. He struggled as a man condemned to death struggles in the hands of the executioner knowing that he cannot save himself. And every moment he felt that, despite all his efforts, he was drawing nearer and nearer to what terrified him.

> Suddenly some force struck him in the chest and side, making it still harder to breathe, and he fell through the hole and there at the bottom was a light.[7]

Existentially, once the mind is focused on death as the ultimate absolute, we have to follow its path to the bitter end. But there, in the darkness of the abyss, shines a light that gives hope. As Faust climbs down into the underworld, Mephisto promises emptiness and the Void, eternal nothingness. But Faust's prophetic answer, "In your nothing I hope to find my All," reveals the power of the living dialectic that turns Nothingness into salvation. In the center of the void, Ivan finds true love and compassion. Feeling the head of his young son next to his bed with his hand, Ivan

> opened his eyes, looked at his son, and felt sorry for him. His wife came up to him and he glanced at her. She was gazing at him open-mouthed, with undried tears on her nose and cheek, and a despairing look on her face. He felt sorry for her too.

[6] *Kraseman, Keith ed., Questions for the Soul (Massachusetts: Copley, 1997) p. 528.*
[7] *Ibidem pg. 533.*

"Yes, I am making them wretched," he thought, "They are sorry, but it will be better for them when I die." He wished to say this but had not the strength to utter it. "Besides, why speak. I must act." – And suddenly it grew clear to him that what had been oppressing him was all dropping away at once from two sides, from ten sides, and from all sides. He was sorry for them, he must act so as not to hurt them; release them and free himself from these sufferings.[8]

Compassion turns darkness into light. "In place of death there was light. . . What joy!" Ivan exclaims, turning himself from a mere suffering man into a shining bodhisattva, a bearer of the light of hope.

Equipped with syllogism and logic the scrutinizing human mind can only see absurdity in death, and ultimately in life as well. The *memento mori* of the middle ages had left Christian culture a suffering, martyred, and crucified Christ as the prevailing image. But during the Catholic Middle Ages, human works could at least still be seen as liberating milestones to God. The Protestant reformation robbed work of that spiritual meaning. Salvation henceforth was an act of grace and of grace alone. The rediscovered Aristotelian logic and the new scientific mind discarded the possibility of a passionate involvement with the universe, until ultimately the whole world was sacrificed on the altar of science. Once science had driven out all spirits from nature, the world appeared hostile, dark, and empty. In this mechanical universe, there is no redemption. Even human labor, the source of creative involvement for pagans and a way to God for earlier Christians, now turns into a Sisyphusian task.

To illustrate this dispirited world, a grandmother in Georg Büchner's *Woyzeck,* tells a fairy tale most fitting for the new cold age of science:

Once upon a time there was a poor little girl who had no father and no mother. Everyone was dead, and there was no one left in the whole wide world. Everyone was dead. And the little girl went out and looked for someone night and day. And because there was no one left on the earth, she wanted to go to Heaven. And the moon looked down so friendly at her. And when she finally got to the moon, it was a piece of rotten wood. And so she went to the sun, and it was a piece of faded sun-flower. And when she got to the stars, they were little golden flies, stuck up there as if they were caught in a spider's web. And when she wanted to go back to earth, the earth was an upside down pot. And she was all alone. And she sat down there and she cried. And she sits there to this day, all, all alone.[9]

Human labor, in ancient times the source of pride and creativity, during the industrial age had been turned into a source of suffering, a meaningless activity, a Sisyphusian task. In the ancient myth, the cunning Sisyphus, defying the gods, was able to trap *thanatos* and hold him hostage. Ares, the god of war, was the only one who could subdue Sisyphus and set *thanatos* free. As a result Sisyphus was condemned by the gods to die. Once in the underworld he was again able to trick the gods and return back to the living. When his time finally came, Sisyphus refused to return to Hades. Hermes himself had to take over the punishment for this act of defiance. Sisyphus was punished for his bad faith by being condemned eternally to

---

[8] *Ibidem, pgs. 533/34.*
[9] *Op. cit. Büchner, Woyzzeck, pg 133.*

roll an enormous boulder up the slope of a mountain. Each time it nearly reached the summit, it rolled down again.

Jean Paul Sartre's close friend, Albert Camus, turned this ancient myth into a modern metaphor, illustrating the attempt to find ultimate meaning in a post-Kantian world. Any work, whether it is doing one's daily chores or searching the stars for a sign of intelligent design, is affected by the absurd. It is like rolling a bolder up a hill only to see it fall back down. Kant's conclusion that the thing itself can never truly be known ended two thousand years of ontological transparency that had begun with the Greek masters; and he ripped the ground out from underneath any metaphysical speculation. Any work that one dedicated to the grand task of understanding God and the world was further on condemned to the absurd. Sisyphus is the absurd hero.

> His scorn of the gods, his hatred for death, and his passion for life won him that unspeakable penalty in which the whole being is exerted. This is the price that must be paid for the passions of this earth.[10]

In the absurd hero, Camus skillfully combines ancient wisdom with modern heroism. For the existentialist Camus, after the night of Gethsemane a new morning is allowed to dawn, grown not from metaphysical speculations concerning absolute truth, not even as a result of a relentless examination of one's life as Socrates had commanded, but grown out of the very passions of this earth. Camus reaches back to the wisdom of the ancients. He proposes to overcome suffering by boldly declaring victory. Such victory for the absurd hero is found in the very passions of the Earth: "Sophocles' Oedipus, like Dostoevsky's Kirilov, . . . gives the recipe for absurd victory."[11] In the face of absurdity, the absurd hero knows and tells us that "Despite so many ordeals, my advanced age and the nobility of my soul make me conclude that all is well."

This realization is the utterance of the absurd faith that is allowed again to appreciate the little things in this world. "It drives out of this world a god who had come into it with dissatisfaction and a preference for futile sufferings. It makes fate a human matter, which must be settled among men."[12]

This is the triumph of the absurd that lets Kafka's Gregor Samsa, as a beetle, appreciate the simple music his sister is playing in a way he had never appreciated it before. "The absurd man, when he contemplates his torment, silences all the idols. In the universe, suddenly restored to its silence, the myriad wondering little voices of the earth rise up."[13]

The absurd philosopher realizes the futility of relentless self-examination and the futility of the universal command. These trends in Western thinking have been the root of myriad misjudgments, violence, and suffering. People have pitted themselves as masters against others and the mind has positioned itself outside of the material world and as the dominator over it. Once we again realize that in our separateness all is connected, our whole being finds a new focus toward understanding the other in compassionate love. The highest mission of the mind is not to find truth, to discover self and dominate, but to transcend, communicate, and

[10] *Op cit, Kraseman, pg 543.*
[11] *Ibid. pg 544.*
[12] *Ibid. pg. 545.*
[13] *Ibid.*

relate. This is ancient wisdom, standing at the end of a two-thousand-year-long history of Western philosophy and boldly opening up a small door of escape. Consciousness has come full circle.

The reason why those less developed, less refined people – those whom Western civilization liked to call savages – seemed to suffer less was not their less refined mind, but their closer relation to nature and the earth. They had not yet lost their connection with the wonders of the Earth, revering it as a Goddess. When death is interpreted as a returning to the womb from which one will be reborn in the fullness of time, death loses its tragic uniqueness, the cause for so much alienation and suffering.

For we moderns, the return to paradise is not easy. It may have to follow the path into the depth of Gethsemane. But in recognizing that pursuit as absurd, we can short cut the way and embrace transcendence. We can begin the joy of discovery by compassionately seeking the other. In this pursuit we thankfully do not have to rely on achievements of Western philosophy and civilization alone. Eastern philosophy can teach us ancient techniques of empowerment and self-realization, without which true communication with the other, in a non-cognitive way, is not possible. Eastern practices, which today have been incorporated successfully in many ways into our daily lives, can teach us to overcome the alienating dualism of mind over body and lessen the blow of suffering.

A number of Western philosophers, most notably Walter Benjamin, have discovered that the secret of true transcendence lies somewhere hidden in the experience of the Now moment. This realization is an intrinsic part of any meditative experience and can also be found at the heart of the Empowerment movement. The psychology of Now has been researched more recently by Chicago University psychologist Mihaly Csikszentmihalyi in *Flow: The Psychology of Optimal Experience*.[14] The experience of Now is put to practical use through techniques made available by the new science of neuro-linguistic programming. Techniques taught by the Empowerment movement are also useful to get a practical handle on refocusing temporal suffering and developing a new outlook on life. I have outlined this extensively in my book, *Compassion*.

Ken Wilbur was once visiting Germany with his wife who was dying. The well-known writer and mystic supposedly walked into a pub one night, feeling all sorry for himself and for his wife.

> "My whole fucking life is a shambles," he thought. He wandered into a pub and started drinking. Sensing his distress, a group of German men pulled him off his bar stool and made him dance a polka with them. Alternately crying and laughing as he danced, Wilber felt his self-pity washing out of him. "I would like to claim that my big satori. . . came from some powerful meditation session with blazing white light," Wilber wrote. "But it happened in a little pub with a bunch of kindly old men whose names I do not know and whose language I did not speak."[15]

According to Eastern philosophy, the universe just *is*. Suffering is the result of interpretation. The more we examine life, the more intense our suffering will become. In the West, Hegelian

---

[14] *Mihaly Csikszentmihalyi in Flow: The Psychology of Optimal Experience.*
[15] *John Horgan, Rational Mysticism, (Boston: Houghton Mifflin Co., 2003) pg. 234/235.*

dialectic came close to this recognition, but was in the end not able "to jump the fence." Following Hegelian dialectic, but with a scientific eye on unraveling the secrets of materia neo-Marxist philosophers such as Theodore W. Adorno, the above mentioned Walter Benjamin and perhaps Maurice Merleau-Ponty recognized the value of the dialectical way to escape Hegel's unhappy consciousness by submersing into the Now. Dialectic, Merleau-Ponty once said, is an extended bridge over the abyss. No one knows what is on the other side. The unhappy consciousness is the result of relentless examination that leads to refined suffering. Trusting that the unexamined life also is good and worth living is its dialectical Other, a second way well worthwhile to explore.

First published in SKEPSIS, © International Center of Philosophy and Interdisciplinary Research, Athens and Ancient Olympia, Greece. Reprinted with permission.

■ 2. COMPASSION AND THE WISDOM OF NATURE

"Now people of conscience the world over have a clear choice between Religion and Spirituality; Fundamentalism and Wisdom; A Punitive Father God and the Mother-Father Creator of Justice and Compassion; Fascism and Control vs. Letting the Spirit Work; between a preferential option for the rich and powerful (cf. Opus Dei) and a preferential option for the poor (as in liberation theology)."

– Rev. Dr. Matthew Fox

While collecting my thoughts for this paper, I asked myself, "What is the meaning of compassion? How can we let the spirit work? I have just spent a day wandering through the exhibit halls of Next Fest, the yearly exhibit of futuristic projects sponsored by *Wired Magazine* in Chicago. Next Fest is a parade of cutting-edge technological innovations – the human spirit at work. This exhibit is perhaps the closest we human beings can come to being co-creators of the world.

Next Fest is an exhibit of human co-creation at its best. I stared into the eyes of a cloned cat, her donor cat sleeping in a cage next to her. How long will it be, before we will meet the first cloned human being? I stand in line to smile and frown into a lens connected to a computer which can recognize human faces and tell their emotions. The computer lens picks out faces, frames them on a screen and recognizes whether you are happy or sad. So far it's only a game, but soon these cameras will be mounted on every street corner insuring the safety of us global citizens. Will it really make the world safer? Crime has been going down for the past four years in America's big cities. Is this cause for optimism?

At home I pick from among over 200 TV channels and I pick the one thing that interests me – the live aid concerts that happened in eight locations around the world simultaneously. These rock performers have made it their goal to convince the leaders of the world to finally end global poverty. Does it really need rock-n-roll to spread this message? Why aren't all the churches united in this endeavor to eliminate hunger and poverty?

Another show I choose to watch is a reality show called Thirty Days. People from diametrically opposite walks of life trade places with each other for a month. A vegetarian new age couple from California trades places with a black, inner city, junk-food eating and TV-addicted family. Children and family pets are not included in the exchange. Another episode brings two yuppie real estate brokers from New York to a commune called Dancing Rabbits in rural Missouri where they trade places with a couple of pagans. The initial culture shock often turns into real learning; although arranged as a game, these people learn real life skills and they learn to see the world through the eyes of the other. I wonder how it would be to exchange places with a gorilla living behind bars in a zoo. Seeing and experiencing the world through the eyes of the other is one of the basic qualities lacking in many people today. Can technological innovations or television help us develop these qualities so sorely needed to foster compassion?

At the trial of Adolf Eichman, Hannah Arendt observed that Eichman completely lacked the ability to see the world through the eyes of another person. This condition made him incapable of compassion. Compassion is the ability to experience the world from the standpoint of the other. It is the capacity to become truly dialogical, not just as an intellectual exercise in the pursuit of winning an argument, but in a fully existential way. This disability was at the core of Eichman's character, and it is more widespread today than anyone can imagine.

In order to solve a problem, it was customary among some Native American tribes to employ an exercise designed to practice seeing the problem through the other person's eyes. Adversaries would stand in a circle with defined points on the periphery. Then each would get the chance to explain the situation from his or her perspective. After that, they all changed places. Participants now were asked to explain the situation from what they had heard about the other position. They were encouraged to adopt not only the thought patterns of the other perspective, but also experience the other perspective emotionally. Wise elders expected that through this exercise common ground could be found and a compromise achieved. Could modern technology help us to revive this ancient custom?

If our goal is to develop a compassionate relationship with nature, we need to find ways to trade places and to see ourselves and the world through nature's eyes. Only if we can achieve this on a more or less regular basis – as an exercise beginning in early adolescence – will we be able to experience the natural world authentically and develop a sense of her inherent wisdom.

On first consideration, trading places with the natural world seems almost trivial. We as human beings are part of nature. Looking through our eyes at the world is looking with nature's eyes at itself. But this process is trivial only on the surface. Our philosophy, our culture and even our emotional condition steps into this relationship and creates artificial barriers between us and the natural world. What should be most familiar to us has become most estranged. We as human beings are alienated from our natural sources. This condition has become alarmingly real, especially in recent human history. So in order to reestablish a sense of communication with our natural sources and heal the rift, we first need to understand how this fracture developed.

The first source of alienation came from philosophy. On its path to ever increasing enlightenment and reason, the awakening human mind set itself apart from the rest of nature. The very act of naming things by name is often seen as the first violation of nature. Language, according to Derrida, represents the first act of violence against the individuality and uniqueness of each natural object. By positioning oneself as *self* and attaining self-consciousness, human beings, according to Adorno, initiated a process of domination that began with men dominating women and God dominating the universe. It ended with humans dominating the rest of the natural world.

This first step, attaining a consciousness of *self*, was an inevitable step in the pursuit of enlightenment. It nevertheless set an irreconcilable barrier between human beings and the rest of nature. This coming to awareness and finding oneself as a person appears in all its inevitability as a cornerstone of enlightenment. Although philosophically an inevitable step toward autonomy, it is also the mark of the fall of man.

In Christian theology this fallenness reappeared as original sin which separated human beings from God. Christianity literally left human beings in a state of limbo, existing in this world as strangers always on the way to their real home with God. But humans could not be with God in heaven either, at least not in our material existence, and not without a redeemer sent specifically by God for that purpose. To the Christians of the Middle Ages, the world appeared as a halfway house, a wayside inn. If you make yourself too comfortable in this place, you are sentenced to eternal damnation. All good, according to Augustine, comes from the knowledge of the Divine, which he called *sapientia* or wisdom. Knowledge of the world, in contrast, Augustine called *scientia*, from which the word science developed. Knowledge of God always superseded the knowledge of this world. In God was all wisdom, in this world was none. Augustinian dualism, as practiced in the Christian Churches, made wisdom inherent in nature all but impossible.

There were, of course, exceptions and rare moments of insight into the mysteries and the wisdom of nature. These exceptions could even be found within the restrictive confines of the church. At the fringes of the official church, a tradition of mystics survived and at times even thrived. Names like Hildegard von Bingen, Bernard of Clairvaux, Meister Eckhart and Saint John of the Cross remind us of a deep mystical tradition that flourished often against the edict of the official church. Rather than finding the divine in church structure and the gospels, these mystics set out to find God by ecstatic immersion into the very depth of the material world. According to mystical tradition, which dates back to prehistoric pagan times but was revived again throughout the ages, the divine is dispersed in the very materiality of things.

While official Church doctrine teaches how to encounter the Divine in the scripture and/or through the teachings of the Church, mystics generally believed that they had privileged access to the divine spark within the material world. One of the giants of Christian theology, Thomas Aquinas, turned silent for the last year of his life, perhaps because he had lost faith in reason, being able to comprehend and to access the Divine. He may have had a mystical insight that caused this scholastic master of the word to abandon words forever. Many other mystics claimed that words are an inadequate rendition of their visions. But with words we communicate; perhaps language is all we have.

While mystics of all ages and faiths labored to explore the unknown depth of the material world in search for spirit, and while these pioneers tried to develop techniques that could guide the traveler, the official church in Rome continues to deny any value of such individual and collective exploration. As late as the 1990s, the Pope denounced the practice of Yoga.

In Judaism, the ability of the mind to merge with the Divine became a desired practice in the Cabalistic movement. These Jewish mystics went so far as to rewrite the creation story to express their faith in the divine depth of the material world. Gershom Scholem, a contemporary Jewish scholar, did extensive research into the history of Jewish mysticism. Scholem reported about the school of Isaac Luria, which arose in Palestine as a transplant of Spanish Cabalism after the exodus of the Jews from Spain at the end of the Middle Ages. Luria added a new version of the creation of primal humans to the existing symbolic creation stories of the Cabala – a version that lent itself to a clearer and more vivid interpretation of mystical reality and underlined the need for mysticism and redemption. In a world of impermanence and insecurity and full of yearning for redemption and the coming of the Messiah, Luria's symbolic story provided a vehicle for active involvement of humans in the process of salvation.

According to Luria, when God created man sparks of divine energy broke out of the first man's eyes. Clay vessels that were supposed to catch the sparks broke in the process. The fragments of the clay vessels, interspersed with sparks of the divine, tumbled through empty space. From the pieces of the clay vessels, the things of this world came into being. The sparks of the divine scattered, leaving divine goodness in the world. Divine spirit and soul was present in both people and things. Thus, Lurianic Cabalism saw the sparks of the divine exiled from their true home and calling out for redemption. Shekhinah, the presence of God in the world, was the feminine side of God. Shekhinah was exiled and wandered in sorrow, crying for redemption. Redemption was known as Tikkun, or the restoration of the primordial harmony. By uniting oneself to God in Kawwanah – or mystical intentionality – and by uniting oneself to those sparks of the divine in people or things, one could lift those sparks out of their cramped imprisonment and free them to rejoin the divine.

From these Judaic sources, Hegel got inspiration for the dialectical model as a living excursion of the mind into the other. Adorno utilized the left Hegelian interpretation of the Hegelian dialectical model, which took its vitality from Hegel's aesthetics rather than from his philosophy of history and right. Adorno, following Marx' reversal of the dialectical poles, combined Marx' dialectical materialism with a good dose of Nietzsche's aesthetical encounter, which is found in artistic immediacy. From this Adorno developed his unique aesthetic of negative dialectics. It allowed him to develop a non-ideological model for the exploration of spirit as an aesthetic exercise, though there are only a few occasions where Adorno actually addressed this issue directly.

The second major reason for the separation of our mind from its natural sources is found in science. Newtonian science, the science behind the advances of the industrial age, is the reason for treating the whole universe like a machine. In the introduction to Ilya Prigogine's ground breaking book, *Order Out of Chaos,*[4] Alvin Toffler depicted the world of classical science as "a world in which every event was determined by initial conditions that were, at least in principle, determinable with precision. It was a world in which all the pieces came together like cogs in a cosmic machine." During the Nineteenth and most of the Twentieth Century, the image of a "simple, uniform, mechanical universe" not only shaped the development of science, but influenced most other areas of human development. We even shaped our social orders (the large bureaucracies that governed most modern industrialized nations) like giant machines, their "checks and balances clicking like parts of a clock." The achievements of the technological mind confirmed "the image of the universe as an engineer's giant Tinker toy."[6]

In this Newtonian universe there was no place for spirit. No wisdom can be expected to come from the slick performance of a machine. Even the human body was dissected by science as if it was nothing but a sophisticated mechanical puppet that responded to stimuli. Behaviorist psychology almost succeeded in explaining the mind itself as only a responsive computer, a machine that even lacks a ghost to manipulate it. Some cultural anthropologists who observed these trends were rather alarmed, and some philosophers, leading among them the young Walter Benjamin, warned about this incredible alienation of the mind. In his best known work, *The Art Work in the Time of Technical Reproducibility,* Benjamin speculated on whether the human mind, once driven into total alienation and exile, would find enough residual strength to reappear, after the dark night of alienation, on the other side, rejuvenated and refreshed like the phoenix rising from the ashes. This work is a testament to Benjamin's philosophy of hope. It found its energy from the trust in the living dialectic, which in Adorno's aesthetics is present as an imperishable residue in all art, if not in all things.

As the art object comes to life in the act of creation, it regains some of its original uniqueness and individuality, which all things possessed in the prehistoric, primordial world, before human language caused separation. Such art creation becomes a mystical encounter with the world of things. It restores material things to their proper place in the universe, a place that had been lost to the advances of the controlling, rational mind and to the dominating grip of science.

Advancing technology and the ruthlessness of the capitalist marketplace, especially as it played out during the industrialization process of the 19th century, joined with the image of the human being as a cog in a machine. In this process, human labor lost its earlier, creative function and became thoroughly alienated. In the public schools of industrialized societies, children of workers were trained and conditioned to serve as the next generation of workers for hire. As human creativity in the factories had to be replaced by repetitive functionality, creative work in schools was replaced by repetitive drills of meaningless data. Learning as the drilling and repetition of facts was, unfortunately, reaffirmed and enforced by empirical science and positivistic education. Mystery ceases to have importance, or even exist, where numbers and facts are the only thing that counts. Bureaucratic accountability replaces the creative spark of genius.

Even after the marketplace and its demands had long changed, and industrialization had given way to information, public schools often missed the cue to change as well. They held on to outdated repetitiveness and functionality, rather than attempt to stimulate creativity and foster a joyful work ethic.

The German word for working tells the story of this alienation of human work long before Marx defined its philosophical essence. I first learned of the original word for work in the German language by listening to a broadcast of a reporter who had interviewed an Amish woman in America. The German reporter asked the old woman whether she would mind if her son left the farm and their community to live in the world of technology. In her old German dialect the woman replied that she would not mind as long as her son continued "to create the earth and trust in God." German television felt obliged to subtitle the German words and translate her words into modern day language. The subtitle in the modern German read: "as long as he works/creates the land and trusts in God." The old German word for working is *schaffen*, which means to create. The same word is used in the Bible for the creation of the world by God. Work, for those traditional religious communities, is the closest human beings can come to the creativity of God, the creator. The new German word *arbeiten* does not carry any such connotation but elicits the idea of a work ethic full of repetition, pain and sweat.

Work as *arbeiten* is supported by the Christian creation myth. *Arbeit* as sweat and toil is supposed to be the result of the expulsion from the Garden of Eden and of original sin. We should not forget that this interpretation of the Garden story is neither traditionally Jewish nor is it originally Christian. It is an understanding that was created by Augustine to provide an explanation for the presence of evil in the world. When the Catholic monk, Mathew Fox, reminded the Christian church of the original Christian message, which he called Creation Spirituality – in contrast to the Augustinian message of sin and fallenness – Fox was branded a heretic by the Roman authorities and harshly asked to leave the church. So deeply is the Church convinced that life has to be pain and sweat, that it initially took a stand against using any form of pain control, even during child birth. Only Holy Mary could have experienced pain-free child birth because she was considered to be free of original sin.

Let me tell you of my own experience with pain-free child birth. First of all, no child birth is completely free of pain. I have experienced this first hand from being actively involved with the birth of my five children. But I have also learned that the experience of pain is subjective, a matter of interpretation, and pain can be minimized by active training of the body, which in the so-called pain-free child birth is taught using techniques developed in Eastern religions.

While for many centuries the Western world was intensely focused on control over people, Eastern philosophers investigated and practiced control of the body through the mind. The control they developed is not a dominator control but a control that lets go, an unpossessive control, a control that consists in giving up control, as contradictory as this may sound. The Lamaze method of painless child birth has made use of these techniques and adopted those which are appropriate to bring the process of child birth under control.

From being an active participant in child birth, I learned another important lesson about the wisdom of nature. A woman's body, in dialogue with the unborn fetus, knows better than any gynecologist when it is time for birth. The mother's job is to listen to the signs of nature and let nature take its course as it has done for eons. There are good reasons why simple people speak of Mother Nature in an almost reverent way, and why in contrast, philosophers such as

Francis Bacon have compared nature with an unwilling woman who needs to be subdued – a whore who must be forced to reveal her secrets. It is not nature who stalls in revealing her secret wisdom; it is we humans who have lost the ability and the will to listen.

I learned the same lesson from being an organic farmer for more than a decade. On our farm in southwestern Michigan, the soil nourished and grew a variety of crops without human intervention. Often it was an act of listening and observing the signs of nature which taught us the right companion plants to use to find the most effective natural antidote to disease, and to intervene, not on a schedule dictated by the chemical companies, but rather to follow the signals of Mother Nature. Even though farming was an experience of incredibly hard work, it was also an experience of the bountiful wisdom inherent in nature. I always looked at farming as an art, not as a business observing the laws of the stock exchange. The aesthetics inherent in the experience of natural farming taught me the importance of dialoguing with nature. In a deep sense this is spiritual activity – the living dialectic at work.

I found this same spiritual reward from working with actors in the Whole Art Theater, which I had founded in rural Michigan. Here, I established an experimental theater with five actors over a period of almost 15 years. Together we developed plays for children and plays for adults who had not lost a sense of wonder that lies at the base of all art. In our small company I followed the rules for theater that had been set out by such theater giants as Bertolt Brecht, Jerzy Grotowski and Konstantin Stanislawki. In our plays we were in search of the truth that lies somewhere right underneath our very skin, as Stanislawki often proclaimed. From Grotowski and the Living Theater we had learned to treat the stage as a sacred place and each performance as a celebration and as a sacrifice.

I have never forgotten the time we played in a home for so-called retarded children. I was on stage playing Jack and the Beanstalk, a favorite American children's play. The giant, played by myself, had just lost the golden hen and was crying. A child came up on stage, and bending over to look me in the eyes, she said: "You don't have to cry! Everything will be okay." A few days later we played for a suburban school in Kalamazoo. Most children came from affluent families employed by the Upjohn Company. During the scene with the golden hen, a boy barely seven years of age, shouted out: "It's fake gold anyhow! I don't see what all the fuss is about." Does advancing civilization necessarily mean disillusionment and does this disillusionment necessarily have to turn into a lack of compassion? Does the advancement of the awakening mind have to turn into alienation? I don't believe so.

How can philosophy help? From my perspective, I can discern a few details. I believe that philosophy has failed and will always fail to deliver absolutes, whether they are called forms, ideas, laws or universals. We all have only our own perspective. From that personal perspective we can make some pretty good assumptions about the way things are, but whoever harbors a secret hope to gain absolute knowledge sets himself or herself up for failure. Even a judgment about the state of humanity is in itself a sign more of the author's arrogance or depression than it is a verdict of the real state of affairs. Consider, for instance, Stanislaw Lem's proposal when he says: "People basically suffer from either shortsighted stupidity, or farsighted stupidity." If Lem gets confused by the prospect of having to watch a mere 30 different programs on television, wait until he has the choice of several hundred. This is, of course, a far cry from the two official TV programs that were available under the former repressive regime. Lem should know that intelligent machines will know what you like to watch and make those difficult choices for you.

Greek philosophers made a bold leap of faith when they assumed that the whole world, yes, even the whole universe, can be understood free of contradiction. Of course, they had no idea how vast this universe really is and how incomprehensible. Today after having been confronted with black holes, quantum conundrums and a theory of scientific chaos, we have come to the conclusion that we will never know it all and that unsolved mysteries will forever remain hidden behind the veil of distant galaxies covered forever by a cone of time beyond which our information will never travel. The only thing we know for sure is that the world continues far beyond our event horizon. We have long lost the trust of the ancient and not so ancient – that eternal laws govern this universe and all falls into place. Do we therefore have to become fatalistic and depressed? Or do we have to embrace irrationality and promote war and terror?

From the beginning, predicting the future has been at the heart of philosophy and was later transferred to science. There is a direct line from the Oracle of Delphi to the five proofs of God. The critiques of Kant robbed the absolute basis from underneath all philosophical predictions. But by that time science had fully replaced philosophical speculation. When they first appeared, Newton's laws of motion were instantly celebrated as the fulfillment of all human dreams. The future seemed to be as predictable as the past. This scientific optimism found its expression in the invention of La Places demon, a giant Turing machine that potentiality could do all the calculations necessary to predict the future.

Far from being an exact mathematical science, future prediction today is still quite spotty, even anecdotal. Without the possibility of creating a comprehensive philosophical system to explain the universe, philosophers resorted again to storytelling and anecdotes to come closer to their cherished goal – the truth. In a similar way, scientists today often rely on anecdotes and fiction writers, instead of laboratories and experiments, to gaze into the future.

At the Next Fest I had the chance to converse with the American science fiction writer, Philip K. Dick. Philip K. Dick (PKD for short) died on March 2. 1982. He appeared at Next Fest as an android, created by Hanson Robotics and sponsored by the Fedex Institute. When PKD's daughter visited her android father, she was impressed and shaken by the life-like creation. When I met PDK, he seemed exhausted and drained, perhaps tired answering the same questions over and over again. A young attendant showed us a piece of the rubber material his skin was made of. The exhibitors had left the back part of his brain exposed so people would not get confused. Is this the beginning of a dream come true or just a negligible scientific game? Are Hanson Robotics and the Fedex Institute part of the great human enterprise of what Kuczynski has called "co-creating the world," or is this robot nothing but a sophisticated barbie doll with PKD's features?

In regard to our assessment of the future as either pessimistic or optimistic, I believe that one of the most important recognitions of the past century is the importance played by our emotions.

It is not the sum total of cognitive input that makes us look into the future with either optimism or pessimism, but our emotional makeup. Our emotions play a far greater role in our assessment of the future than formerly believed. On one hand, this recognition may be almost trivial because it is a truism for the average person. On the other hand, since scientists and philosophers in the Western tradition generally believed that the universe was built like a rational machine that followed certain knowable laws, emotions played only a small role for scientists and were a hindrance to clear knowledge for philosophers.

By Western tradition the world was divided into an inanimate and animate realm, and emotions played only a role in the realm of the animate. The vast realm of the inanimate (the material world) was directed by iron laws of necessity. For the rational human mind it was now only needed to figure out whether on the large scale these laws of nature would produce a positive or a negative balance. With new scientific advances all such speculations have been found lacking. The cosmic game will forever be unknowable, the outcome uncertain. In spite of Einstein's hope that God does not play dice, there will always be an element of chance in the way the universe operates, at least from our human perspective. Perhaps there is another perspective altogether, but as of now this perspective seems to be unknowable.

Therefore the predictions of the future we make are largely influenced by the state of our emotions. Modern psychology and the human empowerment movement have developed ways to direct and influenced our emotional state. Neuro-linguistic programming has developed techniques to optimize our outlook on the world. Critics may say that this is all just changing the packaging, the surface, the appearance. But I believe that our beliefs matter, whether we look into the future with optimism or whether the future appears grim and dark. To some extent this is up to interpretation. It has been known for some time now, scientifically known, that human life on earth is in trouble, that the earth is in trouble. The signs can no longer be ignored. But as long as ideologues and fanatical pessimists run the world and hold the corridors of power, not much will change. The World Watch Institute calculated in the middle of the nineties the effects of human activities on earth and found them catastrophic. They found back then that all the scientific facts were know that would necessitate a change, but little was done, because the masses lacked motivation. At the Second Parliament of World Religions in 1992 in Chicago, world leaders of all the churches decried the catastrophic state of the ecology, and demanded a new covenant of all religious people to save the earth. More than a decade later, little has changed and churches have continued their divisive activities, set more on saving individual souls than on saving the planet for future generations.

In my youth back in the Sixties it was still commonly assumed that some nearby planet like Mars could easily be colonized and would give refuge for humans once earth was destroyed. Today that dream has become much less likely as well. I still believe that space exploration is as necessary a step for human beings as it once was for life to leave the oceans and live on dry land. But going from here to there won't be easy.

Finally, I don't think many people still consider that life itself is or ever was a freak cosmic accident as traditional science would have us believe. In universalist circles I often hear it said that "matter is pregnant with life." What sense could this assumption have if we do not somehow accept an inherent wisdom imbedded in the natural world? How could this pregnancy have ever come to terms, successfully if nature had no clue what he/she/it, was doing? According to traditional science there is no wisdom in nature. This is why it is urgently necessary to review our traditional understanding of nature. We need a new philosophy of nature which includes some form of animism. There is a long line of Western philosophers who one way or the other defended an animistic, or panpsychic view of nature. This view assumes that there is a will to life, an élan vital if you want; a spiritual force within the seemingly dead material world just like there is a possibility for the real grown man or woman already present in the egg and the sperm before they even unite.

Negative dialectic has left open the possibility to accept mystery in the Other. Through artistic creation we can become aware of this amazing force. All human work will someday become aesthetic creation. Some promoters of solidarity had proposed this to happen during those historic days of liberation from totalitarian joke. But history made a different turn, and dreams did not yet come true. But let us not give up the dream of being co-creators. This is the strongest asset of universalism that as a meta-philosophy it insists on active participation of its members, not to create a new system, but to create the world.

The wisdom of nature will remain closed to us as long as we approach nature with cognition alone. The aging Goethe had written this realization into his Faust story. The Earth spirit that had appeared to Faust in the gloomy confines of his study disappears when Faust's apprentice Wagner enters and disturbs the master's trance. "You are like the spirit you comprehend not me" the vanishing spirit whispers before dissolving into nothing. Eastern yoga and mediation techniques make it possible to achieve the goals of the mystics. Today we have scientific ways to investigate subjective consciousness. We are able to make use of these experiences as many have done in the past. The psychologist Stanislav Grof, for instance, has documented this research and its results in numerous publications. I have called this research into the depth of the emotional existence of the material world the Third Enlightenment. It will ultimately be a scientific combination of the Eastern Enlightenment of the Now and Wow moment, enlightenment as a flash of insight with the Western Enlightenment committed to emancipation and reason. As indicated here, philosophically this new Enlightenment is best described in dialectical terms, as a living merger of opposites. This merger contained in the living dialectic also proposes a new methodology.

Instead of the reductionist methodology of the past we need to adopt a system oriented methodology. As Arthur Koestler has pointed out many decades ago, nature is a system of systems, subsystems nested within larger system much like a Russian doll. Each system extends to the outside as part of a larger system and again to the inside where it is a host for myriads of subsystems. In cognitive terms we need to use dialectical language to describe the relationships of these systems with each other. Each is autonomous and dependent; each functions as a negation and as an affirmation of the other; each is part of the other while simultaneously experience the other as different.

In evolutionary terms this system-within-system thinking proposes a whole new explanation for the hierarchical evolution of complexity and life. I have called this evolutionary progression

Collective Orchestration. At all levels, animate and inanimate alike, particles and organisms come together to achieve tasks they cannot do in isolation. Smaller level systems create a larger system to maintain evolutionary goals. What is new today is that we can assert these same processes among all levels of nature, not only at the level of living things. Once accustomed to a system analytical view we realize that Collective Orchestration is nearly as ubiquitous as procreation and mating. At rare occasions orchestrated units remain connected and build a new system of higher complexity, which translates into a higher dimensional taxonomic existence. This is the evolutionary vehicle to create higher forms of life. The underlying motif or drive is guided by system awareness. In emotional terms systems feel a higher level of satisfaction when cooperating than when being isolated. This is true at the lowest level of space/time quanta and at the highest level presently occupied by human beings.

It then appears that nature is comprised of living systems, from space/time to human beings. These systems are self organizing. Their inherent senses guide them to cooperate and assimilate. As they experiment in cooperation, some experiments turn out to be successful, others fail. Evolutionary laws propel those successful systems to establish themselves and thrive, others who are less successful, perish. As there is wisdom in evolutionary selection, there is an underlying wisdom inherent in each system. This system wisdom is guided by the pleasure and pain each individual system experiences. At the lowest level this may only be a sense of wanting to be rather than not to be.

So when I started out with the intention to let the spirit work, I need not talk about a metaphysical transcendence, a divine spirit, though for the believer there may be no difference. The spirit works within the natural world, organizing lower level systems to ever higher levels of complexity, making materia pregnant with life, finally giving birth to life and leading life to ever higher complexity, even to cosmic dimensions.

First published in Dialogue and Universalism, © *Polish Academy of Science. Reprinted with permission.*

▨ 3. TOWARD A NATURALISTIC FOUNDATION OF COMMUNITY

When we consider human history, especially as it has played out over the past centuries, there appears to be little hope for a resurgence of healthy communities. Yet I contend that vital communities are the single most important factor in achieving the kind of global society that can produce healthy individuals and inspire human life on earth to be creative and fulfilling. Societies must help each person, not just the privileged few, to be the best he or she can be, and each person must in turn help society to be the best it can be. This simple truism was at the base of the Greek masters' ethical ruminations and must be considered again today, as the world moves toward increased globalism and away from the nation-state system which dominated the recent past.

A revitalized concept of community is indispensable if we should ever hope to reach Rudi Siebert's vision of a reconciled society, what he has called Future III. Instead we are coming ever closer to living in societies resembling Siebert's horror vision of Future I, the totally administered society. In the developed countries of the industrialized West, participation in the democratic process is ever decreasing, as citizens feel, more often than not, that they are being manipulated, cheated, and tricked into wars. They often feel that their hard-earned wages are being wasted, that their tax contributions, far from helping their needs and the needs of the *polis*, are being turned into weapons of mass destruction or being used to feed the hungry coffers of multi-national corporations.

On the other hand, I believe that the project of Western moral philosophy, has by and large failed, having not been able whatsoever to anchor ethical reasoning within the confines of the individual's ontology. While the latest attempts of prominent philosophers such as Jürgen Habermas to develop an ethical framework from an analysis of communicative praxis are promising and point in the right direction, I believe that to achieve a real paradigm change it will require a new foundation of community. Such an idea of community can only come from a re-evaluation of our current philosophies of nature and the development of a naturalistic approach to the necessity of community as a prerequisite for human happiness.

Globalization today is on everybody's mind. Which of three alternative futures will this global society ultimately become? In a recent publication on *Democracy and the Quest for Justice*,[1] Tatiana Alekseeva, head of the Department of Political Theory at the Moscow State Institute of International Relations, reflects on the philosophical, political, and religious problems of globalization. She has developed a bold vision for a future global society, a vision well worth considering. She claims that a global society must be based on the "principles of cooperation, mutual help, and justice."[2] Alekseeva continues:

> Not competition between ideas and ideologies, but solidarity, not the clash of civilizations, but their mutual supplementary, not the "balance of power," but mutual help in terms of Martin Heidegger's existential of human being ought to become the main features of the new international order.[3]

With this vision in mind, Alekseeva analysis current trends in Russia and America. For the immediate interaction of nations, Alekseeva envisions a development along the lines of Rawls' concept of "overlapping consensus," which would be the result of different opinions and ideas flowing together into a unifying whole, rather than the development of a new meta-ideology. In spite of this caveat, Alekseeva concludes that, "The 'breakthrough' to a new understanding of the world order may not be possible at all on the level of the so-called theories of the 'medium level.' What is needed is a revolution in philosophies and world views."[4]

Alekseeva contends that "many Russian philosophers have started to reflect on the problems of the paradigms of world society and global problems." On the international stage, Alekseeva believes that a number of prominent philosophers, such as Noam Chomsky, J?rgen Habermas, John Grey, and Klaus Hoffe, have all expressed a renewed interest in the sphere of world politics. But perhaps a little discouraged, she concludes that "for now such reflections are only the beginning of a new paradigm." [5]

In this article I will explore how a new scientific understanding of the processes within the natural world could reshape our understanding and need for community and promote a spiritual stance. The traditional understanding of community limits the usefulness of the communal concept to human beings who live in communities for mutual support. According to the Abrahamic religions, man was created as an individual and as such lives as a separate unit before God. Woman was given to Adam almost as an afterthought. This creation story goes against any naturalistic foundation of community. In spite of overwhelming evidence indicating that the vast majority of primal people have lived in and valued communities, in the mythological context of the Abrahamic world religions, community is simply not important. [6]

The real sources of the Ten Commandments could, with a more refined historical interpretation, be understood as the culmination of the condensed wisdom of the ages. But instead of being conceived as an outgrowth of communal wisdom, the Decalogue is reported to have been delivered directly from God to one man, Moses. In spite of the distinct efforts of the Christ of the New Testament to rescue what he could of a sense of community among his followers, Christianity has not succeeded in fostering and developing a vital concept of community. Christian communities have sprouted, of course, and spread to all corners of the globe. But because of Christianity's otherworldly orientation, the Christian concept of community has not been able to survive the unconditional victory march of enlightenment and secularization. Over time, the civic community was able to replace the religious community, confining any vestige of a former community spirit to religious activities on Sundays, and ultimately preparing the way for the totally administered society, Siebert's Future I.

On its march toward individualism, and in full conformity with the enlightened goal to promote the autonomous individual, Western-style civic societies set out to support their individualistic standards by founding an ethics on the basis of rationality. But in the totally administered, alienated societies of the industrialized world of the 20th century, reason itself quickly turned into instrumentalized rationality. Within the frame of this instrumentalized rationality, it suddenly appeared even reasonable when the subordinated individual, ordered to do so by society, committed horrific crimes against humanity. Society, on the other hand, sees no wrong in neglecting the plight of the poor and hungry masses. In the name and under the pretense of spreading democracy, it invades sovereign countries in order to appropriate their national resources and set up shopping malls and industrial parks to feed the ever-demanding needs of the multi-nationals. Such behavior is defended by referring to Darwin's law of survival and justified by declaring one's own version of democracy to be "on the right side of history" and as "part of God's plan." In other words, those in power declare themselves the good guys while declaring the other side as evil.

With no hope on the horizon, people everywhere, perhaps sensing a lack of healing community, flee back into the arms of nearly forgotten institutions and old religions, only to find them hollowed out and meaningless, victims of the same process of secularization. But instead of looking back in an attempt to rescue ancient values, I sense hope in looking forward and employing science itself on the road toward a society of tomorrow.

Scientific methodology, with its emphasis on openness, empirical testing, and trust in verification could help in developing and promoting a concept of community, free of ideological force. Such a society could focus again on providing a good, decent, and happy life here on earth, not unlike the kind of life secular society, at least in principle, had at one time attempted to provide, as enshrined in the so-called American Dream. But far from promoting only the acquisition of material values, after the paradigm shift in regard to our concept of nature is completed, this new society would most emphatically be able to fulfill Siebert's Future III, especially its other part, namely keeping open the door to the totally Other. This new society would balance and reconcile the material thrust toward happiness with the scientific recognition of the inherent spirituality of all of nature. This new spirit would clearly be different from Hegel's concept of the spirit of the people (der Geist des Volkes) in not being limited to one nation or one culture, nor even only to human beings, but rather being recognized as a common quality in all animals, plants, and the so-called inanimate world. . This new spirituality would also be different from the nature soul (Natur Seele) of the romantics, because far from being a romantic notion it would be thoroughly scientific and thus within the reach of empirical verification or at least successfully withstanding a pragmatic test.

This new philosophy will not only keep "the door open to the wholly Other" but also offer a bridge for our emotional involvement with the world as the Other and with others: human beings, animals, and plants. I claim that such an involvement is the basic ingredient for spirituality, if spirituality means entering into a compassionate dialogue with the Other in all its shapes and forms. Vaclav Havel once described this dialogue with the totally Other as the only means of survival for the human race. He said:

> ...in today's multi-cultural world, the truly reliable path to coexistence, to peaceful coexistence and creative cooperation must start from what is at the root of all cultures and what lies infinitely deeper in human hearts and minds than political opinion, convictions, antipathies, or sympathies: it must be rooted in self-transcendence. Transcendence, as a hand reached out to those close to us, to foreigners, to the human community, to all living creatures, to nature, to the universe; transcendence as a deeply and joyously experienced need to be in harmony even with what we ourselves are not, what we do not understand, what seems distant from us in time and space, but with which we are nevertheless mysteriously linked because, together with us, all this constitutes a single world. Transcendence as the only real alternative to extinction.[7]

On first sight science, community, and spirituality seem to belong to entirely different worlds. Scientists often cringe when their vocabulary, their discoveries, and their inventions are used in what they consider the softer academic fields or worse yet, in the public arena. But perhaps without its specific consent, science has always been used to support and explain claims that were made in the social realm and the humanities. Thus, Newton's contribution to science, which became known as Newtonian Science, gave birth to the philosophy of Deism. A totally mechanical universe was presided over by a disinterested deity who had started the world like a giant clock, but now left it alone and to its own devices. This made possible the classical understanding of the universe as a machine.

In the introduction to Ilya Prigogine's ground breaking book, *Order Out of Chaos*,[8] Alvin Toffler depicted the world of classical science as "a world in which every event was determined by initial conditions that were, at least in principle, determinable with precision. It was a

155

world in which all the pieces came together like cogs in a cosmic machine."[9] During the 19th and most of the 20th century, the image of a "simple, uniform, mechanical universe not only shaped the development of science, but influenced most other areas of human development. We even shaped our social orders (the large bureaucracies that governed most modern industrialized nations) like giant machines, their "checks and balances clicking like parts of a clock." The achievements of the technological mind confirmed "the image of the universe as an engineer's giant Tinker toy."[10]

Within this framework of Newtonian science, there was no room for spirituality and no sense of community. God could be declared dead without causing uproar. As the Newtonian mechanism on the one hand inspired a rational concept of society, on the other hand it encouraged the idea of a rational ethics, serving the individual by providing meaning and serving the state by producing law-abiding citizens.

During the first part of the 20th century, the mechanical interpretation of nature resulting from Newtonian science was first challenged by new insights into the smallest particles of nature called quanta. Quantum Theory seemed to say that, contrary to Newtonian certainty, nature at a fundamental level appeared to be quite inconsistent. Observations made on quantum objects such as photons and electrons seemed to contradict the laws of traditional physics. What was observed could not be explained with the tools of that physics. The most famous example is the dual character of the smallest particles which appear to be waves and particles alternatively in experiments, depending on what the observer sets out to find. This is not possible under the traditional laws of mechanics. A particle in the macro world of our experience cannot also be a wave. In the famous Copenhagen Agreement (1932), a considerable number of scientists of that period agreed to settle the question about the true nature of microscopic particles, such as electrons and protons, by accepting this contradiction as unsolvable. This interpretation of the quantum world became a cornerstone of the so-called standard model, even though several recognized scientists of the time, among them most prominently Albert Einstein, disagreed with this solution.

Another important influence of quantum theory on the general world view of the time was what became known as observer dependence. Classical physics is objective. There is no place in Descartes' theoretical explanations for an observer or even a subjective mind. Processes in classical physics develop regardless of whether they are observed or not.[11]

Quantum Theory seemed to offer a completely new role for the observer. Referring back to the famous wave/particle duality, it was generally assumed that the quantum world behaves like a wave when not observed and turns into particles when observed. The moment of observation became known as quantum collapse: the collapse of the wave into a particle through observation. This phenomenon placed a completely new emphasis on the importance of the observer and thus on the subject in an otherwise objective, physical world. This led to far reaching research into subjectivity and a reevaluation of the role of consciousness.

Another observation at the quantum level has had great impact on everyday world views. At the quantum level, the whole world appears to be intrinsically connected. This phenomenon came to be known as quantum wholeness. Scientifically, this is derived from the fact that certain quantum systems appear to communicate with each other over spatial distances instanta-neously, at a speed faster than the speed of light. Much has been made of this phenomenon. In a world dominated by rampant disconnectedness, super individualism, and alienation, wholeness and connectedness are values we all yearn for, and even cherish. For instance, in the recent aftermath of the Asian Tsunami, scientists scrambled to find an explanation as to why so few animals died in the disaster, as compared to the human toll. The question of whether animals are somehow more closely connected to natural events than we human beings are was on everyone's' mind.

For many people, especially those in the New Age movements, the implications of quantum theory, especially what it seems to say about wholeness and connectedness, are easily aligned with one of the key elements of the Eastern Buddhist experience. At the level of the spiritual experience of *nirvana*, the encounter with emptiness is often associated with a simultaneous experience of total connectedness with the universe. The self-conscious mind, which even pre-philosophically continuously asserts "I am not the Other", is seen as the strongest obsta-cle to the goal of Eastern enlightenment. In the extreme, this view leads to the denial of the natural world, whose center, of course, is my own self. According to ancient Hindu tradition, which is becoming ever more popular among certain groups in the West, the world is *maya*, a veil of illusion. Enlightenment can be reached when we lift the veil and experience every-thing as one. This same experience of emptiness and simultaneous connectedness is reported and verified by numerous mystics in the Western tradition as well. Mystics are people who have experienced the divine in the world of things by submersing their minds into the world, rather than escaping from it. While this kind of mysticism and the mystical tradition in general are certainly valuable parts of the human experience of transcendence, they add little to our experience of community. [12]

Interestingly enough, a number of key scientists involved in the formulation of quantum mechanics have also come to the conclusion that the nature of the quantum world supports the idea of things as an illusion. Werner Heisenberg is the most prominent among them. This, too, was interpreted by many to mean that everything outside of myself is not really real, and that the most important spiritual task consists in eliminating concerns for one's own self. The goal is to reach a state of mind in which nothing matters. Non-attachment promises to be the ultimate liberation. This kind of philosophical stance does not lead to spirituality or community, but rather points toward a dark pessimism, a la Schopenhauer.

The end of the 19th century had seen a tremendous decline of certainty about enlightenment and trust in reason. Intellectuals had lost their confidence in the power of the human mind and had succumbed to irrational fears of final doom. This was a direct result of the implica-tions of the Second Law of Thermodynamics. This law, discovered during the 19th century, said that any system left to its own devices will go toward decreased order, a virtual death sentence for the universe. In the 20th century, this sense of general pessimism was again supported by an apparent uncertainty governing the objects of the quantum world, a fact formulated in the famous Uncertainty Principle. This principle states that a quantum object can never be described with any sense of accuracy when stating its location and its velocity at the same time. Even though quantum theory deals with an utterly strange world seemingly far removed from our experience, quantum uncertainty was quickly interpreted to be a direct blow to the understanding of physical principles in the macro world or the world we know intimately.

On the surface, this effect would seem utterly strange and unexplainable. Why should the one have such an effect on the other? On closer inspection, these two worlds are not at all separated. There is no such thing as the macro world independent and away from the micro world. The two worlds are intricately interwoven, one nested inside the other. What sense could it possibly make that the two were ruled by a completely different set of natural laws – and yet, there it was. It is well known that Einstein himself never accepted this and searched for a hidden solution to the quantum conundrum to the end of his life. His famous edict, "God does not play dice," has become proverbial.

A final scientific discovery was made in 1984 by the Nobel Prize winning Russian physicist Ilya Prigogine in *Order Out of Chaos*. His formulation is what has become known as chaos theory. The most important implication of chaos theory resulted yet again in a sense of general unpredictability of natural phenomena.

To the great dismay of many scientists who would have liked science to provide the kind of security that philosophy had given up searching for, this new scientific theory now most definitely extended the uncertainty of the micro world to virtually all processes taking place and processes that defined the macro world. Many scientists hastened to soften the damage by pointing out that their conclusions from chaos theory are not at all anti-deterministic, but the damage was done. The new concept of deterministic chaos was supposed to counteract the fact that chaos theory was indeed a theory that showed the general unpredictability of natural phenomena at all levels. The idea of deterministic chaos never captured the popular imagination like chaos theory itself had done. In fact, on closer inspection deterministic chaos only seems to state the obvious: once a quantum event has run its course, all individual steps become totally causal and logical, exactly as in an event of classical nature. But that is a little bit like saying, "Once the bad guy has killed, I know he is a killer." Classical predictability strives for something much more causal and convincing. The classical scholar would like to be able to determine, by analyzing the DNA of a person, whether he has the potential to be a killer, and will indeed eventually kill. That is what is meant by classical determinism.

As a direct result of chaos theory, physicists now had to admit that even those systems studied in the field of classical mechanics can behave in an intrinsically unpredictable manner. In principle, such a system may be perfectly deterministic, but in practice its behavior is completely unpredictable. In broader terms, a system is chaotic if its trajectory through space/time depends with a high degree of sensitivity on the initial conditions: that is, if small causes can produce large effects. This phenomenon became popularized as the famous Butterfly Effect. In fact, it now became evident, that all living systems belong to this group of open, dynamic systems that can be subject to chaotic disturbances under the influence of the Butterfly Effect. Hence, classical mechanics can predict the trajectory of mechanical objects, but is incapable of fully predicting the actions of any living systems, such as the flight of a bee, or the path through the day of any human being, simply because living things can alter their path.

According to classical physics, scientists assumed that small causes will always produce small effects and large causes large ones. With this assumption in place, many small conditions in the observed world could be ignored; and yet scientists believed that they could make reliable predictions. Today we know that natural systems are non-linear, which means that they are sensitive to initial conditions; but to know all the initial conditions of a process is impossible. Therefore, scientific theory has to accept a level of uncertainty in all its predictions. When we look today to science to provide answers to global questions, we must keep this distinction in mind: theories derived from scientific observation and scientific facts cannot claim to be universally true in the old, traditional sense. In fact, it is clear today that universal, absolute truth claims have always been vehicles invented and used by those in power to establish and maintain control. Such claims for truth have rightly been called ideologies, and as tools used to gain or maintain power, are in need of deconstruction.

Many of the implications of quantum theory and chaos theory can perhaps only indirectly be used to support a naturalistic approach to community and spirituality. For instance, New Age and some feminist theories have borrowed from quantum theory's concept of wholeness and connectedness to assist their causes. But perhaps more often the combined effect of unpredictability and uncertainty found in both quantum theory and chaos theory produced an irrational fear of the future and a totally pessimistic stress on life's general meaninglessness. This negates rather than supports the idea of community and spirituality.

At the same time, the legacy of Western civilization with its history of totalitarian systems, disregard of individual freedoms, and mass exploitation appears also to be pointing away from collaboration, collectivization, and connectedness, though these are obviously necessary features of any functional community. When the walls that had separated a collective and totalitarian system from the rest of the world came down not so long ago, the global village applauded. The momentous dissolution of one of the two superpowers is almost old history now, but the fear and resentment of forced wholeness and top down orchestrated cooperation lingers on.

But over the past few decades, almost unnoticed, these same scientific theories that seem to provide support for a pessimistic world view have also changed the general focus of research from individual components to research into systems and wholeness itself. When in 1944, Erwin Schrödinger first published his short but consequential essay *What is Life?*,[13] little was known about collective behavior of particles and individuals on the small and the large scale. Reductionism was the standard of scientific inquiry. By investigating and analyzing the smallest member of a group, scientists expected to get information about the composite set that they were investigating. The principles of System Theory, Cybernetics or Synergy were not yet understood.[14] No one had heard of a Science of Complexity either.

Asking the same question today over sixty years later, new theories and whole new sciences have been developed to assist us in understanding complex phenomena such as life, community, and perhaps also spirituality from equally complex perspectives. Instead of trying to understand the riddle of life and communal practices by reducing the problem to its individual components — for Schrödinger the individual cell or the DNA within each cell — we have learned to investigate complex arrangement of those smaller units in a holistic way. Today we should have a better understanding of how the very complexity might be the source of sophisticated, new, and dynamic properties such as life. We should be able to develop new insights into why community is a vital part of each natural system. We should also be able to provide detailed reasons why communication, the essence of spirituality, is present at all levels of the natural world and why this will also help the human community to fulfill its ultimate cosmic mission.

When investigating the structure of complex systems we realize more and more that the world is comprised of layers and layers of such complex systems. Each is nested within myriads of others and all are interdependent in more ways than we can fathom. As Arthur Koestler pointed out many decades ago, each individual system is a whole at one level and a part of a larger whole at another level.[15] My first insight into wholeness and systems came from studying aesthetics. Studying at the Frankfurt School with Theodore W. Adorno during the 1960s, I learned about theories of classical and modern art and music. One of Adorno's main aesthetic questions was this: what makes a piece of art whole? Was this only a subjective matter of experience or was there something inherent in the piece of art that suggested wholeness? With his attention firmly focused on the transition from classical to modern music, the question of wholeness in Adorno's aesthetic theory was paramount. Wholeness was one of those ancient qualities which Aristotle had required of a good piece of art. To express their opposition to such ideological aesthetics (an aesthetics that insists on wholeness even if life seems anything but whole), modern artists and composers had often made it their mission to destroy – structurally and through content or lack thereof – the very wholeness of a piece of art. What was this elusive wholeness and could one really ever escape it?

Following Aristotle's command to achieve wholeness and believing in the mission, classical composers had laid down structural and mathematical requirements to guarantee the completeness and wholeness of a musical piece. Was it possible to leave out certain requirements or to contradict them? Would a piece of art then be less than whole? To describe the transition of a piece from the level of disconnectedness to a level of wholeness, Adorno used new terminology. He called this a qualitative transition (qualitativer Umschlag).

Qualitative transition was also used to explain the emergence of a synthesis when in the dialectical triad two opposites combined to jointly emerge as a new unit but at a higher level, containing the earlier opposites and somehow superseding them (Aufhebung). The dialectical model was a first conceptualization of a collective process that today is called phase transition by physicists and bifurcation by system theorists. Philosophically this model might still be useful as an explanation or a visualization of the qualitative advance of natural systems when a certain critical mass or threshold is reached.

During a discussion at a theater festival in Poland in the Seventies, the question came up as to whether dialectics could last beyond death. At the time I intuitively affirmed this question, but had no real grasp of its meaning. I have now come to the conclusion that in nature there exists a system of qualitative advancement quite independent of human cognition. In some sense then, this would be a natural dialectic that persists beyond death. In a paper delivered at the Consciousness Conference in Tokyo[16] in 1999, I began using the term Collective Orchestration to describe the largely functional aspect of such a dialectical transition. Further inspired by Hiroomi Umezawa's[17] use of the collective mode to explain complex collective brain functions, I began exploring Collective Orchestration as a mechanism of qualitative advance occurring in all natural systems. Collective Orchestration is synchronized behavior of otherwise independently existing individuals for the purpose of achieving tasks that are not achievable by each individual in separation. Through Collective Orchestration, individuals collaborate to achieve a qualitatively higher state of existence. Collective Orchestration describes a system of evolutionary advance that as of now has not been fully explored.

In *What is Life? The Next Fifty Years, Speculations on the Future of Biology*,[18] a number of evolutionary biologists reflect on Schrödinger's heritage. The biologist Stuart Kauffman emphasizes the importance of collective dynamics in the emergence of life. He says: "The ultimate source of order and self-reproduction may lie in the emergence of collectively ordered dynamics in complex chemical reaction systems."[19] Kauffman asserts that

> . . . development and evolution, while requiring the stability of organic molecules, may also require emergent ordered properties in the collective behavior of complex, non-equilibrium chemical reaction systems. Such complex reaction systems, I shall suggest, can spontaneously cross a threshold, or phase transition, beyond which they become capable of collective self-reproduction, evolution, and exquisitely ordered dynamical behavior. The ultimate sources of the order requisite for life's emergence and evolution may rest on new principles of collective emergent behavior in far from equilibrium reaction systems.[20]

This is the kind of Collective Orchestration I had in mind. Collective Orchestration can be understand as the process not only for life to emerge, but for qualitative advance of all dynamical systems, beginning with the continuity of space/time to the complex organizations of corporations and galaxies. This will also have profound implications for our discussion of community.

Chaos theory put the concept of self-organization into the center of scientific discussion. Self-Organization is a key concept in understanding processes of Collective Orchestration in the so-called inanimate world. Scientists currently explain events of self-organization when they occur among inanimate things as a simple move of a system toward a state of lower energy consumption. They use this description of an otherwise difficult to explain process in order to preserve the traditional materialistic view of nature.

In order to be able to fully integrate the process of self-organization into the inanimate world, I would like to propose the acceptance of a view common to virtually all primal people and most non-Western traditions. This is the view that the whole world, including the so-called inanimate world, is indeed permeated with some level of mind or consciousness. It has alternately been called panpsychism, panexperientialism, or quantum animism. In this view, awareness does not start at the level of one-cell organisms, animals, or even only human beings, but a rudimentary level of awareness exists at the deepest level of the material world. At the basic level, this awareness of a particle may be as little as having a preferred state, being *on* rather than *off*. It might mean being open to certain combinations and being closed to others. Within the terminology of Transcendental Perspectivism, I have called this awareness an inside-out view, a minimal kind of perspective present at all levels of the natural world.

The idea of locating consciousness within *materia* is not new. In *The Spirit of Materia,* the French nuclear physicist Jean Charon identified electrons as the most likely carriers of mind and spirit.[21] Charon claimed that the basic building blocks of materia and spirit directly connect on a material level. As an extension of Albert Einstein's theory of relativity, which, according to Charon left no room for spirit in the universe, Charon proposed a "Complex Theory of Relativity" which includes the possibility of consciousness.

According to the traditional mechanistic view of the universe, the laws of nature causally determine, and therefore, predict everything. This view, according to Charon, failed to address spiritual phenomena, driving out the last of whatever spirit remained from mythical times. Only after the more flexible quantum theory replaced the mechanical worldview were we able to rethink the position of consciousness or spirit in the composition of the universe. Quantum theory replaced the stringent logical order proposed by the strict geometricazation inherent in traditional science with a new order of probability.

Charon claimed that another space/time complements the space/time of our immediate experience. In that complementary space/time, the coordinates are reversed. Every electron is an entity with its bulk existing in that other space/time. Charon used the image of an ocean and the airspace above it to explain his speculation. The ocean corresponds to our world. The airspace above the ocean reflects this other reality, the realm of spirit. Each electron, according to Charon, lives in the airspace above the ocean and only touches the surface of the ocean at one point. This single point is the only appearance of an electron in this world. This other space is a spiritual world where information is stored by the infinite multitude of electrons. Each electron, according to Charon:

> represents an autonomous individuality, which has its very own space/time. This space/time differs from ours substantially. Each electron forms a separate micro-universe. Its time is cyclical, which allows it to recollect all past events of the space it consists of. All events within this micro-universe develop with increasing negentropy. All this is evidence for our conclusion that the electron contains a spiritual space/time.[22]

Negentropy is the ability of mind to overcome the disintegration of materia by systematic organization. Electrons, according to Charon, have the ability to form systems with other electron without any external help; and they can develop hierarchical orders of ever higher complexity through increased information.[23] He claimed that his research into the physics of elementary particles showed that electron have the ability to store information. They have a system of remembering and retrieving such information, and they communicate and cooperate with other electrons to create and operate complex systems.[24] This creation and operation of systems counteracts the entropic decay that otherwise rules the material world. Similar to the binary model of storing information that computers use, Charon suggested that the negative or positive spin within each electron constitutes the mechanism of electrons to store information. The exchange of information between electrons, said Charon, is connected with the electric magnetic properties of electrons. Contrary to the functional character of computer chips, however, electrons have the freedom to enter into relations with other electrons. The free exchange of information and affection between the elementary particles of materia, Charon said, is similar to the exchange of affection human beings experience as love.[25]

When Charon's book was first published in 1979, scientists had not yet discovered the science of chaos. Charon had little support for his thesis of a self-organizing tendency among elementary particles. Chaos theory put self-organization in the center of the discussion as a common property of chaotic systems, which includes the systems of smallest particle. Today the idea of a self-organizing quantum world does not seem so far fetched. In *The Life of the Cosmos,* Lee Smolin, a physics professor at Pennsylvania State University, connects self-organizational processes observed on the large scale of galaxies with those observed on the quantum scale.[26] He asks, "Is it not possible that self-organization through processes analogous to natural selection is, indeed, the missing element without which we have so far been unable to construct a quantum theory of cosmology?"[27]

Philosophically the idea of allocating consciousness to all nature, even at the level of the smallest particles, is not at all new. In 2003, the *Journal of Consciousness Studies* dedicated a whole issue to the topic of panpsychism. David Skrbina, a researcher at the University of Michigan and the editor of the journal issue, is in the process of publishing a book on the subject.[28] In his introductory remarks Skrbina says:

> . . . the view that all things have a mind, or a mind-like quality – has been held by a surprisingly large number of the greatest thinkers in the history of western civilization. And not just in ancient times, but virtually throughout the whole of the past 2500 years. Even in the modern era of philosophy (since 1500CE), one finds nearly three dozen major philosophers advocating some variation on the panpsychist theme. Additionally in the 20th century we find another two dozen or so prominent physicists, biologists, and others supporting a similar view. Clearly these individuals found something compelling about panpsychism.[29]

Skrbina then discusses the various forms of panpsychism and how throughout the history of Western philosophy various philosophers expressed panpsychic views and tendencies. It is perhaps needless to say that within the newly emerging studies of consciousness this discussion has become of vital importance, because the panpsychist solution could bridge the age old gap of mind and matter and avoid further dualisms. From Plato through Leibniz to Whitehead and Chalmers, philosophers of all times have defended this view, but panpsychism remained at the fringes of Western thought.

Looking into the 21st century, Skrbina notes a considerable increase in discussions around this topic, seeing it as the "very hallmark of a new anti-mechanistic worldview." Skrbina concludes:

> ...panpsychism has much to offer even beyond the confines of academic philosophy. It is not only a viable alternative conception of mind, but it promises to realign our

thinking toward a more compassionate and ecological outlook on nature. Certainly one of the contributing factors to our present environmental (and some would add, spiritual) crisis is an entrenched system of mechanistic values, and any value system that sees nature as consisting of dead and insensate particles is ripe for exploitation. As many have observed, a panpsychic world view can serve as the conceptual framework for a new system of sympathetic and ecological values, one that may form a new basis for action.[30]

Panpsychism, when it refers to the awareness of the smallest particles, is often called quantum animism. It sets the basis for a compassionate relationship within the universe. Scientifically, quantum animism makes the phenomenon of self-organization in the inorganic world much more plausible. Some level of self-organization has also been observed in computer simulations that mimic fundamental systems. As in the game of life, some basic logical units are programmed to relate to each other following a set of very simple rules. But all these systems operate only after an outside mind or control center, in most cases a computer operator, has designed the system according to those rule and then set the system in motion. This is not unlike the deistic universe in which God has set the parameters and then, in an initial bang, set the whole thing in motion. Without this outside originator, the system would be utterly incapable of self-organization.

The whole thing changes when we assume that at the lowest level logical units operate and relate to each other without any outside stimuli. Charon demonstrated this by using electrons as examples. This is quantum animism in action. Self-organization then makes immediate, intuitive sense. Quantum animism provides the background for the possibility of meaningful communication within the natural world. What is still lacking is an organizational principle that explains how less developed units evolve into ever higher ones of increasing complexity and flexibility. Such a principle sets the foundation for a new theory of community.

Traditional wisdom would suggest that evolutionary forces are the motor of advancement at the micro level of life as well as at the macro level of life. But traditional science only allows evolution to set in at the level of life. The blind tumbling of particles, following the laws of nature, is supposed to be the norm for the rest. With the acceptance of quantum animism, we are able to extend evolutionary forces into the inanimate world.

We are able now to take a closer look at Collective Orchestration and how this organizational principle will affect a naturalistic understanding of community. Collective Orchestration is based on cooperative aspects of systems and the advancement of systems through cooperation. Cooperative organization among living individuals has been observed in various forms. Take for instance a small volvox which has been called one of the seven wonders of the micro world.[31] A volvox is a small, round animal that lives in the water and is made up of individual cells of algae. When food supplies fall short, separate algae cells have been observed organizing into a volvox. This gives the individual cells an advantage in survival. Connected, they are able to propel themselves in a way similar to an octopus and capture food inside the sphere. The algae cells operate in a unified manner, just as the cells in a larger organism do. Even staunch defenders of evolutionary survival theory admit that this is a clear example of increased complexity. Increasingly complex organizations of cells, combined with favorable mutations, can result in higher forms of life.

A similarly stunning example comes from the same murky world of one-cell organisms. At the threshold of what we generally call life, at the level where chemistry meets biology, one-celled organisms called dictyostelium live alone and isolated for most of their existence. As individual particles they do not even qualify as "alive." Like a virus, they barely have an existence of their own. As much as scientists can tell, each of these tiny particles is identical with the other. But a strange mutation occurs when a qualified number of these creatures experience a deficiency in food and space. Scientists have observed how they suddenly group together to cooperate in a formerly unknown way. Collectively, they form one large, multi-celled organism with head, tail, and digestive system. Each cell takes over a specific function within the new organism. They evidently group together to achieve goals that they could not achieve by themselves. In the case of the dictyostelium, the new body enables this collection of individual cells to move to new feeding grounds. They accomplish this in several meta-morphic stages:

> After several hours, the Dictyostelium slug goes through another change. The back end catches up with the tip, and the slug turns into a blob. The blob stretches upward a second time, and now some amoeba produce rigid bundles of cellulose. They die in the process, but their sacrifice allows the blob to become a slender stalk. Perched atop the stalk is a globe, bulging with living amoebas, each of which covers itself in a cellulose coat and becomes a dormant spore. In this form the colony will wait until something – a drop of rainwater, a passing worm, the foot of a bird – picks up the spores and takes them to a bacteria-rich place where they can emerge from their shells and start their lives over. [32]

Today scientists have no idea what makes some cells become tails, others heads, and yet others, digestive organs. There is no observable DNA in the original units. As far as science can say, they are identical. Yet, at the moment of unification they "know" or perhaps even "choose" their places. Scientists have speculated much about this phenomenon. Is there a hidden vari-able, something that has so far evaded the observing scientist?

In nature, it appears, autonomous individuals can collaborate in a synergistic way when nat-ural conditions make such collaboration advantageous or necessary. Once they achieve this cooperation, development levels off and can remain static, at least for some time. We can observe such plateaus in evolutionary development at all levels. They have been called forms, universal categories, classes, species, or populations depending on the cognitive frame and the theory behind it.

What are the energies behind synergistic behavior? What natural power orchestrates such community formation? Is it possible that at one time an organized colony of these amoebas did not disperse again after they had found new feeding grounds but stayed together as one organism, forming the new beginning of a higher form of life? Remarkably, scientists have noticed that dictyostelium are similar to the cells that make up the human system. Millions of other bacteria and microbes have not become part of our complex system. Why is it that these community creating dictyostelium have become part of the success story of life? Could this collective orchestration be the tool with which nature proceeds and climbs up the evolutionary ladder to ever new plateaus?

Collective orchestration is also a well-known occurrence among insects. When a new hive forms, bees join together in a swarm. They leave the old habitat and collect around the queen, often hanging from a tree. The collective slapping of the bees wings produces a temperature in the center of the blob that differs from the temperature of each individual bee. This is the optimal temperature for the queen to conceive new life.

For living organisms the traditional interpretation of such organizational phenomena, on the surface at least, appears adequate. Why is there a need for a new approach? While it is intuitively correct to assume that living creatures have a tendency to organize for the purpose of survival, this is, according to standard theory, not at all intuitive to assume at the inorganic level. Here blind chance, governed by the laws of nature, is the general rule.

Stephen Strogatz, a mathematician who recently published a book on the subject of synchronized behavior, observed that Collective Orchestration occurs in nature on many levels. Technically such synchronized behavior is made possible through so-called oscillators. An oscillator is a pulsating device mostly used for the purpose of generating a signal. Coupled oscillators are systems of such devices with two or more members that are communicating with each other. Often their communication results in synchronized behavior. Strogatz observed:

> Groups of fireflies, planets, or pacemaker cells are all collections of oscillators entities that cycle automatically, that repeat themselves over and over again at more or less regular time intervals. Fireflies flash; planets orbit; pacemaker cells fire. Two or more oscillators are said to be coupled if some physical or chemical process allows them to influence one another. Fireflies communicate with light. Planets tug on one another with gravity. Heart cells pass electrical currents back and forth. As these examples suggest, nature uses every available channel to allow these oscillators to talk to one another. And the result of those conversations is often synchrony, in which all the oscillators begin to move as one.[33]

Synchronicity in its simplest form occurs when two things keep happening simultaneously for an extended period of time. According to Strogatz, "such persistent sync comes easily to us human beings, and, for some reason, it often gives us pleasure. We like to dance together, sing together, play in a band."[34] The surprising fact is that this includes synchronized behavior among non-living, non-animate things. He says:

> ...when sync occurs among unconscious entities like electrons or cells, it seems almost miraculous. It's surprising enough to see animals cooperating – thousands of crickets chirping in unison on a summer night; the graceful undulating of schools of fish – but it's even more shocking to see mobs of mindless things falling into step by themselves.[35]

Strogatz observes that all these occurrences of synchronized behavior follow the same mathematical pattern described by oscillators. They are also perfect examples of how natural systems, animate and inanimate, self organize into more complex creatures: Strogatz observes:

> ...the fireflies organize themselves. No Maestro is required, and it doesn't matter what the weather is like. Sync occurs through mutual cuing, in the same way that an orchestra can keep perfect time without a conductor. What's counterintuitive here is that the insects don't need to be intelligent. They have all the ingredients they need – each firefly contains an oscillator, a little metronome, whose timing adjusts automatically in response to the flashes of others. That's it. [36]

That's it? All that is needed, says Strogatz, is "a little metronome, whose timing adjusts automatically?" I have difficulty following such simplification. If things in nature occur automatically we are bound to ask for the causes, the mechanism. There are no metronomes in nature. Strogatz marvels at the inventiveness of evolution:

> The heart's natural pacemaker is a marvel of evolution, perhaps the most impressive oscillator ever created. A cluster of about 10,000 cells called the sinoatrial node, its function is to generate the electrical rhythm that commands the rest of the heart to beat. Unlike most of the cells in the heart, the pacemaker cells oscillate automatically – isolated in a Petri dish, their voltage rises falls in a regular rhythm. Evolution has produced a more reliable, democratic system in which thousands of cells collectively set the pace. Of course, democracy raises its own problems. Somehow the cells have to coordinate their firings. [37]

What are the options to explain such evolutionary inventiveness? What could be the reasons for "mindless things falling into step by themselves?"

When scientists first observed synchronization among supposedly non-sentient lower animals, their accounts were met with disbelief. Says Strogatz: "These phenomena are so incredible that commentators have been led to deny their existence, attributing them to illusions, accidents, or perceptual errors. Other observers have soared into mysticism, attributing sync to supernatural forces in the cosmos."[38] But Strogatz does not stop here. He asks: "Can perfect synchrony emerge from a cacophony of thousands of mindless metronomes? In 1989 my colleague, Rennie Mirollo, and I proved that the answer is yes. Not only can it work, it will always work, under certain conditions."[39]

What are these conditions? As a mathematician, Strogatz finds a mathematical answer: "...at a deeper level, there is a connection, one that transcends the details of any particular mechanism. That connection is mathematics. All the examples are variations on the same mathematical theme: self-organization, the spontaneous emergence of order out of chaos."[40] Strogatz and his colleagues actually built a computer model of synchronizing oscillators to prove their point: mindless coupled oscillators really synchronize. He describes the results:

> It was spooky – the system was synchronizing itself. Defying skeptics who had argued that firefly sync was impossible in principle, that such a thing was "certainly

contrary to all natural laws," the computer was showing that a mob of mindless little oscillators could fall into step automatically. The effect was uncanny to watch. An onlooker couldn't help but feel that the oscillators were deliberately cooperating, consciously striving for order, but they were not. Each one was responding robotically to impulses fired by others, with no goal in mind.[41]

Without going into further detail on how Strogatz set up this experiment, it suffices to know that his results are impressive. Proving that coupling oscillators can indeed be found at various levels of nature and that these systems all follow the same mathematical description is no small accomplishment. It certainly gave my own research into Cooperative Systems and Collective Orchestration a solid foundation. Ultimately Strogatz, however, fails to probe deeper into the phenomena he began to investigate. His conclusion: "For reasons we don't yet understand, the tendency to synchronize is one of the most pervasive drives in the universe, extending from atoms to animals, from people to planets."[42]

Strogatz brought awareness to the ubiquity of synchronization at all levels of natural systems. While the process of synchronization itself is perhaps less visible in the inorganic, material world, its effects are everywhere. We only have to think of the various forms of crystals, in frozen water as ice and as snowflakes, in salt formations and in precious metal formations. Of course, the inorganic world presents itself to us mostly in the form of less synchronized aggregates.

To probe into the source of inorganic synchronization we need to enter deep into the microscopic world of quanta. Collective Orchestration may here present an exiting new insight into the complex world of fields, perhaps giving a whole novel approach to the understanding of quantum field theory and electromagnetic fields. In the light of Collective Orchestration, these coherent fields of quanta are organized systems of quanta, which in their higher order are capable of performing functions that were impossible for the lower order individuals.

The presence of a higher functionality in collective fields is evident when we consider the multiple functionality of a laser beam when compared to individual photons. The inability to explain the larger, ordered state of a system by examining the individual members of the system, atoms, neurons or whatever, first led the Japanese physicist Hiroomi Umezawa to the recognition of a collective mode. His students, Mari Jibu and Kunio Yasue, in *Quantum Brain Dynamics and Consciousness*[43] explain the nature of a laser beam the following way:

> A laser is a device that can emit a specific form of light in which numerous photons with a definite wave number display the same wave motion as that of the electro magnetic field. This is accomplished by a collective motion of the electrons, called the collective mode, in a large number of atoms interacting with the electromagnetic field. Recall that a global harmony or order emerges in the matter field and the electromagnetic field, that is, electrons and photons. Due to the presence of this global order, the creation and annihilation dynamics is so elaborately tuned that an extremely large number of photons can be created in a single wave motion of the electromagnetic field with a definite wavelength and phase. Then, ideal monochromatic light made of only specific wave motions of the electromagnetic field with a single and definite wave length and phase can be produced by a laser. This is a laser beam.[44]

From laser surgery to star wars systems, we are of course all aware of the many uses found for laser beams in modern technology. But Collective Orchestration may be able to bridge another explanatory riddle on a yet deeper level, perhaps probing into the last frontier of science, the nature of space/time itself. In Quantum Brain Dynamics and Consciousness, Yibu and Yasue ask the provocative question of whether the scientific community has "lost interest in the cryptic mechanism of nature lying concealed behind Schrödinger's wave equation and in Born's probabilistic interpretation?"[45]

The reality behind quantum mechanics remains unknown to this day. It was Hideki Yukawa, named a Nobel laureate for his discovery of meson theory, who sought the yet unknown reality behind quantum theory. Yukawa looked for this reality in the discontinuous structure of space on the extremely fine, sub-microscopic scale. He initiated a revolutionary school of thought in his theory of elementary domains. According to Yibu and Yasue:

> The first and second questions in the domain of basic research – "What is reality?" and "What is the world?" – are believed to have been answered by quantum theory and the general theory of relativity, respectively; however, we do not know why the fundamental assumptions or principles of those theories – that is, Schrödinger's wave equation, Born's probabilistic interpretation in quantum theory, and Einstein's equation in the general theory of relativity – are true. The assumptions or principles have been proven to be correct, but the scientific community does not know why they are valid... if we wish to put aside our conventional way of describing natural phenomena in order to achieve a true understanding of reality, we need to probe deeper for yet unknown physical objects behind the assumptions or principles of both quantum theory and the general theory of relativity.[46]

Jibu and Yasue's description of a basic space/time assembly entails the presence of a "collective mode." They say: "The world consists of an infinite number of discrete elements of space called elementary domains, and Reality is given by the transfer or exchange of energy between those elementary domains."[47] These elementary domains are the foundational units of our space/time. They are one-dimensional strings that extend and build space/time. They constitute the individual elements of the evasive Higgs field. By cooperating with each other, these elementary domains collectively orchestrate to construct a continuous space/time. In other words, elementary strings self-organize and compact themselves into large scale assemblies. First they form continuous space and then further compact forms such as solids – photons, electrons, and all the elementary particles. These again self-organize and collectively build molecules and cells. Thus the material world is assembled from the ground up through a process we should recognize as Collective Orchestration.

According to Yukawa, "the essence of the perceptible world is nothing but the ongoing transfer and relocalization of energy as elementary domains."[48] Thus evolution is a self-organizing, self-creating activity that begins as elementary domains or elemental nothingness and eventually compacts into increased orchestration to end up being stars and galaxies and you and me. The evolutionary tool that makes this possible is Collective Orchestration, by means of which nature produces higher dimensional entities with an over-arching new order that cannot be explained from the level of the lower dimension. No recourse to design and mystical sources is needed in order to explain the order around us. The lower elements of such individuals are kept in cohesion by a higher dimensional order, recognizable only from that higher plateau. What has been overlooked so far is the fact that our human consciousness, while living in a three-dimensional physical body, actually views the world not from that third dimension, but from a platform much higher, closer to that of the twelfth dimension. These many dimensions are actually needed to have, and to realize, a world experience of three dimensions. The higher dimensions provide the inner structure projected into the third.

In my book, *Compassion*, I asked: "Could collective orchestration also drive human collaboration? Could the same collective orchestration cause human beings to form communities? Is there a subconscious awareness that through collective orchestration the whole human race will reach a level of realization, a new dimension of awareness, which we cannot reach individually? If so, nurturing human communities could be one of the most burning missions of humanity on earth."[48]

Once panpsychism, quantum animism and collective orchestration have become part of the way science views the universe, I am convinced that humanity will finally evolve to a new level of cooperation, both with each other and with the rest of the natural world. This just might help bring about the bold vision of Tatiana Alekseeva, in her dream of a new global community enabling a new non-ideological philosophy based on the principles of self-organization, cooperation, solidarity, and mutual respect. It may finally bring about the kind of reconciled society that Siebert envisioned in his *Future III*. Even if today we still seem to be far from realizing such a vision, the tools are at hand to move toward it.

© *Werner Krieglstein, presented at the Inter-University Center, Dubrovnik, "Future of Religions" 25th – 29th of April, 2005. Dubrovnik, Croatia.*

1. *William Gay and Tatiana Alekseeva, eds. Democracy and the Quest for Justice, Russian and American Perspectives, (Amsterdam: Rodopi 2004)*
2. *pg 18*
3. *Ibid.*
4. *Ibid.*
5. *pg 19*
6. *Islam might be mentioned as an exception. The Quran and especially the Prophet's interpretative texts give detailed instructions about the operation and conduct within a Muslim community. But community here is also not so much seen as the source of the ethical norms, but its enforcer, not as an end but as the instrumental means to otherworldly fulfillment.*
7. *Werner Krieglstein, Compassion, A New Philosophy of the Other, (Amsterdam: Rodopi 2002) pg. 5*
8. *Ilya Prigogine, Order Out of Chaos. New York: Bantam Books, 1984. pg. xii*
9. *Ibidem*
10. *Ibidem*
11. *This is true in spite of the enormous role the observing self in the Cartesian world. Descartes anchored his proof of existence on the absoluteness of the observing mind. By placing the Self in the realm of spirit his philosophy created the ultimate ideological split, known as Cartesian dualism.*
12. *Thomas Merton who as a trappist monk saw the contradiction between individual mystical pursuit and the need for community. When discussing the Desert Fathers Merton once said: "They were among the few who were ahead of their time, and opened the way for the development of a new man, and a new society. . . The eigteenth and nineteenth centuries with their pragmatic individualism . . . prepared the way for the great regression to the herd mentality that is taking place now. The flight of these men to the desert was neither purely negative nor purely individualistic . . . They did not reject society with proud con-tempt, as if they were superior to other men. On the contrary, . . . they fled from the world of men (because) in the world men were divided into those who were successful, and imposed their will on others, and those who had to give in and be imposed upon. The Desert Fathers declined to be ruled by men, but had no desire to rule over others themselves. (Thomas Merton, The Wisdom of the Desert, (Gethsemani, 1960) 4-5.*
13. *Erwin Schrödinger, What is Life? (Cambridge, Cambridge University Press, 1967)*
14. *See W Ross Ashby, Introduction to Cybernetics, 1956 and Ludwig von Bertalanffy, General System Theory, 1968.*
15. *Arthur Koestler, Janus: a summing up (New York: Random House, 1978)*
16. *Werner Krieglstein, From Aristotle's Universals to Umezawa's Collective Mode. Is the Vacuum really a Proper Locus?*
17. *Mari Yibu and Kunio Yasue, Quantum Brain Dynamics and Consciousness, Amsterdam: Benjamin, 1995.)*
18. *Stuart A. Kauffman, "What is Life? Was Schrödinger right?" in What is Life? The Next Fifty Years, Speculations on the future of biology, eds. Michael Murphy and Luke A.J. O'Neill (Cambridge: Cambridge University Press, 1995) pgs. 83-114.*
19. *Ibid. pg. 85.*
20. *Ibid. pg. 84.*

21. Jean Charon, Der Geist der Materie. Wien: Zsolsnay, 1979.
22. Ibid. pg 85.
23. Ibid. pg 88.
24. Ibid. pg 90.
25. Ibid. pg182.
26. Lee Smolin, The Life of the Cosmos, (Oxford University Press, 1997).
27. Ibid. pg 292.
28. David Skrbina, Panpsychism in the West (May 1, 2005)
29. David Skrbina, "Panpsychism as an Underlying Theme in Western Philosophy" in Panpsychism, Journal of Consciousness Studies Vol 10, No 3 (2003) pg 5.
30. Ibid. pg 43
31. http://www.microscopy-uk.org.uk/mag/indexmag.html
32. Carl Zimmer, "The Slime Alternative" Discover, (September 1998), p. 88.
33. Strogatz, pg 3.
34. Steven Strogatz, Sync, The Emerging Science of Spontaneous Order, (New York, Hyperion Books, 2003) pg 2
35. Ibidem.
36. Ibid. pg 13.
37. Ibid. pg 15.
38. Ibid. pg 3.
39. Ibid. pg 14.
40. Ibidem
41. Ibid. pg 22.
42. Ibid.pg. 14.
43. Yibu and Yasue, Quantum Brain, 1995.
44. Ibidem
45. Ibid. pg 27.
46. Ibidem
47. Ibid. pp.28/29
48. Ibid. p. 29
49. Krieglstein, pg 85.

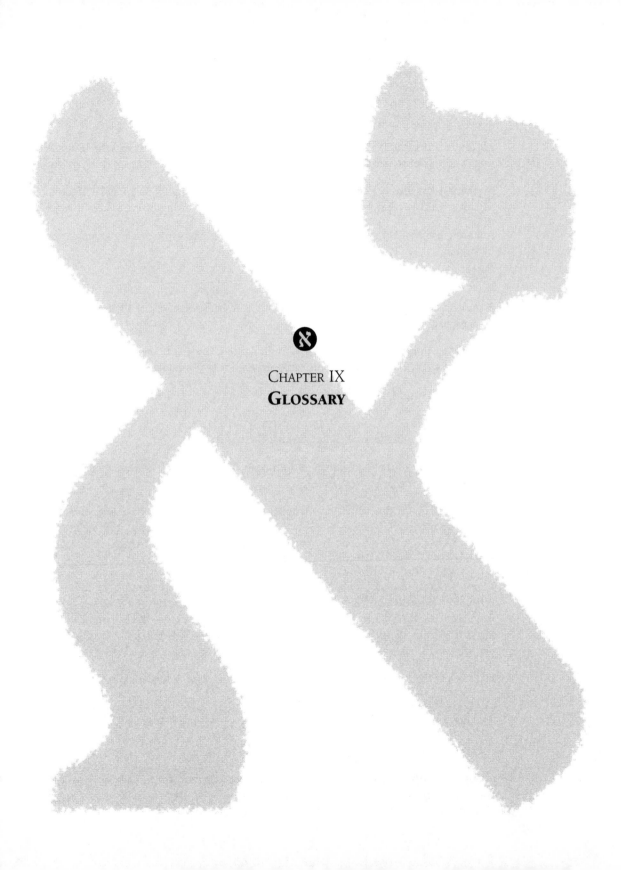

CHAPTER IX
GLOSSARY

Absolute: A neutral name for God, Allah, Jehovah etc. Aristotle also used the term the unmoved mover to describe god as the ultimate principle.

Aesthetics: A relatively new term (17th century) for an old discipline going back to the Greek idea of artistic perception, to set this type of perception off from logical or cognitive knowing.

Animism: The view of virtually all early civilizations that the world around them was inhabited by spirits.

Analytical: Investigating things separately.

A priori: The mind knows certain truths without having experienced them. This is the basis for Rationalist philosophy.

Archai: first things, self evident concepts, similar to a priori, but an older term used by Aristotle. In a syllogism a judgment can only yield true results if based on valid archai.

Art(ist): For Aristotle the artist helps to promote universals, for Plato art was three times removed from the truth.

Atheism: The belief that one can prove that there is no god

Autonomy: One of the main values of European Enlightenment. It means being in charge of your affairs, giving your own law.

Aryans: A nomadic people, falsely assumed by the German fascists to be members of only one identifiable tribe. They were the first to tame horses, built chariots and preferred male gods who lived in the sky. Their common language, one of the first written languages, was Sanskrit.

Atom: Greek for indivisible. Until the beginning of the twentieth century the atom was believed to be indivisible as the Greeks speculated. Now scientists could now make models of an atom and knew it had an internal structure. This gave them the first indication that it might be further divisible. Einstein was the first to suggest this possibility until it was first performed at the University of Chicago in 1934.

BCE: Before Current Epoch. This is a way to mark the time before the birth of Christ (BC).

Categorical Imperative: Kant's major contribution to deontological ethics. It goes something like this: Act always so that the principle of your action could be made into a general law.

Cause: (see the Four Causes)

Chaos: is the opposite of order. Western civilization has a negative image of chaos as destructive, meaningless, even as evil. Modern physics has shown that chaos is a necessary natural state of a system in the transition to a new order.

Chronos: The Greek god of time.

Canon: A selected list of authors chosen to be the representatives of a time, era, or a whole civilization.

Dharma or dharmic values: A Hindu system of values derived from nature. Ancient Hinduism knows of peripheral laws and core values. Peripheral laws must be reviewed from time to time, in order for core values to be accepted and succeed.

Deduction: Second step in Aristotelian logic, applying universals or essences to individual members of a group, proceeding from general ideas to individuals.

Democracy: Rule by the people. Not a preferred way of governance according to the Greek philosophers.

Deism: The belief that God created the world, but then left it alone. The world is like a machine, more precisely like a clock, once wound up, it just keeps ticking. The watch maker is no longer interfering, perhaps not even needed any more. This philosophy greatly aided the development of science.

Deity: Another way to speak about God (from Latin dues = God).

Deontological: Duty ethics, absolute laws tell you how to act, as a philosophical ethics developed by Kant.

Determinism: The belief that everything is predestined, there is no free will.

Dialectic: A progression of opposites rather than a linear progression. The dialectic triad already used by the Greeks was the progression of thesis, antithesis, and synthesis. For the Greeks this was a device to develop an argument in a speech. Hegel used it much more broadly as a progression of the universe.

Dialectical Materialism: While materialism is the philosophy based on the primacy of materia, dialectical materialism teaches that materia, from the beginning was pregnant with life and consciousness.

Dilemma: A situation where you have to choose between two alternative courses of action. Often neither of the choices is completely satisfying.

Discourse: A systematic, logical approach to solve problems. Most philosophical texts are written that way. The bible in contrast is written in a narrative form. In the bible problems are solved by giving examples and telling stories.

Dualism: The world consists of two opposing substances like mind and body, spirit and materia. It was first proposed by Plato, but finely developed by Descartes.

Dionysus: Known as the god of wine, of ecstasy, and of altered states of mind.

Eco-philosophy: A philosophical concern for preservation of the environment and a critique of its destruction, which was often supported by Western philosophy and religions.

Egalitarian: Men and women have equal chance to advance in society.

Einstein, Albert: (1879 to 1955) Probably one of the greatest geniuses ever alive. During his school years he was not a particularly good student and became a patent clerk in a Swiss office. Papers he soon published changed our understanding of time, space, light and the universe. Immigrated to the United States fleeing Hitler's Europe he became a professor at Princeton.

Electi: The inner circle of members at the Pythagorean School. They were sworn to secrecy and loyalty.

Eleusinian XE "Eleusinian" Mysteries: A festival regularly held in Athens still at Aristotle's time around the fall equinox (September, October.) It was a festival celebrating the Goddess in all her different forms, dating back to ancient times when Goddess worship was the rule. Aristophanes talks about the need for purity and abstention from all evil for those who wanted to participate in the festival.

Empiricism: A philosophy influenced by science. Everything we know comes from sense experience. At birth the mind is an empty slate. Empiricism rejects innate ideas.

Enlightenment (European): A period in European history that emphasized human reason, self determination and empowerment. The values of the European Enlightenment were enshrined in the French and in the American Revolution.

Enlightenment (Eastern): Like a flash of insight, a moment of total clarity, of feeling to be connected with the universe.

Epistemology: Theory of knowing. How do we know something?

Essential: What a thing is by nature, the part that never changes, your soul. According Aristotle, it is the universal part of an object.

Essentialism: a philosophy following Aristotle's view that everything has an unchangeable soul or essence. The philosophy developing as an opposite is existentialism.

Ethics: Goes back to the Greek word ethos, which means habit, or behavior. Doing the right thing only once or a few times does not result in ethical behavior. An ethical character is the result of continuous or long term right action.

Existentialism: The philosophical belief that there are no essentials, universals, or essences.

We are thrown into this world without guides. We must decide our own fate.

Evil: For the Greeks it was the absence of knowledge. Hence their emphasis on education and rehabilitation.

Feminism: A modern movement critical of Patriarchal rule. Feminism has criticized Western philosophers for their misogynist views and Western philosophy for its male bias.

Feudalism: Hierarchical stratification of society dominant during the Middle Ages. The king is on the top and the peasants are the base. Feudalism continues social stratification first developed by Plato in the Republic.

Four Causes: Aristotle's way to explain change. Efficient Cause brings fourth the object, is the author or creator, the Material Cause is the stuff out of which an object is made, the Formal Cause is the shape or form into which it is transformed and the Final Cause is the ultimate purpose of an object.

Frankfurt School: The Frankfurt School was never a real physical school. It describes the school of thought that came out of the teachings of Theodor Adorno and Max Horkheimer, two professors who taught philosophy and sociology at the Goethe University in Frankfurt/ Germany until the late Sixties. I was a student of both of them.

Golden Age: Described by the Greek historian Hesiod as an age in which people lived in harmony with each other and with nature. Hesiod divided time into five ages: the Golden age, ruled by Chronos, in which people lived extremely long lives 'without sorrow of heart'; the Silver age, ruled by Zeus; the Bronze age, an epoch of war; the Heroic age, the time of the Trojan war; and lastly the Iron age, which for him was the corrupt present.

Happiness: The final goal of everything living.

Hesiod: A Greek historian who lived in the 8th century BCE. He refers to himself as a farmer in Boeotia, a region of central Greece, but other than that we know little about him. His poetry codified the chronology and genealogy of the Greek myths.

Hierarchy: A divine or holy order of things. Hieros is the Greek word for holy. There are many hierarchies in nature. People at all times created hierarchies among themselves.

Hinduism: One of the oldest, still practiced religions in the world today. It originated in India in ancient times. The main books of Hinduism, the Vedas, were developed around the same time philosophy developed in Greece. Modern Hinduism is a merger of Aryan religion and the original religion existing in India before the Aryan invasion. This old religion revered women and female Gods. As a result of the caste system that was introduced by the Aryans Hinduism today knows little respect for woman. There is much indication that in Pre-Aryan times, Indian civilization was structured very similar to that of the ancient Minoans. It was a more egalitarian society with a highly developed sense of community.

Idealism: First there was an idea. From this everything else developed.

Ideology: A set of ideas to explain everything, usually spread by force or manipulation.

Ideology Critique: Major tool of the Frankfurt School to deconstruct false absolutes and oppressive theories. In connection with critical theory it also taught how to "think outside the box."

Induction: First step in Aristotelian logic, collecting objects and classifying them according to essential characteristics. This is also the way to initially discover essentials.

Instrumental Value: According to Aristotle an instrumental good is a good you achieve in order to achieve other goods. For instance you earn money in order to buy things.

Intrinsic Value: A good you achieve for its own sake

Justify: Means to give a good reason for something you do or intend to do. To justify can have a negative meaning: to make excuses for your actions.

Logic: A systematical exploration of what is, making your verbal statements consistent with nature. It is also the attempt to make language as concise as mathematical symbolism. Today logic is often only used to prove the inherent consistency of a statement.

Manicheists: Followers of the prophet Mani who believed that the universe and the human soul were the battle ground between good and evil forces. These forces were so powerful that the human being had little choice but to follow them.

Maryolatry: Mary worship in the Christian church.

Materia: The stuff out of which everything is made. Modern physics is not sure any longer that such a material exists.

Materialism: A philosophical view that the world began with one substance: materia.

Meta-philosophy: A philosophical movement that wants to be more than a simple philosophy, providing a system to explain the world. It wants to be an umbrella for the evolution of diverse thoughts, multiple voices, plurality of ideas.

Methodology: The way you conduct research and write a research report

Minoans: Were the ancient inhabitants of the Island of Crete. They left a large collection of art works, which show that Minoan life was largely peaceful. They seem to have equal opportunities for males and females to advance in society.

Misogynist: Hostile to women

Monism: Everything started from one single substance (for instance spirit or materia).

Mythology: A set of stories to explain natural occurrences using supernatural means.

Natural Law Theory: First developed by Thomas Aquinas. It assumes that the Laws of Nature do not contradict the laws provided by God in the Bible.

Negative Dialectic: Developed by the Frankfurt School, mainly Adorno, to indicate that in the progression of opposites the first step comes out of the unknown, out of a negation of the antithesis. This is mostly an aesthetic device, but ultimately refers to everything. In order to get into the depth of things, the mind must take a plunge into the unknown, momentarily denying its own reality.

Neo-Platonism: The adjustment of Platonic philosophy to fit early Christian doctrine and ideas. The most important neo-Platonist was Augustine.

Newton, Isaac: (1642-1727) Discovered and explored the basic laws of nature and gave them a mathematical foundation. With this he established a solid scientific foundation for the exploration of nature and provided the backbone for what became known as philosophical deism.

Newtonianism: A world view based on Newton's laws of nature. It became the basis for the philosophy of Deism.

Norms: The modern equivalent of Platonic forms or Aristotelian universals.

Objective: You believe the world exists independently of being observed

Olympus: Was the heaven of the Greek gods. It was thought to be located on Mount Olympus, a high elevation in the Northern part of Greece.

Ontology: Asks the question "What is? What really exists? What is real?" Ontos is the Greek word for being. You already know the second part; Logos means thought, spirit, meaning, or science. Ontology is the science of being.

Oracle of Delphi: was a sacred place for the Greeks. Ordinary Greeks and famous leaders alike made pilgrimages to this place high up in the mountains near Athens. Here a priestess was ready to give answers to their important questions. She was supposed to be inspired by the Gods. Fumes that came out of the ground put this holy woman into an altered state of mind.

Other: The philosophical Other is everything that is not you, your self, your thinking mind. But to the reflecting mind, even its own self can become the Other.

Pantheism: The belief that God is everything and everything is God. There is a newer version of pantheism called pan-entheism. This view says that while being in everything God is simultaneously different from everything.

Pantheon: The temple in which the Greeks kept their gods. There was always an open place for new arrivals. This was the alter for the unknown god. The Greeks found new gods to add to their Pantheon, whenever they encountered a new civilization in their travels. Instead of

179

obliterating their histories they added them to their own.

Perfection: For Aristotle the final goal of every change in the world, Aristotle's reason for why things change.

Perspectivism: Transcendental Perspectivism is a new philosophy trying to promote the recognition of valid different perspectives and to promote communication with all these perspectives. It is based on feminist standpoint theory, assuming that every subject in the universe has a unique perspective. Transcendental Perspectivism assumes that the whole universe is alive and filled with subjective perspectives.

Philosopher King: In the Republic, Plato proposes that a philosopher should be head of state.

Philosophy: The love of wisdom. It is composed of the two words, philos and Sophia. Philos is the Greek word for friend, or lover. It is still found in the modern words Philadelphia and Philip (the city of brotherly love and the lover of horses).Sophia is Greek for wisdom.

Polytheism: The belief in many gods. Primal people were generally polytheist. Gods or spirits, they believed, inhabited the natural world around them. This view is also called animism. Only later people projected their gods primarily into the sky. This made their deities portable. Examples of modern day polytheistic religions are Hinduism and Jainism.

Pragmatism: An American philosophy based on the idea that true is what works. American Pragmatism is based on scientific principles. It greatly influenced education in America.

Premise: First part of Aristotelian logic, major and minor premise lead to conclusion

Pythagoras: Born in Samos 530 BCE. He founded a society at Kroton (in southern Italy). The Pythagoreans were a religious community and a scientific school. Because of its extreme secrecy the community was met with mistrust by the surrounding people. In his old age Pythagoras had to flee from Kroton to Metapontion, where he died. He never left anything in writing about his ideas. The date of his death is also not known. His main accomplishment was to project that the universe was constructed from numbers. This view has gained recent recognition by some modern physicists.

Quantum Theory: The scientific theory that deals with the smallest particles out of which everything is made. These were assumed to be atoms until atoms were split into smaller particles. Science today believes that the smallest particles are matter and waves at the same time. On an even smaller scale matter and energy seem to be interchangeable.

Rationalism: A philosophy based on the idea that the mind knows things that it does not need to experience. The mind knows *a priori*.

Reductionism: Reducing an object to its smallest parts. By understanding the smallest part the scientist hopes to understand the whole.

Relativism: No absolute values guide our actions. For a total relativist there is no moral universe.

Second Law of Thermodynamics: Deals with the flow of energy from an ordered state to a less ordered state. This is also called entropy. In an open system, energy will always flow in only one direction. We know this direction from experience. It sets for us what is called the arrow of time.

Secularism: Separation of church and state. This is an ongoing process that began at the end of the Middle Ages.

Self-evident: Something that is very obvious to the mind. An a priori truth or an archai must be self-evident.

Skepticism: Doubting that any absolute truth can be known or even exists. But keep in mind that the truth that is meant here is an absolute truth, a truth no one can doubt. You can understand this easiest by looking at a mathematical statement such as 1+1=2. If you doubt that this statement is true you end up in remedial math. The basic position of philosophy is skepticism.

Socrates: Often considered the father of philosophy. He taught philosophy by asking many questions. He was born in 469 and died in 399 BCE.

Subjectivism: Beginning to philosophize with the reality of the subject, with your subjective experience. This is the opposite of objectivism, beginning to philosophize with objective experiences.

Syllogism: main tool of Aristotelian logic. You know it from Math class: if a = b and b = c then a = c.

Synthesis: Seeing things together as wholes rather than as parts

Symmetry: Put a drop of ink on a piece of paper and fold the paper through the center then open it up and you have a perfect symmetrical image. Look in a mirror and you see a symmetrical image of yourself. There are many symmetries in nature. Think of symmetries within your body. Ancient people considered symmetrical things as beautiful. Do you?

Teleology: A major concept in Aristotle's philosophy. Everything is striving for perfection. In Aristotle's view all humankind was striving for perfection.

Thales: Born in Miletus in Greek Ionia in 620s BCE. He died in 546 BCE. Aristotle identified Thales as the first person to investigate the basic principles of nature. Thales is considered to be the founder of the school of natural philosophy. He proposed theories to explain events of nature, the primary substance, the support of the earth, and the cause for change. His questioning approach freed natural events from godly intervention. He founded the Milesian school of natural philosophy and was the first to develop a precursor to the scientific method.

Theory of Relativity: Einstein's formulation for the curvature of space (general theory of relativity)

and the behavior of objects moving at or near the speed of light (special theory of relativity).

Theory: Comes from the Greek word *thean*, which means something like to gaze like when you squint your eyes and see a whole group of people at once. It shares this word with the term theater. In theater the Greeks expected to be shown how things and events are mysteriously connected with each other, rather than just observing the surface of things. In modern usage, theory is closely connected with a scientific hypothesis. The Theory of Relativity is one example.

Theory of Evolution: Charles Darwin's scientific theory of evolution replaced Aristotelian essentialism in the 19th century. Instead of things evolving toward perfection, according to a master plan (intelligent design), in biology living things evolved through natural selection.

Thermodynamics: The study of the patterns of energy change. "Thermo" means energy, and "dynamics" means patterns of change. In other words, thermodynamics deals with energy conversion and the stability direction of change of molecules. The First Law of Thermodynamics deals with the flow of energy and says that energy can never be destroyed.

Thomistic: Philosophy based on Thomas Aquinas.

Transcendental Perspectivism: (see Perspectivism)

Truth: For Plato forms or ideas, for Aristotle the universal within each thing. For Pragmatists an idea that works.

Universal: A good or value that is the same for anyone and anywhere in the universe.

Universalism: As a new meta-philosophy universalism is the attempt to develop a basic theory for a new global world.

Utilitarianism: An ethics based on the idea that good is what provides happiness for the majority of people.

Value: Something you hold dear, something you believe in, you are willing to make sacrifices for. Think of some values you believe in.

Wisdom: A combination of knowledge and experience. It is not much used today any more. Reflect about what kind of people we call wise? In ancient times young people had to go to older people to get information. Whom or better what do we consult today when we have a question? What kinds of animal do people call wise? Why do you think an owl is called wise? An owl was actually the bird of Athens. Athene, the goddess of wisdom, was often pictured with an owl on her shoulder. Do you think there is wisdom in nature?

Zeno's Paradox: Try to figure out whether the following mathematical sum ever reaches 1 and how this relates to Zeno's paradox: $1/2 + 1/4 + 1/8 + \dots = 1$?

Zoroastrianism: A religion founded in ancient times by the prophet Zarathustra. It was the dominant world religion during the Persian empires (559 BC to 651 AC) and had a major influence on other religions. It is still practiced world-wide, especially in Iran and India.